INSPIRE / PLAN / DISCOVER / EXPERIENCE

PROVENCE
AND THE CÔTE D'AZUR

PROVENCE
AND THE CÔTE D'AZUR

CONTENTS

DISCOVER 6

EXPERIENCE 58

NEED TO KNOW 204

Left: Weathered painted shopfront in Marseille
Previous page: Sunset over Gordes

DISCOVER

Pont St-Bénézet over the Rhône, Avignon

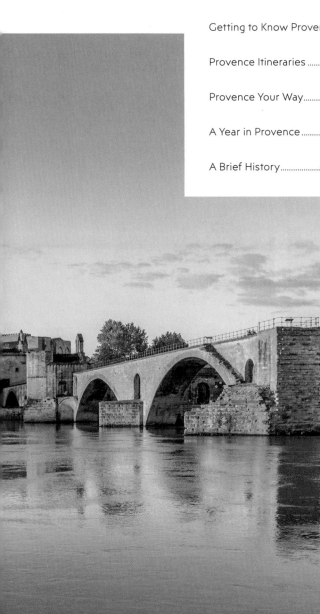

WELCOME TO PROVENCE

Fragrant fields of lavender and relics of ancient realms. Restaurants that rank among the world's finest and glamorous Riviera nightspots. Lush vineyards, snow-capped peaks and sun-soaked beaches: this region has it all. Whatever your dream trip to Provence entails, this DK Eyewitness Travel Guide is the perfect companion.

1 Les Arènes, Nîmes.

2 Basket filled with freshly picked Provençal lavender.

3 Yacht docked in the harbour at Monte Carlo.

4 Sunflower field in Vaucluse at sunset.

Provence might just be France's most alluring region. Its cities have something to seduce every visitor, from the vibrant streetlife of Marseille and Nice to the sun, sand and bling of Riviera resorts such as St-Tropez and Cannes. Roman amphitheatres, papal palaces and medieval abbeys hark back to the power and glory of vanished empires, and fabulous galleries celebrate the work of some of the greatest artists of modern times.

Stretching from the sunny shores of the Mediterranean to the snow-capped peaks of the French Alps, Provence's amazing diversity of terrain and terroir make it a paradise for foodies. Vineyards produce luscious reds and extraordinary bone-dry rosés. From mountain pastures and fishing harbours come culinary treasures like truffles, saffron and a cornucopia of seafood. Lovers of the great outdoors are spoiled for choice, too: hikers can watch the sun rise from the summit of Mont Ventoux, kayakers can tackle the rapids of the Gorges du Verdon, and wildlife watchers can spot flamingos on the lagoons of the Camargue.

With so many different things to discover, Provence can seem overwhelming. We've broken the region down into easily navigable chapters, with detailed itineraries, expert local knowledge and colourful, comprehensive maps to help you plan the perfect visit. Whether you're staying for a weekend, a week, or longer, this Eyewitness guide will ensure that you see the very best the region has to offer. Enjoy the book, and enjoy Provence.

REASONS TO LOVE
PROVENCE

Magnificent Roman architecture, picturesque vineyards, excellent cuisine and fine modern art: there are so many reasons to love Provence and the Côte d'Azur. Here, we pick some of our favourites.

1 PALAIS DES PAPES

Within the white limestone walls of Avignon's Palais des Papes, echoing vaulted chambers and serene courtyards evoke the power and the glory of a succession of pious yet cunning medieval pontiffs *(p158)*.

SUN, SEA AND SAND 2

Whether you are looking to be pampered at a private beach club or splash around with the kids, Provence's beaches have something for everyone *(p32)*.

3 DIVINE WINES

From the Châteauneuf-du-Pape vineyards in the Rhône valley, the hinterland of Côtes de Provence and the sandy coasts of Camargue come complex red wines, flinty rosés and luscious *vins doux (p40)*.

4 CELEBRITY SPOTTING

Ever since the 1950s, the beaches of St-Tropez, Antibes, Juan-les-Pins and Monaco have been bywords for celebrity glamour. If you're hoping to photograph the stars, Cannes is the place to be when the world's greatest film festival is in full swing *(p70)*.

ABBAYE DE SÉNANQUE 5

Vast sunflower prairies and purple lavender fields surround the serene Abbaye de Sénanque *(p170)*, where blossoms create a bee-buzzing haze of colour, scent and sound around the cool medieval cloisters.

ROMAN ARENAS 6

At Roman arenas like those at Arles *(p134)* and Orange *(p168)* it's easy to imagine audiences roaring as gladiators battled to the death. These days, events range from concerts to operas.

WILD WETLANDS 7

Flocks of flamingos, storks and other waterfowl patrol the shallow lagoons and reedbeds of the Camargue delta, where sturdy half-wild white horses and black cattle roam (p138).

RIVER CRUISING 8

The mighty river Rhône has shaped Provence's culture for millennia. Cruising down its waters while sampling fine cuisine is an experience to remember forever (p23).

9 LIVE MUSIC

Nice hosted the world's first great international jazz festival in 1948 and the tradition continues with a year-round calendar of events held at stunning venues, from medieval chapels to Roman theatres (p48).

10 PARC NATIONAL DU MERCANTOUR

Raptors soar above alpine peaks in the Parc National du Mercantour *(p80)*, where adventurous visitors can ride whitewater rapids and abseil down rugged limestone crags.

FINE SEAFOOD 11

Colourful fishing boats still pootle out to sea from Provence's pretty village harbours, returning with squid, anchovies, grouper and many other fruits of the sea for you to savour at the best quayside restaurants *(p38)*.

GREAT ARTISTS 12

The landscapes and colours of Provence inspired artists like Picasso, Matisse and Cézanne, and turned harbours like Cassis and St-Tropez into havens for creative adventurers *(p36)*.

EXPLORE
PROVENCE

This guide divides Provence into five colour-coded sightseeing areas, as shown on the map below. Find out more about each area on the following pages.

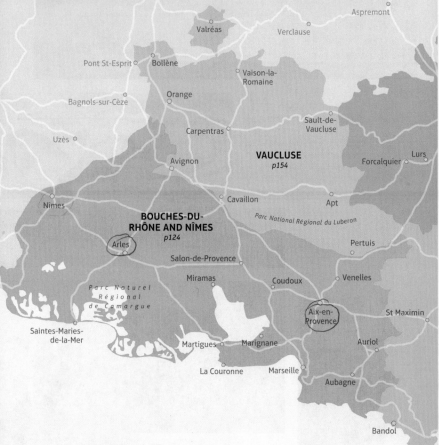

FRANCE

Lalley

Aspremont

Valréas

Verclause

Pont St-Esprit   Bollène

Vaison-la-Romaine

Bagnols-sur-Cèze

Orange

Sault-de-Vaucluse

Uzès

Carpentras

VAUCLUSE
p154

Lurs

Forcalquier

Avignon

Cavaillon

Apt

Nîmes

Parc National Régional du Luberon

BOUCHES-DU-RHÔNE AND NÎMES
p124

Arles

Pertuis

Salon-de-Provence

Miramas

Coudoux

Venelles

Parc Naturel Régional de Camargue

Aix-en-Provence

St Maximin

Saintes-Maries-de-la-Mer

Martigues

Marignane

Auriol

La Couronne

Marseille

Aubagne

Bandol

M e d i t e r r a n e a n
S e a

| 0 kilometres | 25 |
| 0 miles | 25 |

N
↑

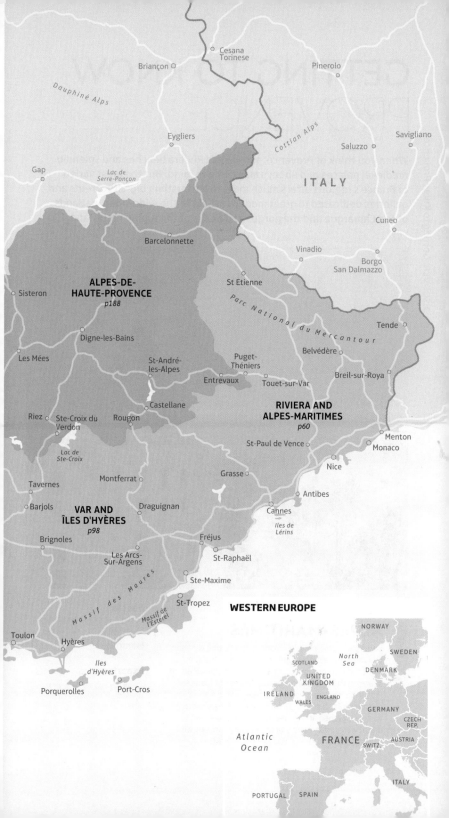

Briançon

Cesana
Torinese

Pinerolo

Dauphiné Alps

Eygliers

Savigliano

Cottian Alps

Saluzzo

ITALY

Gap

*Lac de
Serre-Ponçon*

Barcelonnette

Cuneo

Vinadio

Borgo
San Dalmazzo

St Etienne

Sisteron

**ALPES-DE-
HAUTE-PROVENCE**
p188

Parc National du Mercantour

Tende

Digne-les-Bains

Belvédère

Les Mées

St-André-
les-Alpes

Puget-
Théniers

Breil-sur-Roya

Entrevaux

Touet-sur-Var

Riez

Ste-Croix du
Verdon

Rougon

Castellane

**RIVIERA AND
ALPES-MARITIMES**
p60

Menton

*Lac de
Ste-Croix*

St-Paul de Vence

Monaco

Tavernes

Montferrat

Grasse

Nice

Barjols

**VAR AND
ÎLES D'HYÈRES**
p98

Draguignan

Antibes

Cannes

Brignoles

*Iles de
Lérins*

Les Arcs-
Sur-Argens

Fréjus

St-Raphaël

Ste-Maxime

Massif des Maures

St-Tropez

WESTERN EUROPE

Toulon

Hyères

*Massif de
l'Estérel*

*Iles
d'Hyères*

Porquerolles

Port-Cros

NORWAY

SWEDEN

*North
Sea*

SCOTLAND

DENMARK

UNITED
KINGDOM

IRELAND

ENGLAND

WALES

GERMANY

CZECH
REP.

*Atlantic
Ocean*

FRANCE

SWITZ.

AUSTRIA

ITALY

PORTUGAL

SPAIN

GETTING TO KNOW
PROVENCE

When you think of Provence, sun-kissed Riviera beaches and splendid medieval palaces and abbeys may come to mind. But the most varied of France's regions offers much more, from bustling big-city streets and galleries dedicated to great modern artists to the wide-open wetlands of the Camargue and the gorges and peaks of the Alpine hinterland.

PAGE 60

RIVIERA AND ALPES-MARITIMES

Superyachts in upmarket marinas testify that this is still the world's most glamorous coastline, and the favoured retreat of plutocrats and movie stars. Finding space on the beaches of Cannes, Antibes or Juan-les-Pins in summer can be a challenge. Escape a short distance inland and you'll find breathtakingly pretty villages perched above steep gorges. Plunge deeper into the hinterland and you can explore canyons with soaring eagles and year-round alpine resorts.

Best for
Celebrity-spotting, sunbathing, hiking, skiing

Home to
Nice, Cannes, Monaco

Experience
Hiking through the Vallée des Merveilles in the Parc National du Mercantour

PAGE 98

VAR AND
ÎLES D'HYÈRES

The Var encapsulates all that Provence has to offer in one handy package. Midway along a rugged coastline interspersed with sandy beaches, St-Tropez is the ultimate resort, with smart cafés around its bustling old harbour. Offshore, the Îles d'Hyères offer underwater adventure. Toulon, further west, is Var's big port city, with a lively artists' quarter. Just inland are the thickly wooded slopes of the Massif des Maures, while grand abbeys and vineyards nestle in the foothills of the Haut-Var.

Best for
Market shopping, swimming and snorkelling, wine-tasting

Home to
St-Tropez, Îles d'Hyères, Toulon

Experience
Diving and snorkelling around Île de Port-Cros

→

PAGE 124

BOUCHES-DU-RHÔNE AND NÎMES

The Bouches-du-Rhône is full of contrasts. Flamingos wade and black cattle roam in the wild Camargue wetlands not far from the throbbing streets of Marseille, France's biggest seaport. Reminders of the heyday of the Roman Empire can be seen in Nîmes and at the Pont du Gard nearby. The towns of Arles, Aix-en-Provence, Tarascon and St-Rémy-de-Provence, and the serene Silvacane and Montmajour abbeys, have a rich medieval heritage.

Best for
Sightseeing, beachcombing, city life

Home to
Nîmes, Aix-en-Provence, Marseille, Arles, Camargue

Experience
Seeing flamingos, half-wild white horses and black cattle on a four-wheel-tour of the Camargue wetland

PAGE 154

VAUCLUSE

The lonely summit of Mont Ventoux, inspiration for painters and poets for centuries, looms over the Vaucluse as a challenge to cyclists and hikers. Scattered below its slopes and along the Rhône and Durance rivers are Roman and medieval relics, such as Orange's Théâtre Antique and the Palais des Papes in Avignon. The hilltop ruins of Châteauneuf-du-Pape castle overlook vineyards, while the Abbaye de Sénanque is surrounded by swathes of purple lavender. There are pretty walks in the Dentelles mountains or through orange and crimson canyons in the Luberon.

Best for
Roman and medieval heritage, wine-tasting, shopping for antiques

Home to
Avignon, Villeneuve-les-Avignon, Théâtre Antique d'Orange, Mont Ventoux

Experience
Sampling fine food and wine on a Rhône river cruise

PAGE 188

ALPES-DE HAUTE-PROVENCE

The most peaceful part of Provence is a region of rugged alpine foothills where the upper Durance and the Verdon rivers have carved dramatic deep canyons beneath limestone cliffs, forming an area of exceptional natural beauty. The gentler lowlands around the town of Valensole make up France's biggest lavender-growing area. Mighty fortresses built to guard Provence's eastern frontier loom over strategic mountain passes, and the air is said to be the clearest in all of France.

Best for
Getting away from it all, dramatic scenery, whitewater sports

Home to
Gorges du Verdon

Experience
A day trip on the Train des Pignes from Entrevaux to Digne-les-Bains

←

1 La Maison Carrée.

2 Sculpture of matador Nimeño II at Les Arènes.

3 Jardins de la Fontaine.

4 Raising a glass of rosé at Le Cheval Blanc.

Provence is a treasure trove of things to see and do, and its relatively small size means that you can navigate the region easily. These itineraries will inspire you to make the most of your visit.

1 DAY
In Nîmes

▍ *Morning*

Start the day with a self-guided tour of Les Arènes *(p128)*. Built almost 2,000 years ago, the tiers of seats within this ring of arched walls are still used for concerts and other spectacles. Afterwards, stroll up boulevard Victor Hugo to place de la Maison Carrée to discover the Maison Carrée *(p129)*, said to be the world's best-preserved Roman Temple, and watch a fascinating multimedia presentation, *Nemausus: the birth of Nîmes*, which focuses on the story of the Roman Empire in Provence. Pause for a coffee on place de la Maison Carrée, then cross the square to the gleaming Carré d'Art *(p129)* to glimpse challenging 20th- and 21st-century works of art.

▍ *Afternoon*

For lunch, head for Nîmes's covered market, Les Halles, where Aux Plaisirs des Halles *(4 rue Littré)* offers a fusion menu that combines nouvelle cuisine with traditional favourites like brandade. Then walk through the serenely beautiful Jardins de la Fontaine *(p129)*. The main highlight of this tranquil space is the ruined 2nd-century Temple of Diana. Its white marble columns stand among lawns, greenery and pools and splashing fountains fed by underground springs. The temple was built on a site that was likely a place of worship for Celtic people long before the Roman conquest.

Finish the afternoon by making your way up wooded slopes to the summit of Mont Cavalier. Despite its name, at 114 m (374 ft) high, it's less a mountain, more a low hill, and not a particularly challenging ascent. At the top, the 32-m (105-ft) Tour Magne, the most impressive of a ring of Roman towers that once guarded Nîmes, adds enough altitude for a spectacular sunset view. On the way back, pause for a photograph at the Castellum. Despite its name, this tower built into the Roman ramparts was not a castle; it was the reservoir for water which flowed to Roman Nîmes over the Pont du Gard aqueduct *(p145)*.

▍ *Evening*

Dine at Le Cheval Blanc *(1 place des Arènes)*, where the menu features traditional cuisine and an excellent selection of wines. After dinner, join Nîmois locals at the lively Bar 421 *(37 rue Fresque)* to round off your day in Nîmes with a nightcap and some live music.

←

① Palais des Papes, Avignon.

② River cruise on the Rhône.

③ Painting in the Musée du Petit Palais.

④ Meal at Christian Etienne.

2 DAYS

In Avignon and Villeneuve-lès-Avignon

Day 1

Morning Grab coffee and croissants at one of the cafés on the place du Palais, then head to the Palais des Papes *(p158)* as soon as it opens to avoid the crowds. Take a self-guided audio tour of the serene halls and courtyards, then stroll to the end of the famously curtailed Pont St-Bénézet *(p160)* for a mid-river photo opportunity. Next, walk through the historic centre to the bustling Les Halles *(p159)*. Sip a pre-prandial glass of rosé on place Pie, then take your pick of amazingly fresh seafood at La Cabane d'Oleron *(p160)*, tucked away in a corner of the market hall.

Afternoon Admire masterpieces of early medieval art in the Musée du Petit Palais *(p159)*, then visit the grandiose Cathédrale Notre-Dame-des-Doms *(p160)* before walking through the flower-filled hillside gardens of the Rocher des Doms *(p163)* for a sunset view of Avignon and the mighty river.

Evening Take a dinner cruise on the Rhône to enjoy the sight of the floodlit palace and bridge while savouring traditional dishes and vintages from Châteauneuf-du-Pape *(www.mireio.net)*.

Day 2

Morning Rent a Vélopop bike *(p211)* to ride across Pont Daladier to Villeneuve-lès-Avignon *(p164)*. After no more than 20 minutes of pedalling, your first stop is the Tour Philippe-le-Bel *(p165)*, a formidable landmark that once marked the boundary between the French realm and the Papal territory of Avignon. Climb the 176 steps to the viewing terrace at the top of the tower for an unbeatable panorama. Next, ride through Villeneuve to walk through the lavender-fragrant gardens of the Abbaye de St-André, within the impressive medieval ramparts of Fort St-André *(p164)*.

Afternoon Take a leisurely lunch break in the sunny courtyard at Les Jardins d'Été. Afterwards, visit the Chartreuse du Val-de-Bénédiction *(p164)*. The cool, echoing cloisters and gardens, shaded and scented by cypress trees, are a pleasant place to linger on a hot afternoon before cycling back to Avignon.

Evening Back in town, treat yourselves to dinner at Michelin-starred Christian Etienne *(p160)*. Located in a 12th-century villa overlooking the Palais de Papes, this restaurant serves exquisite tasting menus.

2 WEEKS

A Grand Tour of Provence

▌ Day 1

Arrive on an early flight to Nice and pick up a hire car to make the two-and-a-half-hour drive to Avignon. On your way, stop at the famous Châteauneuf-du-Pape vineyards to stretch your legs with a walk to the ruined papal château, which offers great views of the surrounding countryside.

Make a second stop at Villeneuve-lès-Avignon *(p164)*, grabbing an alfresco lunch at one of the lively cafés on place Jean-Jaures. Wander through the Chartreuse du Val-de-Bénédiction, a vast Carthusian monastery, before taking a short walk to the Tour Philippe-le-Bel. Ascend this majestic medieval tower before crossing the Rhône to your final stop in Avignon.

Treat yourself to a refined meal at Christian Etienne *(p160)*, Avignon's only Michelin-starred restaurant.

▌ Day 2

Explore Avignon – follow the first day of the Avignon itinerary *(p23)*

▌ Day 3

It's a short 40-km (25-mile) morning drive to Arles from Avignon, so stop off en route in Tarascon *(p146)* for coffee and a peek at the gleaming white ramparts of King René's 15th-century Château Royal de Provence *(p146)*. Once in Arles, your first stop must be Les Arènes *(p134)*, the 20,000-seat Roman theatre that is still used for concerts and other spectacles. Then go back to the future at the Luma Foundation *(p136)*, an amazing slice of futuristic 21st-century architecture.

In the afternoon, take a guided tour of the Cryptoportiques *(p134)*, an underground labyrinth carved 20 m (60 ft) beneath the limestone bedrock some 2,000 years ago. Afterwards, wander through Les Alyscamps *(p137)*, a vast necropolis that Romans believed was haunted.

To see Arles after dark as Vincent van Gogh saw it, visit the Place du Forum and the Restaurant-Café Van Gogh *(p137)*, still painted just as it was when it inspired his *Café Terrace at Night* (1888).

1 Food at Christian Etienne.

2 Tour Philippe-le-Bel,
Villeneuve-lès-Avignon.

3 Camargue flamingos.

4 Café in Aix-en-Provence.

5 Miroir Ombrière, Marseille.

Day 4

Set off early to drive down the Rhône on the D35, passing through the seemingly endless reedbeds, lagoons and rice fields of the Camargue fringes. Make time to stop and see stunning flocks of flamingos and other fowl at Étang de Fangassier *(p140)*.

Stop in Aix-en-Provence *(p130)* for lunch. Stroll through the historic centre, with its elegant 17th- and 18th-century townhouses, to visit L'Atelier de Cézanne *(p131)*, preserved exactly as it was when artist Paul Cézanne *(p36)* died in 1906. Enjoy the view of Montagne Ste-Victoire, the imposing summit on the northern horizon that was one of Cézanne's favourite subjects. Afterwards, carry on to Marseille, a 40-km (25-mile) drive that should take no more than 45 minutes on the A51/A55 autoroute, the fastest way through Marseille's vast urban sprawl.

Aim to arrive in Marseille *(p132)* before sunset, then stroll along the Canebière to pick a café where you can sip a glass of pastis, the city's signature apéritif, before dinner.

Day 5

Begin at the Museé des Civilisations de l'Europe et de la Méditerranée *(p132)* to discover works of art from all the shores of the Mediterranean, then head for the Vieux Port for lunch beside Norman Foster's dazzling Miroir Ombrière building.

Hop on a boat to Château d'If for a fun voyage across the bay to a forbidding island prison replete with legends and true histories.

For dinner, sample bouillabaisse, richly flavoured with saffron and garlic, Marseille's ultimate signature dish, at the excellent L'Épuisette *(p38)*.

Day 6

Drive along Les Calanques *(p153)* to Cassis *(p152)*, where you can stop for a morning coffee. Arrive in Toulon for lunch at harbourside Le St Gabriel *(p110)*.

Stroll through the rejuvenated rue des Arts quarter *(p110)*, then hop on the cable car to the summit of Mont Faron *(p111)*.

Dine on old-school favourites like *magret de canard* (duck breast) at Le Bistrot du Boucan *(p110)*. →

Day 7

Catch a morning ferry to the island of Porquerolles *(p112)* to discover a labyrinthine world of contemporary art at Fondation Carmagnac.

Hire a bike in the afternoon to explore the island's hinterland of pine-scented woods and dunes, and take a dip in the sea before catching the return ferry.

Back on the mainland, Le Lavandou *(p120)*, with its lively club and bar scene, is a great place to unwind in the evening.

Day 8

Begin your day by driving round the picturesque D559 coast road towards St-Tropez, a 40-km (25-mile) drive which takes around an hour. Divert through Ramatuelle *(p121)* to the bay of Pampelonne, then tear yourself away from the beach to arrive in St-Tropez for lunch on the place des Lices *(p103)*.

Walk to the Musée de l'Annonciade *(p102)* to admire works by Signac and other 20th-century greats, then ascend to the ramparts of the Citadelle de St-Tropez *(p103)* to admire the spectacular view.

Glam up for a night at one of St-Tropez's legendary nightspots, such as Les Caves du Roy or the Bar du Port *(p102)*.

Day 9

Follow the coast road that loops round the shore of the Gulf of St-Tropez then head east to Fréjus, a journey of 38 km (23 miles) that takes around an hour. Wander through the old town's quiet streets and visit the Arènes de Fréjus.

In the afternoon, relax in the sun at Fréjus-Plage, just outside the old town, where you'll find plenty of café-bars with loungers and parasols on the beach.

Take a sunset stroll round Port-Fréjus before dinner at a waterside restaurant such as L'Amandier *(19 rue Desaugiers; www.restaurant-lamandier.com)*.

Day 10

Rise early to drive to Cannes *(p70)* through the wooded slopes of the Massif de l'Estérel, along a road that follows the line of the ancient Roman Aurelian Way. The journey takes around 30 minutes.

1 Sailboat at Porquerolles.
2 Musée de l'Annonciade.
3 Street food in St-Tropez.
4 Nice's Cathédrale Ste-Réparate.
5 Port Grimaud.
6 Casino de Monté Carlo.

Explore Les Allées de la Liberté for the colourful flower market (p70), then treat yourself to a luxurious lunch on a lounger at a private beach club on La Croisette, such as La Plage du 45 (p71).

Finish the day with a nightcap on the terrace of The Carlton Bar (p71).

Day 11

Take the 40-minute A8 autoroute from Cannes through Antibes to Nice (p64) and stroll through Nice's Italianate Old Town on arrival. Don't miss the Cathédrale Ste-Réparate with its art-filled chapel.

Stroll along the promenade des Anglais and consider lunch and a swim at a casual beach club along the sea front.

Make your way to the summit of the Colline du Château for the best sunset view over the Baie des Anges.

Day 12

Start your second day in Nice by exploring the grand Baroque Palais Lascaris (p69), with its collection of antique musical instruments.

Head for the elegant Cimiez district to discover works by two great artists who lived and worked in Nice at the Musée Matisse (p66) and Musée Chagall (p64).

Enjoy dinner on the cours Saleya, then spoil yourselves with a nightcap in the bar of the iconic Hotel Negresco (p65).

Day 13

Carry on from Nice to Monaco (p72) along the A8 autoroute. Visit the Palais Princier, and watch for the ceremonious changing of the royal guard at 11:55am.

Lunch at a seaside restaurant such as Quai des Artistes (p74), then explore the Jardin Exotique's desert plants.

Dine at Café de Paris (p74), before spending the evening at the belle époque Casino de Monté Carlo (p73).

Day 14

Drive back to Nice along the impressive coast road that runs through Èze (p93), stopping for lunch and one last swim in the sea at Villefranche-sur-Mer (p92) before heading back to Nice airport.

Moustiers-Ste-Marie

Perched on the edge of a deep ravine overlooking the azure expanse of the Lac de Sainte-Croix, the pretty village of Moustiers-Ste-Marie *(p202)* is famous for its distinctive tin-glazed ceramics. Fine examples can be seen in the Musée de la Faïence, and many shops sell perfect reproductions of delicately coloured 17th- and 18th-century works.

←

View over the rooftops of Moustiers-Ste-Marie, a village famous for its ceramics

PROVENCE'S
PICTURESQUE VILLAGES

Each of Provence's glorious villages has its own character and unique history. Settings are distinctive, too, from the rugged crags that turned hilltop villages into strongholds in turbulent times to the fjord-like inlets of Les Calanques.

Les Baux-de-Provence

Located on the fringes of the Camargue and crowned by a ruined 10th-century citadel atop a limestone spur, Les Baux-de-Provence *(p148)* is the most spectacular fortress site in the region, with red-roofed stone houses that descend in tiers beneath the hilltop castle. From its battlements, the Seigneurs de Baux could be lords of all they surveyed, from the rugged Alpille to the reedy flatlands of the Camargue.

↓ The citadel at Les Baux-de-Provence

St-Paul-de-Vence

It's easy to see why great artists like Picasso and Matisse fell in love with St-Paul-de-Vence *(p76)*. Ringed by ramparts that gaze out over the foothills of the Alpes-Maritimes and the Mediterranean coast, this former farming community is an artistic hotbed, and its narrow streets are lined with upmarket galleries and ateliers.

→

Galleries lining one of the narrow medieval streets in arty St-Paul-de-Vence

Bormes-les-Mimosas

Clusters of yellow blossom make Bormes-les-Mimosas *(p120)* dazzlingly colourful in spring. There are splendid panoramic views from the village's medieval château, below which steep alleyways and centuries-old stone houses appear to tumble down the hillside. Almost 100 different species of mimosas can be found here.

←

Blossom-framed view from the castle at Bormes-les-Mimosas

Cassis

With its clear light, vivid blue water and steep limestone cliffs, this delightful fishing port *(p152)* attracted painters such as Dufy, Derain, Matisse and Peploe, as well as amateurs such as Winston Churchill (who taught himself to paint here). The unspoiled rocky coves of Les Calanques *(p153)* are within walking distance, and beaches include the sweeping sandy crescent of Plage de la Grande Mer. The local delicacy is sea urchins, harvested from the rocky shallows around Cassis, and best served with a glass of the village's famous full-bodied white wine.

←

The pretty port of Cassis, overlooked by a 9th-century château

Mont Ventoux

Known as the "Giant of Provence", this lonely 1,912-m (6,242-ft) peak dominates the Provençal countryside for miles around (p174). In winter it is often snow-capped, while on a clear summers day the treeless limestone summit remains a dazzling white against the deep blue sky.

→

Hikers taking in the view at the summit of Mont Ventoux.

PROVENCE'S
NATURAL
WONDERS

Beyond Provence's sun-kissed Mediterranean shores, a dazzling array of landscapes wait to be discovered. Rugged summits loom above limestone canyons, fast-flowing rivers carve their way to the sea, and the Rhône delta creates a watery world unlike any other part of France.

Gorges du Verdon

France's answer to the Grand Canyon cuts a swathe through limestone cliffs that in some places are up to 700 m (2,300 ft) deep, making it a favourite destination for climbers. The thunderous rapids of the Verdon, which flow for some 25 km (16 miles) through the gorge, are also a big draw for watersports enthusiasts (p192).

→

Panoramic view over the vast Gorges du Verdon

Camargue Lagoons

A unique expanse of wetlands between the channels of the Petit Rhône to the west and the Grand Rhône to the east, the Camargue *(p138)* is home to a dazzling array of wildlife. Flocks of greater flamingos, European beavers, wild boars and migrating and resident birds roam its numerous marshes and reed-beds, while modern-day cowboys (called *gardians*) herd its distinctive half-wild white horses and bulls.

$\rightarrow$

Horses and flamingos in the the Camargue

Îles d'Hyères

Underwater exploration is the big attraction at Port-Cros, one of three tiny but adventure-packed isles just off the Var coast, where rich marine life throngs the rocky seabed of France's first marine national park. On land, the natural forested habitat of Port-Cros and its neighbour Porquerolles is also protected as a national park *(p112)*.

$\leftarrow$

Tranquil sea view from one of the beaches on Port-Cros

$\uparrow$ The snow-capped peaks of the Parc National du Mercantour

Parc National du Mercantour

Vultures and eagles soar above the bare summits and wooded lower slopes of the Parc National du Mercantour *(p80)*, where chamois, ibex and mouflon roam. Some peaks rise to heights of more than 2,000 m (6,500 ft). Beech, maple and sweet chestnut trees cloak the lower valleys, and tall conifers grow at higher altitudes.

Les Calanques, Bouches-du-Rhône

Nestled between Marseille and Cassis, Les Calanques *(p153)* are narrow inlets of turquoise water sheltered by chalk-white cliffs. Often only accessible via boat or on foot, these bijou bays are nonetheless highly popular in Provence. The craggy cliffs are also favoured with climbers, who can often be seen clambering up the rocks.

←

Visitors relax on the picturesque Calanque d'en Vau, near Cassis

PROVENCE FOR
BEACH LOVERS

Those who like the feeling of sand between their toes are spoiled for choice in Provence. You'll pay a hefty premium to be pampered in the private beach clubs around Cannes, St-Tropez, or Antibes, but you don't have to look far to find stunning coves and bays where there's no entry charge.

Îles d'Hyères, Var

Island beaches always feel special, and those on the Îles d'Hyères *(p112)* are no exception. With its pure white sand and azure sea, Plage de Notre-Dame on Porquerolles would not look out of place on Caribbean shores.

→

Steps leading to Plage de Notre-Dame on the island of Porquerolles

Lac de Sainte-Croix, Alpes-de-Haute-Provence

Not all of Provence's best stretches of sand are on the Mediterranean seafront. The man-made Lac de Sainte-Croix *(p193)* has a plethora of family-friendly freshwater beaches that are pleasantly free of marine pests like jellyfish, and offer an array of activities from kayaking to water-skiing.

$\rightarrow$

Golden sandy beaches lining the man-made Lac de Sainte-Croix

Baie de Pampelonne, Var

The beach clubs scattered along Pampelonne, a 5-km (3-mile) crescent of perfect, powdery white sand south of St-Tropez *(p103)*, have been bywords for glitz and glamour for more than half a century.

$\leftarrow$

One of the many luxury beach clubs located on the Baie de Pampelonne

> ⊙ PICTURE PERFECT
> **Deserted Beach**
>
> Walk east from Stes-Maries-de-la-Mer and keep going for the perfect sunset shot of one of the last deserted beaches in Provence, Plage Est.

Camargue, Bouches-du-Rhône

Rainbow-coloured kites swoop over the seemingly endless miles of white sand that stretch eastward from the family-friendly resort of Stes-Maries-de-la-Mer to Plage de Beauduc *(p138)*. This, the emptiest part of coastline in Provence, is adored by beachcombers and naturists. For stunningly beautiful sand dunes, head further along the strip to Plage Piémanson.

Sand dune in Stes-Maries-de-la-Mer, Camargue's capital $\uparrow$

Pont du Gard

This triumph of Roman engineering *(p145)*, with its triple tier of arches made of unmortared limestone blocks, was the tallest aqueduct in the whole of the Roman Empire and carried 20 million litres (5 million gallons) of water every single day from Fontaine d'Eure, just outside Uzès, to Nîmes. Wonderfully preserved, it was added to UNESCO's list of World Heritage Sites in 1985.

→

The colossal 1st-century AD Pont du Gard, with its three tiers of arches

PROVENCE FOR
ROMAN ARCHITECTURE

Provence's portfolio of Roman relics almost outdoes Rome itself. In vast, echoing amphitheatres you can imagine gladiators locked in mortal combat and cheered on by crowds of thousands. Triumphal arches celebrate the Roman Empire's power and glory, and aqueducts, bridges and civic buildings are testament to the genius of Rome's great engineers.

Les Arènes, Nîmes

With its ring of tall, multi-arched walls, the Roman amphitheatre in Nîmes *(p128)* is one of France's most spectacular and best-preserved Roman relics. Built in the 1st century AD, it was used for gladiatorial combat until the collapse of the Roman Empire. Today, it hosts dramatic spectacles such as the Festival of Nîmes.

←

The exterior of the impressive Roman amphitheatre in Nîmes, seen from above

Detail of the ruined ↑
La Trophée d'Auguste

 **TOP
3 FURTHER
ROMAN SITES**

**Théatre Antique,
Orange**
The semi-circular
multi-tiered Théatre
Antique *(p168)* once
seated 7,000 people.

Maison Carrée, Nîmes
Built in the 2nd century,
this is arguably the
world's best preserved
Roman temple *(p129)*.

**Site Archéologique
de Glanum**
A triumphal arch dating
from 10 BC to celebrate
Julius Caesar's victories
is the high point of the
Roman site at Glanum,
where a series of
dramatic memorials
line the roadside *(p147)*.

La Trophée d'Auguste

The white columns of the Trophée
d'Auguste *(p94)* can be seen from miles
around, marking the ancient border
between Italy and Roman Gaul. Built in
the 6th century BC the 50-m (164-ft)
rotunda was partially destroyed
after Rome's fall.

↑ La Trophée
d'Auguste,
looming over
the town of
La Turbie

Yves Klein

Blue is the colour that defines the work of Yves Klein (1928–62). For most of his career, Nice-born Klein concentrated on "monochrome art" using a unique blue pigment of his own invention, now recognized in the art world as International Klein Blue.

Yves Klein's striking *Le Buffle* (1960–61) ↑

Paul Cézanne

Cézanne (1839–1906) spent most of his life in his native Aix-en-Provence. The surrounding landscapes inspired many of his most famous works, which would prove hugely influential for 20th-century art.

→

Cézanne's *Still Life with Apples and a Pot of Primroses* (1890)

PROVENCE FOR
AMAZING ART

Provence's sun-soaked, colour-saturated landscapes and warm climate inspired masters of the avant-garde from Bonnard, Pissaro, Signac and Cézanne in the 19th century to 20th-century titans like Picasso, Chagall, Matisse and Klein.

Paul Signac

Signac (1863–1935) discovered St-Tropez long before the jet set. Along with a group of other artists, many of whom stayed with him in St-Tropez, he developed a unique painting technique that would come to be known as Pointellism.

→

Signac's Pointellist masterpiece *Place des Lices, St-Tropez* (1893)

Marc Chagall

Provence's dazzling colours provided new inspiration for Chagall (1887–1985), who settled in St-Paul-de-Vence in 1949. His work draws on his Russian-Jewish heritage.

Chagall's *Field of Mars* (1954), painted in the artist's studio in St-Paul-de-Vence

TOP 3 WORKS OF ART IN PROVENCE

Nu Blue IV, Matisse
Created in 1952, the most instantly recognizable of Matisse's famous "cut-outs" can be seen in the Musée Matisse in Nice *(p66)*.

La Joie De Vivre, Picasso
Pablo Picasso (1881–1973) portrays himself as a flute-playing centaur in this 1946 painting in the Musée Nationale Picasso, Antibes *(p88)*.

L'Été, Bonnard
This glowing landscape by Pierre Bonnard (1867–1947), is a jewel in the crown of the Fondation Maeght in St-Paul-de-Vence *(p78)*.

Vincent Van Gogh

The exotic culture and landscapes of Provence drove the Dutch genius Vincent van Gogh (1853–90) to create his greatest works during the time he spent in Arles and St-Rémy-de-Provence between 1888 and 1889.

Van Gogh's evocative *Wheat Field with Cypresses* (1889)

Taste of the Sea

Bouillabaisse, Provence's famous fish stew, tops the menu at the region's seafood restaurants. Other items on the menu include shellfish such as mussels and *violets* (sea figs), and fish such as *loup* (sea bass) and sea bream served grilled with herbs.

Top seafood eateries: L'Épuisette *(156 rue du Vallon des Auffes, Marseille)* and L'Oustau de la Mar *(20 quai des Baux, Cassis)*

←

Fresh oysters for sale in a restaurant in Cannes

PROVENCE FOR
FOODIES

From fine-dining establishments in glamorous resorts to authentic family-run village bistros, Provence's chefs produce mouth-watering menus using fresh produce sourced from the region's sun-kissed plains, Alpine pastures, Camargue rice-fields and Mediterranean fisheries.

Dine Like a Local

Locals favour the family-run Provençal bistro for lunch or dinner. You'll find one on any village square or marketplace. The menu is usually simple, with dishes such as steak and moules-frites, and local wines often served by the glass or *pichet* (small carafe).

Superb local bistros: Bistro du Cours *(13 cours Julien, Marseille)* and Le Bistrot d'Antoine *(27 rue de la Préfecture, Nice)*

↑ Chef Mauro Colagreco at the Michelin-starred restaurant Le Mirazur in Menton

TOP 5 TRADITIONAL DISHES

Bouillabaisse
Fish stew containing a dozen types of fish and seafood, always including *rascasse* (scorpion fish).

Boeuf à la Gardiane
Bull's meat stew from Camargue, served with lashings of nutty red Camargue rice.

Brandade de Morue
This purée of salt cod, cream, potatoes and olive oil is a real Nîmes speciality.

Pissaladière
Nice's take on the pizza is very heavy on the anchovies.

Saucisson d'Arles
Salami-style sausage, traditionally made from donkey meat but now usually from pork.

Fine Dining

A hushed, reverent atmosphere prevails in Provence's finest temples of gastronomy. The region boasts a galaxy of fine-dining restaurants in plutocratic playgrounds such as Cannes, Antibes and Monaco, and in the Provençal hinterland.
Best fine-dining spots: Christian Etienne *(see p160)* and Christophe Bacquié *(Hôtel du Castellet, Le Castellet)*

Market Restaurants

Lunch with the locals at a covered produce market such as Les Halles in Avignon *(p159)* is a real treat. The food comes from stalls piled high with local produce, and you'll find restaurants specializing in fresh seasonal ingredients.
Excellent market restaurants: Jon Chiri *(Cuisine Centr'Halles, Avignon)* and Les Tapas de la Major *(Halles de la Major, Marseille)*

↑ Fresh Provençal tomatoes on display at a market stall in Avignon

← Locals dining alfresco at a bistro restaurant in Forcalquier

Did You Know?

To see the full range of local produce it's best to arrive at markets early in the morning.

Châteauneuf-du-Pape

Medieval pontiffs founded the Côtes-du-Rhône vineyards that still produce Provence's best-known red wine. Today, the region's dry, rocky and sun-soaked soils produce 110,000 hectolitres (2.5 million gallons) of the renowned Châteauneuf-du-Pape each year, which is more wine than the entire North Rhône region produces. This heady, intense wine goes best with robust meat dishes (particularly red meat), but can also complement spicier dishes, depending on the blend.

$\rightarrow$

Châteauneuf-du-Pape, bottled sunshine from Côtes-du-Rhône

PROVENCE'S
DIVINE WINES

Stone-dry rosé, best served chilled on a hot day, is the signature wine of the Provençal summer. But Provence's multifarious microclimates also nurture vines that yield muscular reds, delicious dessert wines, and unique vintages from sandy soils.

Beaumes de Venise

The hot sun and arid soils beneath the Dentelles de Montmirail nurture sugar-rich muscat grapes that are fermented into *vins doux naturels* (naturally sweet wines). They can be drunk chilled as an apéritif, or enjoyed as a dessert wine.

$\leftarrow$

Vineyard at sunset in the village of Crestet in the Dentelles de Montmirail

↑ Sommelier pouring Gris de Gris wine from the Camargue

Vins des Sables

Unique to Provence, the Grenache vines that grow on the sandy fringes of the Camargue produce wines such as Gris de Gris that are prized for their steely-pink glint and a bouquet that perfectly complements local seafood.

← A Vin de Sable wine from the Camargue

GRAPE VARIETIES OF PROVENCE

Grapes such as Cabernet-Sauvignon, Syrah, Grenache and Cinsault are all integral to the divine wines of Provence. But alongside these stalwarts of the winemaker's trade are several less well-known varieties like Rolle (perhaps better known as Vermentino) and Tibouren, which imparts an intense, distinctive, almost herbal aroma to the rosé wines of Côtes de Provence.

Côtes de Provence

The vineyards of Côtes de Provence stretch from the rocky, wooded slopes of the Haut Var all the way to the Mediterranean coast. Dry rosé wines made from Grenache and Cinsault grapes predominate.

↑ Juicy Grenache grapes hanging from vines in Provence

Marché les Halles, Avignon

The façade of Avignon's covered market (p159) is an artificial cliff covered with greenery. Within this mecca for foodies, more than 40 stalls display fine fresh produce, cheeses, sausages and shimmering seafood.

→

Vertical Garden by Patrick Blanc, on the exterior of Avignon's Marché les Halles

PROVENCE FOR
MAGICAL MARKETS

A rainbow of colours and a plethora of aromas greet shoppers at markets which – especially on Saturdays – are the social hub of local communities. Stalls are piled high with fresh garden produce, cheese and charcuterie.

Place des Lices, St Tropez

This market square, immortalized by Charles Camoin in his 1925 painting *Place des Lices*, still has some of the atmosphere that the artist captured in his work. Locals shop here on Tuesdays and Saturdays for pastries and fresh fruit and vegetables. Visitors can browse for vintage clothes, accessories, artisan-made pottery and other hand-made arts and crafts.

→

Stalls selling vintage items and crafts on place des Lices

L'Isle-sur-la-Sorgue

Every Saturday morning, the riverside streets of Provence's antiques capital *(p181)* become one huge market, with items spilling onto the road. Dozens of dealers display collectables ranging from prints, paintings and stamps to jewellery, furniture and vintage weaponry. The international antiques fairs, in particular, attract huge numbers of connoisseurs every Easter and in mid-August.

→

Vintage film cameras for sale at the market in L'Isle-sur-la-Sorgue

Marché Forville, Cannes

Canny residents of Cannes shop here from Tuesday to Saturday for the freshest regional produce. Visitors can pick up a range of Provençal treats to take home, from *anchoïade* (anchovy paste) to lavender-tinged honey. On Mondays, the market sells an eclectic range of antiques and bric-a-brac.

←

Bric-a-brac and antique items for sale at Marché Forville

Cours Saleya, Nice

The most photogenic market in Provence, Nice's quayside Cours Saleya flower market explodes with colour and floral scents every morning except on Mondays, when the square is given over to antique and bric-a-brac stalls. Nice has a strong history of flower markets and was the first city to open a wholesale cut flower market back in 1897. Food produce from local farms is also sold at Cours Saleya, but the spectacular flowers steal the limelight.

→

Fragrant peonies on sale at a flower stall in Cours Saleya

Meet Denizens of the Deep at Musée Océanographique

The mission of this museum in Monaco *(p72)* is to raise awareness of the plight of the oceans. The life-size model of a giant squid is bound to impress, and there are charming smaller marine monsters like leafy sea-dragons in the aquarium *(www.oceano.mc)*.

💬 INSIDER TIP
Mini-Trains

Almost every town in Provence has a hop-on, hop-off "mini-train" that slowly weaves around all the key sites. These are a great way to explore without tiring little legs. Some offer audio tours as well. Cheap tickets can be usually be purchased at a stall near the train stop or from the tourist office.

PROVENCE FOR
FAMILIES

Families with children of all ages, from toddlers to teens, are spoiled for choice in Provence. Activities range from rollercoasters to sailing, and for those rare rainy days there are plenty of all-weather attractions, too.

Riding Roller Coasters at Parc Spirou

Loveable cartoon bellboy Spirou stars at this theme park at Monteux, near Avignon *(p158)*, where children can ride thrilling rollercoasters, drop towers and swing carousels, or meet other characters like laid-back cowboy Lucky Luke and bouncy leopard Marsupilami, in person. The immersive comic-book inspired park only opened in June 2018 but has quickly become a favourite for families visiting the area *(www.parc-spirou.com)*.

→

Thrillseekers enjoying the Spirou Racing roller coaster in Parc Spirou

↑ Visitors admiring the aquarium in Musée Oceanographique

Ride a Carousel in Avignon

The pretty painted ponies of the traditional carousel in Avignon's historic square, place de l'Horloge *(p158)*, will delight small children. The square marks the lively heart of the city and is also home to a wide range of open-air eateries.

←

Traditionally painted carousel horses in Place de l'Horloge

Learn to Sail and Canoe at Lac de Sainte-Croix

The lifeguards and sheltered blue waters at Lac de Sainte-Croix's beaches make this inland sea *(p193)* the perfect place for younger family members to learn to sail, pedalo or canoe. Older children can also try their hand at windsurfing.

Families learning to pedalo on the waters of Lac de Sainte-Croix ↑

Ride Rapids in the Gorges du Verdon

The old city of Castellane is the gateway to Provence's grand canyon *(p192)*, where adventurers can ride inflatable rafts, canoes and kayaks along miles of thrilling turbulent white water in the deepest gorge in France. While travelling through the Gorges du Verdon, look out for the vultures, eagles and other birds of prey that inhabit the area.

→

Kayaks and rafts on the Gorges du Verdon

PROVENCE FOR
ADVENTURERS

Provence's rushing rivers, rugged cliffs, and even its clear blue skies offer thrill-seekers a supremely varied choice of adventures all year round. A plethora of specialist agencies based all over the region provide exciting experiences for novices and experts alike.

Climb the Via Ferrata in the Alpes-Maritimes

Metal ladders bolted to sheer cliffs near St-Martin-Vesubie *(p80)* allow novices with a good head for heights to safely ascend precipices that otherwise only expert rock climbers dare to scale. The famous climbing area offers a range of graded routes to suit all abilities. The views from the rocky walls and the swinging bridges are spectacular, with meadows and beautiful lakes to be discovered at the summits.

←

A climber walking across a bridge above the Château Queyras Gorge du Guil

TOP 4 **AERIAL SPORTS IN PROVENCE**

Hot-Air Balloons
🔲 france-balloons.com
Float over Luberon's lavender fields from Forcalquier (p199).

Skydiving
🔲 skydivecenter.fr
Take off from Gap-Tallard in Alpes-de-Haute-Provence.

Hang-Gliding and Paragliding
🔲 aerogliss.com
Soar above the Lac de Castillon from St-André-les-Alpes (p203).

Microlighting
📞 06 62 20 96 82
Take a microlight ride at St-Maximin-la-Ste-Baume (p106).

Slide and Scramble in the Parc National du Mercantour

The craggy Parc National du Mercantour (p80) is one of the birthplaces of the exhilarating sport of canyoning, which involves abseiling and jumping down rocky water-courses. The vertical cliffs here offer challenging rock-climbing routes.

→

Hikers on an alpine trail in the Parc National du Mercantour

Jump Over the Gorges du Verdon

A bungee jump from the Pont d'Artuby is guaranteed to set your pulse racing. Said to be the highest bridge in Europe, only the brave dare to leap 182 m (600 ft) over the plunging Gorges du Verdon (p192).

→

The imposing Pont d'Artuby, a popular bungee-jumping site over the Gorges du Verdon

Chorégies d'Orange

Lovers of opera and classical music flock to Orange each summer for this world-famous celebration of opera and classical music. Big screens display images of performers to complement the amazing acoustics provided by Orange's 2,000-year-old Théâtre Antique *(p168)*. Dating from 1860, this is France's oldest music festival, and it has gained an international following.

$\longrightarrow$

Opera performance of *Lucia di Lammermoor* at the Chorégies d'Orange

PROVENCE FOR
MUSIC
FESTIVALS

Gypsy guitars and violins, hot jazz and cool blues, opera performances and classical music: you'll find all this and more at Provence's many music festivals. All year round, venues from Roman theatres to intimate bars and clubs host performances to cater for all tastes.

Fêtes Latino-Mexicaines

The alpine slopes around Barcelonnette *(p196)* are alive with the sound of mariachi music for one week in August. It's an odd setting for a foot-stamping fiesta, but the region's links with Mexico go back to the 19th century, when locals who migrated to South America brought home a love of Latin-American rhythms.

$\longleftarrow$

Dancing to the sound of mariachi music at the Fêtes Latino-Mexicaines

Le Pèlerinage des Gitans

Flamenco guitars and Hungarian accordion music provide the soundtrack for this unique gathering of thousands of pilgrims from the Gitan, Rom and Manouche communities in Stes-Maries-de-la-Mer in May *(p138)*.

→

Guitarist performing at Le Pèlerinage des Gitans in Stes-Maries-de-la-Mer

Jazz in Arles

For free gigs and street performances, plus big-ticket events starring some of jazz's biggest names, head to Arles *(p134)* for this ten-day event which takes place in mid-May. The 17th-century Chapelle du Méjan is the event's main hub, but there are smaller gigs performed throughout the city.

←

Street performance during Arles's annual jazz festival in May

Nice Jazz Festival

There's something for everyone at the world's longest-established jazz festival in Nice in July *(p65)*, which was first headlined by Louis Armstrong and His All Stars in 1948. Jazz purists head for the open-air Théâtre de Verdure, while the stage on place Masséna hosts acts spanning rock, pop, soul, funk and world music. During the festival and all year round you can catch an excellent range of gigs and some superb late-night jam sessions at ever-popular local jazz bars like Shapko *(5 rue Rossetti)* and Le Jam Bar *(10 rue du Commandant Raffali)*.

→

Jon Batiste and Stay Human performing in the Théâtre de Verdure at the Nice Jazz Festival

Lavender and Sunflower Fields

Make for Vaucluse *(p154)* from June to August for shots of sunflower and lavender fields. Sunflowers face the sun, so aim to photograph them in early morning light. Sault and Valréas are some of the best spots to snap lavender fields.

←

Rows of luminous lavender photographed at Sault in Vaucluse

PROVENCE FOR
PHOTOGRAPHERS

Purple lavender fields, golden sunflower prairies and rugged limestone crags make Provence's hinterland a magnet for photographers, while village markets are rich environments for snappers looking for shots of local life. In smaller coastal towns and villages, the focus is on colourful fishing boats in picturesque harbours, while the region's medieval abbeys and châteaux make imposing subjects for shots that sum up Provence's rich history.

WILDLIFE PHOTOGRAPHY

Keen birders looking for perfect shots of Camargue bird life can set up their tripods in hides connected by walkways among the lagoons of the Parc Ornithologique du Pont-de-Gau *(p138)*. Storks nest on the roof of the park headquarters, and stilts, avocets and a dozen other species wade with flamingos in the shallows. Spring and autumn, when flocks of migrant waterfowl pass through, are the best times to visit

Luberon's Ochre Quarries

Friends back home will think you've been to Mars when you show them your snaps of Le Colorado Provençal *(p176)*. Visit in late afternoon, when the sun brings out the red and orange glow of these weird man-made canyons around Roussillon and Rustel most vividly.

→

Vivid colours of the ochre quarry in Roussillon

Picturesque Harbours

Looking for a postcard-pretty shot of brightly painted fishing boats? Steer clear of bigger commercial harbours and marinas filled with gleaming yachts, and instead seek out bijou villages like Cassis *(p152)*, Stes-Maries-de-La-Mer *(p138)* and Port-Cros *(p112)*, where traditional pastel-coloured quayside houses make an attractive backdrop to images of tiny fishing vessels bobbing up and down in turquoise water.

←

The rustic harbour in the small town of Martigues

Avignon Icons

For an uncluttered silhouette of Avignon's historic skyline and the Palais des Papes, take your longest lens across the Rhône to Ile Barthelasse and the riverside promenade du Chemin de Halage. From here, you can capture great shots of the palace, the famed Pont St Bénézet and the gold Madonna atop the cathedral *(p160)*.

→

The famously truncated Pont St Bénézet in the historic city of Avignon

↑ Citrus fruits for sale at the Marché les Halles in Avignon

Open-Air Markets

Rise and shine on Saturday or Sunday mornings for the evocative images that late-rising visitors miss. Market traders set up their stalls at daybreak as if to tempt photographers to focus on pristine pyramids of scarlet tomatoes and piles of glossy purple aubergines. Crowds of hungry local buyers soon descend, and by midday most of the stalls are empty.

A YEAR IN
PROVENCE

JANUARY

△ **Rallye Monte-Carlo** (*late Jan*). Monaco's high-performance cars hurtle through its streets.
Truffle Festival (*last Sun in Jan*). Provence's prized "black gold" is auctioned and tasted at Avignon's Les Halles marketplace.

FEBRUARY

△ **Carnaval Fête du Citron** (*last fortnight in Feb*). Floats spectacularly decorated with heaps of Menton's favourite citrus fruits are celebrated and marched around town.
Fête du Mimosa (*third Sun in Feb*). Village perché Bormes-les-Mimosas celebrates the region's signature spring blossoms.

MAY

Fête des Gardians (*1 May*). Colourfully costumed Camarguais cowboys (*gardians*) prance through the streets of Arles.
△ **Festival International du Film** (*two weeks in May*). Cannes is packed with paparazzi, stars, producers and directors for the movie business's most prestigious festival.

JUNE

△ **Fêtes de la Tarasque** (*last weekend in Jun*). An effigy of a legendary monster is paraded through Tarascon.
Festival Estival de Musique (*Jun–Jul*). Classical musicians perform at various open-air venues around Toulon.

SEPTEMBER

△ **Fête du Vent** (*mid-Sep*). Rainbow-coloured kites perform breathtaking aerobatics in the skies above Plages du Prado in Marseille.
Jazz dans les Vignes (*Sep–Dec*). Jazz musicians perform in vineyards and villages around Sérignan every weekend from mid-September until December.

OCTOBER

△ **Fête de Sainte Marie Salomé** (*Sun nearest 22 Oct*). In Stes-Maries-de-la-Mer, Romanies gather to pay their respects to Saints Mary Salome and Mary Jacobe. A procession ends in the ritual blessing of the sea.

MARCH

△ **Paris to Nice "Race to the Sun"** *(eight days in early Mar)*. The final leg of the year's first major international cycling race.

APRIL

△ **Feria de Paques** *(Easter)*. Arletans in traditional costume dance the farandole to the accompaniment of tambourin drum and galoubet flute.

Plantes Rares et Jardin Naturel *(last weekend in Apr)*. A delight for gardeners and flower lovers, Sérignan hosts dozens of stalls, guided walks through local gardens and nurseries, exhibitions and workshop sessions.

JULY

△ **Chorégies d'Orange** *(all month)*. Long-established season of opera, classical and choral music in Orange's acoustically perfect Roman theatre.

Festival d'Avignon *(mid–late Jul)*. Avignon hosts France's largest arts festival, with performances in historic venues like the courtyard of the Palais des Papes.

AUGUST

△ **Véraison Festival** *(early Aug)*. Actors in medieval costume bring the past to life with a weekend of music, dancing, jousting and wine in Châteauneuf-du-Pape.

Fête du Jasmin *(first weekend in Aug)*. Floral floats, music and dancing in Grasse.

NOVEMBER

Millévin *(mid-Nov)*. The fabulous vintages of Côtes du Rhône are celebrated in and around Avignon.

△ **Festival International de la Danse** *(biennial, late Nov or early Dec)*. International stars of classical ballet and contemporary dance perform in Cannes.

DECEMBER

△ **Foire aux Santons** *(all month)*. The colourful clay figurines that are an integral part of Christmas in Provence are celebrated and sold in the region's largest pre-Christmas festival in Marseille.

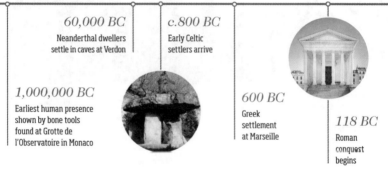

A BRIEF
HISTORY

The great drama of Provence's past stretches from some of the earliest human settlements in Europe to the glitz and glamour of the swinging Sixties and beyond. Celts, Greeks, Romans, Franks, medieval princes and pontiffs have all left their imprint on the region's cities and countryside.

From Stone Age to the Greeks

Rock carvings, fragments of cave paintings and remains of primitive settlements suggest that Provence was inhabited a million years ago by early hunter-gatherers. Nomadic tribes roamed the land for centuries, notably the Celts from the north and the Ligurians from the east. Not until the arrival of the Greeks did trade flourish in a more structured way.

The Roman Empire

Rome conquered Provence in 118 BC, turning it into a prosperous region with flourishing towns like Arles, Nîmes and Orange, as

1 Map of Provence dating to the 1600s.

2 Early horse painting, Cosquer Cave.

3 Detail from a relief sculpture on a Roman arch, Glanum.

4 Medieval engraving of Charles the Bald.

Timeline of events

60,000 BC
Neanderthal dwellers settle in caves at Verdon

c.800 BC
Early Celtic settlers arrive

1,000,000 BC
Earliest human presence shown by bone tools found at Grotte de l'Observatoire in Monaco

600 BC
Greek settlement at Marseille

118 BC
Roman conquest begins

well as imposing monuments like the Trophée d'Auguste *(p94)* and the Pont du Gard *(p145)*. Christ's followers are reputed to have brought Christianity to the region when they landed at Stes-Maries-de-la-Mer in AD 40.

Medieval Provence

With the fall of the Roman Empire, stability and relative prosperity began to disappear. Although Provence became part of the Holy Roman Empire, local counts retained autonomy and towns became fiercely independent. People withdrew to the hilltops to protect themselves from a series of invaders, most notably the Saracens, who were finally expelled in AD 974.

Papal Avignon

When the papacy temporarily abandoned war-torn Italy, Avignon became the centre of the Roman Catholic world. From 1309 until 1377 seven French popes ruled unchallenged. When a new Italian pope, Urban VI, was elected, the French cardinals rebelled. In 1378, they chose a rival pope, Clement VII, thus causing a major schism that lasted until 1403.

↑ Second seal (or emblem) of Raymond VII (1197–1249) who was known as the Count of Toulouse, Duke of Narbonne and Marquis of Provence, from 1222 until his death

536
Provence ceded to the Franks by King Theodahad

1032
Provence becomes part of Holy Roman Empire

1309
Pope Clement V moves Papacy to Avignon

AD 476
Final collapse of the Roman Empire

974
Saracens driven from Provence by William I

War and Peace

Provence became fully part of France with the death of its last Count, René the Good, in 1480. It was thus drawn into 16th-century wars between France and the Hapsburg Empire, and into the Wars of Religion between "heretic" Protestants and Catholics, which resulted in a wave of massacres and the wholesale destruction of churches and their contents. For ordinary Provençal men and women, the next two centuries were relatively peaceful, interrupted by brief skirmishes with England and Savoy.

Revolution, Republic and Empire

Provençal peasants pillaged châteaux and monasteries during the Revolution of 1789. British forces were driven from Toulon in 1793 by the brilliant young Napoléon Bonaparte, who was to visit Provence again in 1815 at the beginning of his last desperate bid to recover his empire. In the less turbulent 19th century, the warm winter climate of the Riviera began to attract foreign visitors and artists. The first railways from Paris opened in the 1850s, and grand hotels and villas started to be built.

↑ 1920s advertisement poster of the Côte d'Azur Pullman-Express.

Timeline of events

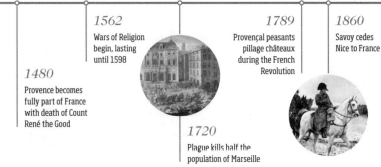

1480
Provence becomes fully part of France with death of Count René the Good

1562
Wars of Religion begin, lasting until 1598

1720
Plague kills half the population of Marseille

1789
Provençal peasants pillage châteaux during the French Revolution

1860
Savoy cedes Nice to France

The Glamorous 1920s

Provence was far from the front lines of World War I, and when peace came the Riviera boomed, attracting bright young things and literary stars like F Scott Fitzgerald and Noel Coward. The party ended with World War II (except for those who collaborated with the occupiers, like the designer Coco Chanel). From 1942 Provence was occupied by the Germans. Liberation began when US and Free French troops landed near St-Tropez in June 1944.

Post-War Provence

After the war, holidaymakers drawn by Provence's summer sun arrived in droves. The first Cannes Film Festival was held in 1946, and film stars and musicians made the Riviera one of the most glamorous places in the world. Expanded airports and high-speed train lines have made Provence even more accessible to sun-worshippers in the 21st century, and the superyachts of billionaires and film stars continue to dock in its marinas. However, the region's environment has suffered from over-development, and new challenges, including racial and political tension, must be faced.

1 René d'Anjou, King of Naples. ↑

2 Painting of the Battle of Toulon.

3 The walk down Cannes Croisette.

4 Yacht at the Monaco Yacht Show, 2015.

Did You Know?
—
Marseille volunteers supported the Republic in Paris in 1792. Their song, *La Marseillaise*, is the national anthem.

1946
First Cannes Film Festival held

1970
Autoroute du Soleil between Paris and Provence completed

1942–44
Germans occupy southern France

2001
TGV Méditerranée link with Paris launched

2019
Nice's second Tramway route opens between port and airport

EXPERIENCE

RIVIERA AND ALPES-MARITIMES

The French Riviera is, without doubt, the most celebrated seaside in Europe. Just about everybody who has been anybody for the past 100 years has succumbed to its glittering allure. This is the holiday playground of kings and courtesans, movie stars and millionaires, where the seriously rich never stand out in the crowd.

But the Riviera is not just a millionaire's watering hole: a diversity of talent has visited, seeking patrons and taking advantage of the luminous Mediterranean light. This coast is irrevocably linked with the life and works of Matisse, Picasso, Chagall, Cocteau and Renoir. It lent them the scenery of its shores and the rich environment of hill villages like St-Paul de Vence. This village has echoed to the voices of such luminaries as Bonnard and Modigliani, F Scott Fitzgerald and Greta Garbo. Today, its galleries still spill canvases on to its medieval lanes.

The Alpes-Maritimes, which incorporates the principality of Monaco, is renowned for its temperate winter climate. The abundance of flowers here attracted the perfume industry and the English – who created some of the finest gardens on the coast. Inland, the mountainous areas of Provence offer a range of skiing activities in superb mountain scenery, and a chance to try traditional Alpine food.

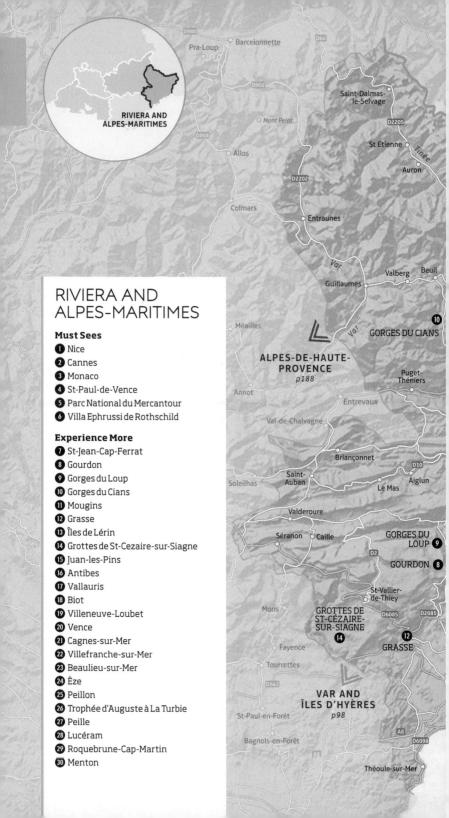

RIVIERA AND ALPES-MARITIMES

Must Sees
1 Nice
2 Cannes
3 Monaco
4 St-Paul-de-Vence
5 Parc National du Mercantour
6 Villa Ephrussi de Rothschild

Experience More
7 St-Jean-Cap-Ferrat
8 Gourdon
9 Gorges du Loup
10 Gorges du Cians
11 Mougins
12 Grasse
13 Îles de Lérin
14 Grottes de St-Cezaire-sur-Siagne
15 Juan-les-Pins
16 Antibes
17 Vallauris
18 Biot
19 Villeneuve-Loubet
20 Vence
21 Cagnes-sur-Mer
22 Villefranche-sur-Mer
23 Beaulieu-sur-Mer
24 Èze
25 Peillon
26 Trophée d'Auguste à La Turbie
27 Peille
28 Lucéram
29 Roquebrune-Cap-Martin
30 Menton

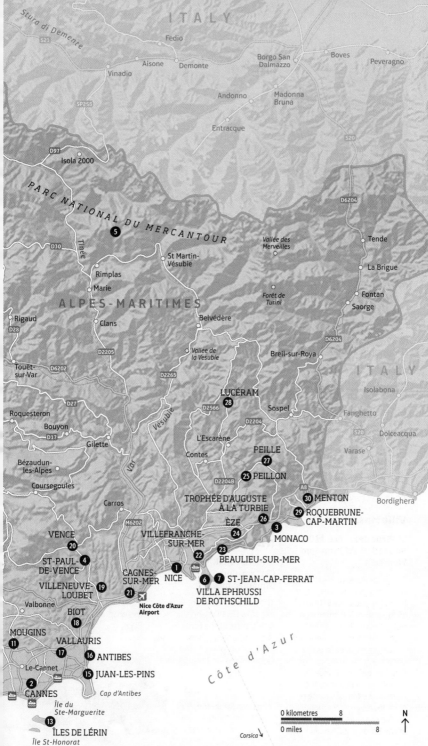

↑ Nice's promenade des Anglais, stretching along the coast

❶ NICE

🅰 G4 ✈ Nice, 7km (4 miles) SW 🚆🚌 Ave Thiers
ℹ 2 promenade des Anglais; www.nicetourisme.com

With the blue curve of the Baie des Anges in front and the white summits of the Alpes-Maritimes as a backdrop, Nice has enchanted visitors since the 19th century, when British, German and Russian aristocrats wintered here, revelling in its mellow climate. Painters, enchanted by Nice's vibrant light, endowed the city with a rich artistic legacy. But Nice is much more than a resort. It's a bustling city with its own distinct dialect and culture.

① Villa Masséna

🅰 65 rue de France 📞 04 93 91 19 10 🕙 11am-6pm Wed-Mon

The golden age of aristocratic tourism in Nice is brought to life in this museum within a 19th-century Italianate villa. Religious works, paintings by Niçois "primitive" painters, and white-glazed faïence pottery are among the exhibits. The villa was built for Prince Victor D'Essling, grandson of Nice-born André Masséna, one of Napoleon's greatest marshals, whose bust has pride of place in the Empire-style main hall.

② Musée d'Arts Modernes et d'Art Contemporain (MAMAC)

🅰 Place Yves Klein 🕙 11am-6pm Tue-Sun 🌐 mamac-nice.org

The enfants terribles of Pop Art, New Realism and the modernists of the École de Nice find a fitting home in this striking complex of marble-faced towers and transparent walkways. Andy Warhol and Yves Klein are among the stars of a collection that celebrates the avant-garde from the 1960s to the 21st century.

③ Musée Chagall

🅰 36 ave Dr Ménard 🕙 10am-5pm Wed-Mon (May-Oct: daily) 🌐 en. musees-nationaux-alpesmaritimes.fr

Paintings from Marc Chagall's Biblical Message series – including five versions of The Song of Songs – form the core of this museum, home to the world's largest portfolio of the painter's work. Three stained-glass windows depict the Creation of the World, and a shallow pool reflects a dazzling mosaic of the prophet Elijah.

→ The Loch Ness Monster by Niki de Saint Phalle at MAMAC

④ 🍽 ☕ 🛍

Hotel Negresco

📍 37 promenade des Anglais ⏰ 24 hrs daily 🌐 hotel-negresco-nice.com

Built in 1912 by gypsy-violin star Henri Negresco, this landmark hotel is even more lavish today than in its heyday. Louis XIII grandeur meets modern amenities in the decadent rooms, and a 16,000-stone Baccarat chandelier hangs in the *salon royal*.

⑤ ♿ Ⓜ 🍽 ☕ 🛍

Musée des Beaux-Arts

📍 33 ave des Baumettes ⏰ 10am-6pm Tue-Sun 🌐 musee-beaux-arts-nice.org

Oil paintings and ceramics by Raoul Dufy steal the show within this charming 19th-century villa, which was once home to a Ukranian princess. Other highlights include sculptures by Rodin (including a copy of his once-shocking *The Kiss*) and works by Bonnard, Vuillard, Van Dongen and 16th- and 17th-century Flemish masters. There's also a collection of 18th-century art from China and Japan.

⑥ Ⓜ 🛍

Musée des Arts Asiatiques

📍 405 promenade des Anglais ⏰ 10am-5pm Wed-Mon 🌐 arts-asiatiques.com

Surrounded by the exotic gardens of the Parc Floral Phénix, the Musée des Arts Asiatiques is a work of art in its own right. Inside Kenzo Tange's dazzling white marble, steel and glass building is an outstanding collection of ancient and modern art from China, Japan, India and Southeast Asia. Cultural activities such as formal Japanese tea ceremonies and Qi Gong exercise sessions are among the highlights here.

NICE JAZZ FESTIVAL

Louis Armstrong and his All Stars headlined at the first Nice Jazz Festival in 1948, as the Riviera emerged from the grim years of World War II and post-war poverty. It was the first big international jazz festival, and more than 70 years on it's still a major event.

The Théâtre de Verdure is the main venue and the six-day event kicks off with a lively carnival parade through the city centre.

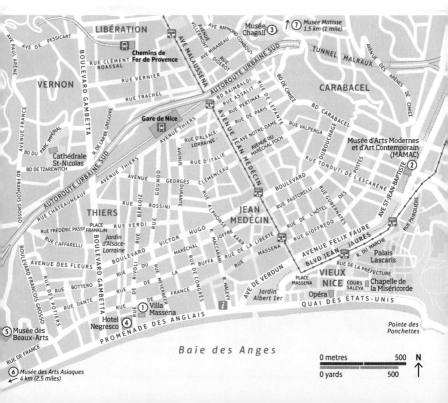

MUSÉE MATISSE

📍164 ave des Arènes de Cimiez, Nice 🚌15, 17, 20, 25 🕐11am–6pm Wed–Mon (mid-Jun–mid-Oct: from 10am) 🚫Public holidays 🌐musee-matisse-nice.org

Henri Matisse (1869–1954) first came to Nice in 1917, and lived at several addresses in the city before settling in Cimiez for the rest of his life. His devotion to the city and its "clear, crystalline, precise, limpid" light culminated, just before his death, with a large bequest of his works to the city.

History of the Museum

Nine years after Matisse's death, the Musée Matisse opened to the public, with the artist's bequest forming the main nucleus of the collection. For decades, the museum shared space with Nice's archaeological museum in the Villa des Arènes, a grand 17th-century villa located next to the Cimiez cemetery, which holds the artist's simple memorial. Since 1993, however, the entire villa, complete with its new extension, has been devoted to celebrating Matisse's life, work and influence. Today, the ground and first floors of this gallery display works from the museum's permanent collection, from which pieces are sometimes loaned out to other museums. The subterranean wing is used for exhibitions devoted to Matisse and his contemporaries.

Works on Paper

Nu Bleu IV (1952) is, for most visitors, the most immediately recognisable of Matisse's works. This is one of the artist's famous "cut-outs", works made from gouache-painted paper that was cut and pasted into unforgettable collages.

In this piece, the artist has tried several compositions in charcoal before pasting down the final lay out.

Paintings and Sculptures

Among the most impressive of Matisse's sculptural works on show is the bronze Torse Debout (1909), a headless female figure given to the museum in 1978 by the artist's son, Jean. The tranquil Liseuse à la Table Jaune (1944), a painting of a woman reading, belies the troubles that beset Matisse during World War II, including a major operation that left him bedridden for a time, and the arrest of his

↑ Jeannette III (1911), one of several bronze sculptures of the subject

←

Matisse's "cut-out" Nu Bleu IV (1952), with its charcoal composition outlines

1941
Diagnosed with duodenal cancer, Matisse undergoes surgery that leaves him bedridden

1947–51
Matisse designs and decorates the Chapelle du Rosaire in Vence

1954
▼ Matisse dies of a heart attack in Cimiez at the age of 84

1917
Matisse relocates to Nice from Paris

1944
Matisse's wife Amélie is jailed for her part in the French Resistance

1945
Matisse's daughter flees to Nice after escaping on her way to a Nazi death camp

wife and daughter for French Resistance work. *Nature Morte aux Grenades* (1947) features ripe pomegranates in one of Matisse's favourite settings, an interior opening onto a window of blue skies.

Matisse in Person

The museum's collection of photographs offers a unique insight into the man and his work. Hélène Adant's photograph, *Matisse in his Studio* shows him drafting the murals for the Chapelle du Rosaire in Vence *(p91)*. A gilded Rococo armchair, the subject of his painting *Fauteuil Rocaille* (1946), is among many of the painter's belongings and painting props on display in the museum.

↑ Exterior of the Villa des Arènes, the setting for the Musée Matisse

↑ Interior of the Musée Matisse, with *Fleurs et Fruits* (1952-3) in the foreground

A SHORT WALK
NICE

Distance 1 km (half a mile) **Nearest tram**
Cathedrale - Vieille Ville **Time** 15 minutes

A dense network of pedestrian alleys, narrow buildings and pastel, Italianate façades make up Vieux Nice (or the Old Town). Its streets contain many fine 17th-century Italianate churches, among them St-François-de-Paule, behind the Opéra, and l'Église du Jésus in the rue Droite. Most of the seafront, at quai des États-Unis, is taken up by Les Ponchettes, a double row of low houses with flat roofs, which was a fashionable walk before the promenade des Anglais was built. To the east of this lies the Colline du Château, occupied in the 4th century by Greeks who kept fishing nets on the quay.

Built in 1650 by the Nice architect J-A Guiberto in Baroque style, the **Cathédrale Ste-Réparate** *has a fine dome of glazed tiles and an 18th-century tower.*

START

The **Palais de Justice** *was inaugurated on 17 October 1892, replacing the smaller quarters used before Nice became part of France.*

Did You Know?

The quai des États-Unis took its name in 1917, after America joined World War I.

RUE DU MARCHÉ

RUE DU PONT VIEUX

RUE E GALLAO

PLACE
ROSSE

RUE COLONNA D'ISTRIA

RUE STE-REPARA

RUE DE LA PRÉFECTURE

RUE ST GAETAN

PLACE
DU
PALAIS

PLACE
PIERRE
GAUTIER

RUE RAOUL

RUE L GASSIN

BOSIO

RUE ALEXANDRE MARI

COURS

SAL

There's an enticing vegetable and flower market on **cours Saleya**, *and it is also a lively area at night.*

RUE ST-F DE PAULE

Built in 1855, the ornate and sumptuous **Opéra de Nice** *has its entrance just off the quai des États-Unis.*

Designed by Guarino Guarinone in 1740, the Baroque **Chapelle de la Miséricorde** *has a fine Rococo interior.*

↑ Tapestries and antique furniture adorning a room in the opulent Palais Lascaris

Sumptuous 18th-century statues of Mars and Venus flank the staircase at **Palais Lascaris***, and Genoese artists decorate the trompe l'oeil ceiling.*

RUE DE LA LOGE

RUE DROITE

RUE ROSSETTI

RUE ST-JOSEPH

O FINISH

RUE BENOÎT-BUNICO

RUE DROITE

RUE DU CHÂTEAU

RUE DU MALONAT

RUE DE L'ANCIEN SÉNAT

RUE BARILLERIE

RUE JULES-GILLY

PLACE CHARLES FELIX

QUAI DES ÉTATS-UNIS

0 metres 100
0 yards 100

N ↑

One of Nice's most unusual architectural features is the row of low white buildings along the seafront, called **Les Ponchettes***. These were once used by fishermen, and are now a mix of galleries and ethnic restaurants.*

↑ View over Les Ponchettes and the quai des États-Unis from the stairs of the Montée Lesage

②

CANNES

Ⓐ F5 ✈ Nice 28km (18 miles) 🚉 4 place de la Gare 🚌 2 place Cornut Gentille ℹ 1 blvd de la Croisette; www.cannes-destination.com

There's a sense of faded glory in Cannes. The Cannes Film Festival, first held in 1946, really put the place on the map. Even when the party is over, the glamour remains in the posh stores, on the swanky private beaches, and in the gaming rooms of the casinos.

①
La Croisette

The long promenade de la Croisette runs parallel to the city's Plage de la Croisette, a palm-lined crescent of imported sand looking out over the gorgeous Bay of Cannes. Its major landmarks are three luxury hotels, the Carlton, the Majestic and the Martinez, where movie industry hacks hang out at Film Festival time. The rest of the year, the hotels are home to less glamorous conferences at the Palais des Congrès, which anchors the western end of the boulevard. Each hotel has its own private beach where, for a hefty fee, visitors can bask in luxury for a while.

②
Les Allées de la Liberté

A statue of Lord Brougham, the British Lord Chancellor who initiated the gentrification of Cannes when he built a villa here in 1834, overlooks this green square just inland from the harbour. Locals play boules or sip coffee in cafés beneath the shady plane trees. The square also hosts a colourful flower market (7am–noon Mon–Fri), stalls selling bric-a-brac, antiques and vintage items (7am–5:30pm Sat & 1st Sun of month), and an array of talented local arts and crafts vendors (8am–1pm Sat & Sun).

③
Rue d'Antibes

Breathtakingly expensive big-name designer boutiques line rue d'Antibes, where the stars shop for shoes, jewellery, handbags and other accessories. Less well-heeled visitors can enjoy window-shopping and may even spot a celebrity.

④
Marché Forville

🏛 5–11 rue du Marché Forville 🕐 7am–1pm Tue–Sun 🌐 marcheforville.com

The air is filled with the smells of coffee, flowers and herbs at this busy open-air market.

> 💬 INSIDER TIP
> **Budget beaches**
>
> Rent a lounger, parasol and locker at one of Cannes' public city beaches – like Plage du Midi, Plage de la Bocca or Palm Beach – and bring your own drinks to enjoy the same sun, sea and sand as the glitzy beach clubs but on a tighter budget

modern building dwarfs the Vieux Port, the original heart of Cannes. It comes into its own as the hub of the Cannes Film Festival, when it hosts the presentation of the Palme d'Or, next to the Academy Award as the film industry's most prestigious honour. In front of the Palais, hand-prints set in pavement concrete immortalize screen icons in the Allée des Étoiles.

Musée de la Castre and Tour de la Castre

⬛ Château de la Castre
📞 04 93 38 55 26
🕐 10am-1pm & 2pm-5pm Tue-Sun (Jul-Aug: to 7pm)

It's worth visiting this quirky museum just for the view from its highest point, the 11th-century Tour de la Castre. Built by the monks of Lérins in the 11th and 12th centuries, the former castle now houses an eclectic collection that includes traditional Pacific Island costumes, Asian artworks and African masks. The Cistercian St-Anne chapel houses a fine collection of antique musical instruments.

↑ Bright lights of La Croisette glittering in the Baie de Cannes

It's a great place to buy local delicacies, and on Mondays it becomes a flea market.

⑤
Palais de Festivals

⬛ 1 bvd de la Croisette
🕐 7am-midnight daily
🌐 palaisdesfestivals.com

Built in 1982 and renovated in 2015, this brutally functional

DRINK

The Carlton Bar
At film festival time the bar of this hotel is a favourite for the movie crowd.

⬛ 58 blvd de la Croisette
🌐 carlton-cannes. commes

Charly's
This purple-lit, vaulted grotto offers a long list of cocktails and fizz, and has an outdoor terrace for warm summer evenings.

⬛ 3 rue du Suquet
🌐 pubcharlysbar.fr

La Plage du 45
Sun loungers line the jetty-like boardwalk of the Grand Hotel's beach club. The cocktail list is a mix of classics and inventive innovations.

⬛ 45 blvd de la Croisette
🌐 grandhotel cannes.com

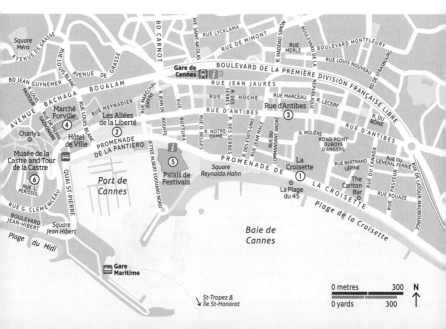

3

MONACO

🅰 G4 ✈ Nice 15 km (9 miles) SW 🚂 Monaco-Monte Carlo, pl Ste-Dévote 🚌 Place des Moulins ℹ 2A blvd des Moulins; www.visitmonaco.com

The mega-yachts of the world's richest men and women dwarf smaller (but still upmarket) vessels in the Port de Monaco, and world-famous sports stars and their consorts hog the VIP tables in the exclusive nightspots of the world's second smallest country. An ambitious €2 billion project to create a new millionaire's enclave on sand dredged from the seabed began in 2016 and is expected to take 10 years to complete. Meanwhile, Monte Carlo, centrepiece of Monaco's royally belle époque heart, still exerts an undeniable charm.

①

Le Rocher

Set on the Rock, a sheer-sided, flat-topped finger of land extending 792 m (2,600 ft) into the the sea, Le Rocher (also called Monaco-Ville) is the historic quarter of Monaco where Europe's oldest ruling family, the Grimaldis, founded their principality in the 13th century. Today, it is a warren of narrow medieval lanes set around the Palais Princier. There are a number of routes up to Le Rocher; the best is via Rampe Major, which starts near the port from place d'Armes.

Timeline

13th–14th century

△ The Genoese Grimaldi family seize Monaco from the Ghibellines, a rival faction

1633–1815

France and Spain recognise Monaco's independence but the principality is conquered by France; in 1814 it becomes protectorate of Sardinia

19th century

France recognises Monégasque sovereignty; the Casino de Monte Carlo opens and is so successful that the principality need no longer collect income tax

20th century

▽ First Monaco Grand Prix held in 1929; Monaco is occupied by Italy and Germany during World War II; Prince Rainier III marries film star Grace Kelly, who tragically dies in a car crash in 1982

21st century

Albert II succeeds to throne in 2005; reclamation project launched to expand Monaco's land area by more than 3 per cent

↑ Sun rising over the bright lights of Monte Carlo harbour

② 🛈

Palais Princier

📍 Place du Palais ⏰ Mar-Oct: 10am-6pm daily 🚫 Grand Prix 🌐 palais.mc

Monaco's seat of government, this castle-palace of the Grimaldi dynasty is built on the site of a medieval Genoese fortress and protected by 17th-century cannons donated by Louis XIV of France. The Compagnie du Carabiniers du Prince (equipped with modern weapons, but still in archaic dress uniform) changes its guards with full military pomp every day at 11:55am. Venture inside to discover wonderful frescoes by 16th-century Genoese artists, the opulent throne room, and the stunning blue-and-gold Louis XV Salon. The cour d'Honneur courtyard, outside, is a lovely setting for summer concerts.

③ 🛈

Casino de Monte Carlo

📍 Place du Casino ⏰ 2pm-4am daily 🌐 casinomonte carlo.com

Monaco owes much of its fame to this spectacular monument

to all that was fabulous about the belle époque of the late 19th century, when this tiny principality came to be seen as *the* place to frolic, flirt and play games of chance for high stakes. Built by the architect of the Paris opera house, Charles Garnier, its dazzling interior is decorated with glittering chandeliers, ostentatious frescoes and gilded bas-reliefs. Edward,

Prince of Wales (later King Edward VII) was just one of its former royal and aristocratic patrons, drawn by the thrill of roulette, baccarat and chemin de fer. The slot machines now in the Salle des Amériques and Salle Renaissance are an egalitarian innovation, and full evening dress is no longer de rigueur, but the casino still strives to maintain a certain decorum.

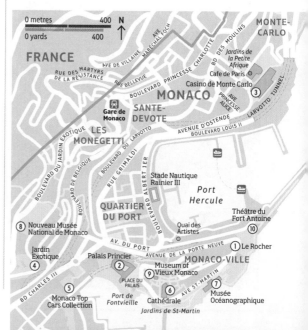

EAT

Café de Paris

This classic brasserie serves refined French cooking and local dishes like *stockfish à la monégasque* under white umbrellas on a flowery terrace opposite the casino.

◻ Place du Casino
Ⓦ fr.montecarlosbm.com

€€€

Quai des Artistes

A classy, contemporary but unpretentious harbourside brasserie that bustles with locals and serves a great selection of seafood and an above-average children's menu.

◻ Quai Antoine 1
Ⓦ quaidesartistes.com

€€€

---

④ 🚶 🛍

Jardin Exotique

◻ 62 blvd du Jardin Exotique Ⓞ 9am–7pm daily Ⓒ 19 Nov Ⓦ jardin-exotique.mc

Clinging to the steep limestone hillside, this garden is filled with weird and wonderful tropical and sub-tropical cacti and other plants imported from arid and unpromising native environments in Africa, Asia and the Americas. It boasts the largest collection of petrophile succulents (plants that grow on bare rock) in the world. But its biggest secret lies beneath the surface. In the Grotte de l'Observatoire, an eerie cavern filled with dripping stalactites, palaeontologists have found evidence of early hominid people from 1,000,000 years BC.

---

⑤ 🚶

Monaco Top Cars Collection

◻ Les Terrasses de Fontvieille Ⓞ 10am–6pm daily Ⓦ mttc.mc

This petrolheads' paradise began as the personal collection of Prince Rainier III. It's one of the world's greatest collections of classic cars, from a quaint 1903 De Dion Bouton to sleek thoroughbreds bearing the hood ornaments and badges of Rolls Royce, Facel Vega, Ferrari, Maserati and Lamborghini. There are also important race and rally contenders from historic Monaco Grand Prix and Monte Carlo Rally events. A specially constructed building displays the cars over five levels.

Tropical and sub-tropical plants in the Jardin Exotique; the Grotte de l'Observatoire lying beneath the gardens *(inset)* ↓

⑥ Cathédrale

📍 4 rue Colonel Bellando de Castro 📞 07 93 15 29 80 🕐 8:30am-6pm daily

The 12th-century church of St Nicholas was replaced in the 19th century by this Neo-Romanesque building in white La Turbie stone. The tombs of princes and bishops surround its 16th-century altarpiece, painted by the renowned Niçois artist Louis Bréa. The much-loved Princess Grace is also buried here.

⑦ Musée Océanographique

📍 Avenue St-Martin 🕐 10am-7pm daily 🚇 Grand Prix 🌐 oceano.mc

A glass-sided, 6-m- (19-ft-) deep shark tank is the centre-piece of this extraordinary clifftop museum. Smaller exotic creatures like the bizarrely charming leafy sea dragons swim in smaller tanks.

MONACO GRAND PRIX

The scream of Formula 1 engines resounds throughout Monaco as drivers hurl the world's fastest racers around its streets in the world's most glamorous motorsports event. First run in 1919, the Monaco Grand Prix is a unique urban circuit that loops for 3.367 km (just over 2 miles) through the principality's streets, where drivers must negotiate 78 twists and turns.

Founded by Prince Albert I in 1910 and directed from 1958 to 1988 by legendary undersea explorer Jacques Cousteau, the museum's ongoing mission is to raise awareness of the plight of the world's oceans and their denizens. The rooftop café also offers superb panoramic views of the coast.

⑧ Nouveau Musée National de Monaco

📍 Villa Sauber, 17 ave Princesse Grace; Villa Paloma, 56 blvd du Jardin Exotique 🕐 10am-6pm during exhibitions only 🚇 Grand Prix, 19 Nov 📞 nmnm.mc

Two spectacular villas house this museum charting the cultural, historical and artistic heritage of the Principality. The Villa Sauber, a fine example of belle époque architecture, hosts a series of entertainment and performing arts exhibits. Villa Paloma, with its lovely Italian garden, displays a fantastic collection of modern and contemporary art, architecture and design.

⑨ Museum of Vieux Monaco

📍 2 rue Emile de Loth 📞 07 93 50 57 28 🕐 Jun-Sep: 11am-4pm Mon-Fr

The paintings, ceramics furniture and costumes on display at this museum aim to preserve national identity and educate visitors about Monégasque traditions.

⑩ Théâtre du Fort Antoine

📍 Avenue de la Quarantaine

This ancient fort has been converted into an open-air theatre showing a wide range of productions in summer.

Did You Know?

Residents of Monaco pay no income tax or inheritance tax, and one in three residents is a millionaire.

④ 🍴 🖥

ST-PAUL-DE-VENCE

🅰F4 ✈Nice 🚆Nice, Cagnes sur Mer 🚌Cagnes sur Mer, Vence, Nice 🛈2 rue Grande 🌐saint-pauldevence.com

Set in alpine hinterland with panoramic views of the Riviera coast, the breathtaking location of St-Paul-de-Vence first drew painters in the 1920s. The outstanding art collection of the Fondation Maeght *(p78)* is St-Paul-de-Vence's most powerful magnet, and a stroll through its maze of medieval streets is a real delight.

①
Place du Jeu de Boules

Venerable plane trees spread their leaves over the place du Jeu de Boules. Any visit to St-Paul-de-Vence must start on this atmospheric space, where locals still like to meet for a friendly game of *pétanque* when the square is not crammed with visitors.

②
Porte de Vence and Ramparts

A 14th-century tower stands guard over the Porte de Vence, an impressive gateway that leads through St-Paul-de-Vence's formidable ring of 16th-century ramparts into the heart of the village. From here, you can walk around the ramparts – originally built to resist assault from Savoy and Piedmont – for a panoramic view of the vineyards and olive groves that cloak the hilly countryside around the village.

③
Rue Grande

Lined with the studios and workshops of local artists and artisans, the rue Grande is St-Paul's main thoroughfare. Running between the Porte de Vence and Porte de Nice, it resembles an open-air art museum where you can ogle the work of cutting-edge talents in the windows of upscale commercial galleries.

④ ✏

Folon Chapel (Chapelle des Pénitents Blancs)

🅰Place de l'Église
📞04 66 28 18 32
🕐10:30am-12:30pm & 2-4pm (May-Sep: to 6pm)
🚫public holidays

Belgian-born artist Jean-Michel Folon (1934–2005) spent much of his life in St-Paul-de-Vence and worked with local artisans to adorn this historic 17th-century chapel with vividly coloured, joyous stained glass windows, graceful sculptures, murals and rich mosaics. The enchanting chapel is immaculately preserved as a celebration of his life and work.

↑ Place de la Grande Fontaine in St-Paul-de-Vence

↑ The medieval village of St-Paul-de-Vence, perched high on a hilltop

⑤
Cimetière

Marc Chagall, who made St-Paul-de-Vence his home from 1966 until his death in 1985, is the most famous resident of the village's cemetery. His modest, cedar-shaded grave is a place of pilgrimage for admirers, who leave coins in a growing pile as visible tribute to a great artist.

⑥ 🄯 Ⓜ
Musée d'Histoire Locale

🄰 Monté de la Castre
📞 04 66 28 18 32 🕔 7:30am-5:45pm daily (Apr-Sep: to 6:45pm)

St-Paul's dramatic history is evoked by waxwork tableaux and life-size effigies created by Paris's Musée Grévin in this small museum. One of the main historic figures featured is Sébastien Le Prestre de Vauban (1633–1707), Francois I and Louis XIV's great military architect, who reinforced much of the village's formidable fortifications to resist attack by France's enemies in 1543–7. A combined ticket for entrance to both the museum and the Folon Chapel is available.

⑦
Place de la Grande Fontaine

A gushing 17th-century central fountain lends its name to this charming square which was once the village's marketplace and communal laundry. Until the 1960s, laundresses would wash clothes and bed linen in stone troughs here within an open-sided washhouse. The square has long been a favourite subject with artists working in St-Paul-de-Vence.

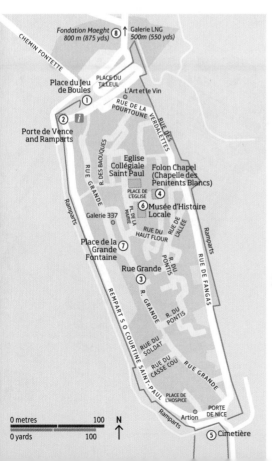

TOP 4
ART GALLERIES IN ST-PAUL-DE VENCE

L'Art et le Vin
🄰 1 rue de la Pourtune
This wine bar and gallery is a perfect spot to savour local vintages and work by local artists.

Artion
🄰 1 pl de l'Église
A Provençal offshoot of a famous Swiss gallery, Artion exhibits work by old masters and world-class modern artists.

Galerie LNG
🄰 11 rempart Ouest
A gallery showcasing colourful pop art and work by 21st-century street artists.

Galerie 337
🄰 29 rue Grande
This modern art gallery features exceptional sculptures, prints and paintings by leading contemporary artists.

⑧ ✦ ▭ ⧄

FONDATION MAEGHT

🏠 623 chemin Gardettes, St-Paul-de-Vence 🕐 10am-6pm daily (Jul–Sep: to 7pm) 🗓 24 & 31 Dec 🌐 fondation maeght.com

Nestling amid the umbrella pines in the hills above St-Paul-de-Vence, this small foundation houses one of Europe's largest collections of 20th-century art.

The Fondation Maeght was established in 1964 by Cannes art dealers Aimé and Marguerite Maeght, who numbered the likes of Chagall, Matisse and Miró among their clients. Their private collection formed the basis of the foundation, and they enlisted the help of their artist friends when designing the grounds: highlights include a courtyard filled with stick-thin Giacometti sculptures, an elaborate sculpture-filled maze designed by Miró, a bold swimming pool by Braque, and a large mural mosaic by Chagall. The Maeghts intended the foundation not as an art museum, but as a forum to present modern art – a place for artists to gather, exchange ideas and exhibit their work. Today, just a fraction of the vast permanent collection is on display at any one time, with a changing programme of popular temporary exhibitions.

These slender bronze figures by Alberto Giacometti inhabit their own shady courtyard.

Georges Braque designed the Les Poissons *mosaic in this swimming pool.*

Cowled roofs allow indirect light to filter into the galleries.

↑ Bold exterior of the Fondation Maeght

Alexander Calder's Les Renforts *(1963) is what he called a "stabile" – a counterpart to his more familiar mobiles.*

Joan Miró's Le Cadran Solaire *(1973) is one of many statues in his multi-levelled maze of trees, water and gargoyles.*

↑ Temporary Giacometti exhibition inside the Fondation Maeght

Did You Know?

The foundation drew Duke Ellington, Samuel Beckett, André Malraux and a galaxy of artists to its early events.

The Chapelle St-Bernard was built in memory of the Maeghts' son, who died in 1953, aged 11. Above the altarpiece is a stained-glass window by Braque.

← Illustration of the building and grounds of the Fondation Maeght, seen from above

↑ *L'Oiseau Lunaire* (1968), a sculpture in Miró's maze

5

PARC NATIONAL DU MERCANTOUR

A F3 **A** Alpes-Maritimes **R** Tende, Fontan-Saorge **bus** St Étienne de Tinée, Auron **i** 23 rue d'Italie, Nice **w** mercantour-parcnational.fr

This alpine wilderness is a paradise for those who love the great outdoors. Covering 70,000 ha (270 sq miles), the Parc National du Mercantour shelters an abundance of wildlife. Tende, overlooking a mountain pass, and Saorge, set in a natural amphitheatre above the river, are gateways to the park.

Vallée des Merveilles

A hike into this valley, with its breathtakingly clear air and pretty alpine scenery, takes you high into the Mercantour and deep into its vanished past. Etched into the rock of Mont Bégo are some 36,000 engravings, dating from around 2,000 BC. The **Musée des Merveilles** displays original and reproduction petroglyphs from the area and puts them in their Bronze Age context.

Vallée de la Vésubie

Two alpine torrents, the Madone de Fenestre and Boréon, merge to become the Vésubie, which cascades through pine forests and meadows, skirting the fringes of the Parc National du Mercantour, before snaking through the Gorges de la Vésubie to join the Var. St-Martin-Vésubie, where the two sources join, is a popular mountain activity centre. There's a spectacular view of the Gorges de la Vésubie at La Madonne d'Utelle, above the fortified village of Utelle.

Foret de Turini

This lush forest seems a world away from the beautiful but barren upper expanses of the Parc National du Mercantour. A humid microclimate and warm Mediterranean breeze nurture thick swathes of beech, maple, sweet chestnut and pine trees, which soar to great heights. Hike to the 2,082 m (6,830 ft) Pointe des Trois-Communes summit for a superb view of the peaks of the Mercantour.

The view over the Gorges de la Vésubie from St-Martin-Vésubie ↑

WILDLIFE OF MERCANTOUR

The multifarious environments and microclimates of the Mercantour provide havens for creatures great and small, from wide-winged raptors and shy mountain herbivores to colourful butterflies in the woodland glades and alpine pastures.

① Ibex and mouflon

Some 1,200 ibex roam the remotest mountain slopes of Mercantour. This nimble, exuberantly horned wild goat shares its habitat with the mouflon, a wild sheep introduced to the region from Corsica.

② Marmots

Look out for these cheeky rodents as they pop out of their burrows to nibble the grass and bask in early morning sun on high mountain meadows.

③ Chamois

Listen for the sound of tumbling pebbles as families of chamois scramble across steep scree slopes.

④ Bearded vultures

With its mighty wingspan of up to 2.83 m (9.3 ft), the gypaete (bearded vulture) is one of Europe's most unmistakable raptors. It's also among the rarest.

Saorge

Once a strategic strongpoint on the borders of France, Piedmont and Savoy, Saorge is a typical *village empilé* (stacked village), where slate-roofed houses rise in tiers high above the river Roya. The backdrop of summits is impressive, as is the nearby **Monastère de Saorge**, set among a wide expanse of terraced gardens. Founded by Franciscan monks in 1633, the monastery is now a cultural centre for writers.

Musée des Merveilles

🅿 😊 🏠 Ave du 16 Sept 1947, Tende 🕙 10am–5pm Wed-Mon 🌐 musee desmerveilles.com

Monastère de Saorge

🏠 Off derrière le Couvent 🕙 10am–12:30pm & 2:30pm–5:30pm daily 🚫 Nov-Jan 🌐 monastere-saorge.fr

Did You Know?

Bearded vultures live almost entirely on bones, which they smash by dropping them in flight.

VILLA EPHRUSSI DE ROTHSCHILD

🅰️ G4 📍 1 ave Ephrussi de Rothschild, St-Jean-Cap-Ferrat 🕐 Feb–Jun & Sep–Oct: 10am–6pm daily; Jul–Aug: 10am–7pm daily; Nov–Jan: 2–6pm daily
🌐 villa-ephrussi.com

Béatrice Ephrussi de Rothschild (1864–1934) could have led a life of indolent luxury, but her passions for travel and fine art led to the creation of the most perfect "dream villa" of the Riviera.

Despite interest shown by King Léopold II of Belgium for the land, Béatrice succeeded in purchasing it and later supervised every aspect of the villa's creation. It was completed in 1912 and, although she never used it as a primary residence, Béatrice hosted garden parties and soirees here until 1934. The villa remains a monument to Béatrice's spirit and vision. Its lavish Neo-Classical façade conceals an opulent interior filled with exquisite antique furniture and art, and a covered courtyard hung with magnificent tapestries.

↑ Exterior of the Villa Ephrussi de Rothschild, set in sumptuous gardens

One of the villa's rooms is devoted to a fine collection of working drawings and sketches by Jean-Honoré Fragonard (1732–1806).

Covered Patio

Béatrice's 18th-century writing desk is the star attraction of her Boudoir.

← Opulent decorations in the State Room

BÉATRICE EPHRUSSI DE ROTHSCHILD

Béatrice was born into one of the richest banking dynasties of the 19th century. Aged 19, she married Maurice Ephrussi, a Russian-French banker. Her fortune enabled her to build this opulent villa. She and Maurice filled it with art and antiques, and Béatrice created her own menagerie in the gardens, stocking it with exotic birds and animals.

The lavish State Room features wooden ornamentation from the Crillon in Paris, Savonnerie carpets, and chairs upholstered in 18th-century Savonnerie tapestries.

EXPERIENCE MORE

7

St-Jean-Cap-Ferrat

◮F3 ⊠Nice ⊜Beaulieu-sur-Mer ⊜St-Jean-Cap-Ferrat 🄸5/59 ave Denis Séméria; www.saintjean capferrat-tourisme.fr

The Cap-Ferrat peninsula is a playground for the rich, with exclusive villas, luxury gardens and fabulous yachts in the St-Jean marina.

King Léopold II of Belgium started a trend for building in the area in the 19th century, when he set his Les Cèdres estate on the west side of the cape, overlooking Villefranche. Further attractive mansions were built nearby for European royalty, industrialists and celebrities. Residents have included the Duke and Duchess of Windsor, British playwright and novelist W Somerset Maugham and singer Edith Piaf. Hedges and gates protect these villas, but one of the finest, the Villa Ephrussi de Rothschild, is open to the public.

There is a superb view from the little garden of the 1837 lighthouse at the end of the cape. A pretty walk leads around the Pointe St-Hospice, east of the port at St-Jean-Cap-Ferrat, a former fishing village with old houses fronting the harbour.

For a fee, you can enjoy one of the town's two private beaches: **Plage de Passable or Plage de Paloma**. Both offer sun loungers, watersports and boat excursions.

Plage de Passable
⊛ ⊜ ◮Chemin de Passable 🄲04 93 76 06 17 ⊙Easter-Sep: daily

Plage de Paloma
⊛ ⊜ ◮1 chemin de Saint Hospice ⊙Easter-Sep: daily ⓌＷpaloma-beach.com

Did You Know?

Europe's first avocados were grown in the gardens of W Somerset Maugham's villa in St-Jean-Cap-Ferrat.

↑ The pretty peninsula of St-Jean-Cap-Ferrat, seen from Villefranche-sur-Mer

← The village of Gourdon, perched on a cliff edge above the Gorges du Loup

the Riviera and the coast. Tumbling between thickly wooded slopes on its way to the sea, the Loup has carved deep cauldrons in the rock, such as the Saut du Loup. Foaming waterfalls, including the 40-m (130-ft) Cascade de Courmes and Cascades des Demoiselles, plunge from steep cliffs. In places, river spray, rich in lime carbonate dissolved from the surrounding rock, has partly petrified trees and shrubs close to the waterside. For fans of wild river swimming, deep blue pools lie between the Cascade de Courmes and the tiny hamlet of Pont du Loup, at the mouth of the Gorges.

---

⑩

Gorges du Cians

🅰F3 ☒Nice ☐Nice, Touët-sur-Var, Valberg **ⓘ**Pl Charles Ginésy, Valberg; www.valberg.com

Among the finest natural sights in the region, these gorges are a startling combination of deep red slate and vivid mountain greenery. They follow the course of the river Cians, which drops 1,600 m (5,250 ft) in 25 km (15 miles) from Beuil to Touët-sur-Var. At Touët, through a grille in the floor of the church nave, you can see the torrent below.

Approaching from the lower gorges, olives give way to scrubland. At Pra d'Astier, the gorges become steep and narrow: in some places, the rock walls block out the sky.

At the upper end of the gorges, overlooking the Vallée

⑧

Gourdon

🅰F4 **ⓘ**1 pl Victoria; www.gourdon06.fr

Built on a hilltop, surrounded by ramparts, Gourdon is a typical *village perché* (perched village), its shops filled with regional produce, perfume and local art. From the square at its precipitous edge, there is a spectacular view of the Loup valley and the sea, with Antibes and Cap Roux in the distance.

There are good views, too, from the gardens of the **Château de Gourdon**, built on the foundations of a Saracen fortress in the 12th century by the seigneurs du Bar, overlords of Gourdon. The terrace gardens – the Jardin à l'Italienne, the Jardin de Rocaille (or Provençal Gardens) and the Jardin de l'Apothicaire – were laid out by André Le Nôtre when the château was restored in the 17th century. Although the château is privately owned and not open to the public, visitors can take a guided tour of the gardens in groups during the summer months.

Château de Gourdon
🚹🚹 🅾Off rte de Caussols ☐May–Aug: by reservation for groups; times vary, check website ☒chateau-gourdon.com

---

⑨

Gorges du Loup

🅰F4

The Gorges du Loup is the most accessible of the dramatic limestone gorges between the hinterland of

→ Pretty arched doorway in the medieval hilltop town of Mougins

du Cians, is the 1,430-m (4,770-ft) eyrie of Beuil. It was first fortified by the counts of Beuil, members of the aristocratic Grimaldi family (p72). They lived here until 1621, despite staff revolt: one count had his throat cut by his barber and another was stabbed by his valet. The last count, Hannibal Grimaldi, was tied to a chair and strangled by two Muslim slaves.

---

⑪

Mougins

🅰F5 🚌 ℹ39 place des Patriotes; www.mouginstourisme.com

This old hilltop town, huddled inside the remains of its 15th-century ramparts and fortified Saracen Gate, is one of the finest in the region. Mougins is a smart address: royalty and film stars have resided here, while Picasso spent his final years living with his wife in a house opposite the Chapelle de Notre-Dame-de-Vie until his death in 1973. This priory house, sitting at the end of an alley of cypresses, is now privately owned and closed to the public.

Mougins is also one of the top places to eat in Provence. Among its many high-class restaurants is the stylish gastronomic restaurant

La Place de Mougins, located right on the main square and home of creative chef Denis Fétisson since 2010.

The permanent collection at the excellent **Musée de la Photographie** features several photographs taken by Picasso, portraits of the artist by other photographers including Robert Doisneau, and works by French photographer André Villers, who helped found the museum.

The eclectic collection at the **Musée d'Art Classique de Mougins** includes Roman, Greek and Egyptian art, alongside pieces by Picasso, Cézanne, Andy Warhol and Damien Hirst. There are also interesting displays of jewellery and Greek war helmets and armour.

Musée de la Photographie
🅰67 rue de l'Église 📞04 93 75 85 67 🕐Daily 🗓Jan, 25 Dec

Musée d'Art Classique de Mougins
♿ 🅰32 rue Commandeur 🕐Daily 🗓25 Dec 🌐mouginsmusee.com

↑ Early distillation methods at the Musée International de la Parfumerie

⑫ Grasse

⌂F4 🚍 🅹Pl de la Buanderie; www.paysde grassetourisme.fr

Once known for its leather tanning industry, Grasse became a perfume centre in the 16th century. Three major perfume houses are still here. Today, perfume is mainly made from imported flowers, but each year, Grasse holds a Jasmine festival *(p53)*. The best place to discover the history of perfume is the **Musée International de la Parfumerie**, which has a garden of fragrant plants. It also displays *bergamotes*, decorated scented *papier-mâché* boxes.

Did You Know?

It takes 1 tonne of jasmine flowers to distil 1 litre (2 pts) of jasmine essence.

Artist Jean-Honoré Fragonard (1732–1806) was born in Grasse and the walls of the **Villa-Musée Fragonard** are covered with his son's murals. The artist's *Washing of the Feet* hangs in the 12th-century Ancienne Cathédrale Notre-Dame-du-Puy, in the old town. The cathedral also houses three works by Rubens.

Nearby, an excellent collection of 18th–19th century Provençal costumes and jewellery can be seen at the fascinating **Musée Provençal du Costume et du Bijou**.

Musée International de la Parfumerie

Ⓢ Ⓟ ⌂ 2 blvd du Jeu de Ballon 🕙 10am–5:30pm daily 🚫 public hols 🌐 musees degrasse.com

Villa-Musée Fragonard

Ⓢ Ⓟ ⌂ 23 blvd Fragonard 📞 04 93 36 52 98 🕙 10am–7pm daily 🚫 public hols

Musée Provençal du Costume et du Bijou

Ⓢ ⌂ 2 rue Jean Ossola 📞 04 93 36 44 65 🕙 10am–1pm & 2pm–6:30pm Mon–Sat (Mar–Oct & Dec: also Sun)

⑬ Iles de Lerin

⌂F5 🚢From Cannes Vieux Port

The scent of eucalyptus and pine greets you as you dis-embark on Ile Ste-Marguerite or Ile St-Honorat, the tiny sister-islands known as the Iles de Lerin. Although just 15 minutes by boat from the bustle of Cannes, the islands reflect a very different history. Tiny chapels dotted around the islands are testament to their Christian heritage, which stretches back to the 4th century, when the Gallo-Roman abbot Honoratus founded an abbey on Ile St-Honorat. Some say that Ste-Marguerite was named after his sister, who set up a nunnery there. The 17th-century Fort Ste-Marguerite served as a prison, incarcerating the "Man in the Iron Mask" from 1687 to 1698. On the Ile St-Honorat, there are some fine coastal views from the 11th-century Monastere Fortifié. Next to it, the Abbaye de Lérins is known for the high-octane Lerina liqueur made by its monks.

PERFUMES OF PROVENCE

Grasse is surrounded by orange and mimosa groves, and fields filled with jasmine, roses and violets. Their rainbow-coloured blossoms are pressed and blended by parfumiers to create the world's most fabulous fragrances.

Grasse did not always smell so sweet. It was originally known for its leather-tanning industry, and it wasn't until the 16th century that local tanners hit on the idea of using floral essences to mask the rank smell of cured skins. When Henri II's queen, Catherine de Medici (1519–89), acquired a pair of perfumed kid gloves made in Grasse they became Europe's must-have accessory. Local entrepreneurs swiftly turned from tanning to perfume-making and the town's fortune was made. Today, there are around 30 parfumeries in Grasse. Artisan parfumiers called "noses" can tell the difference between thousands of basic scents, and it can take them months or even years of experimentation to develop a new perfume. Most guard their secret formulas closely, but a few perfumeries can be visited.

↑ Grasse perfumes, the product of months of careful blending and experimentation

TOP 3 PROVENCE PERFUMERIES

Galimard
🅰 C1 🏠 73 rte de Cannes
🌐 galimard.com
Jean de Galimard, aristocratic parfumier to King Louis X, founded this venerable scent-maker (France's oldest) in Grasse in 1747.

Fragonard
🅰 C1 🏠 20 blvd Fragonard
🌐 fragonard.com
Grasse's most famous perfume house is named in honour of Grasse-born painter Jean-Honoré Fragonard (1732–1806).

Molinard
🅰 C1 🏠 60 blvd Victor Hugo, Molinard 🌐 molinard.com
Founded in 1849, Maison Molinard achieved fame for its innovative scents and perfume flasks. Visitors are offered the chance to create their own scents.

Picking jasmine in a ↑
sweet-scented field
near Grasse

⑭ Grottes de St-Cézaire-sur-Siagne

📍F4 🏠1481 rte des Grottes ⏰Feb-mid-Nov: daily 🌐grotte-saint cezaire.com

Dramatic stalactites and stalagmites festoon the ceilings and floors of these enchanted caverns, which are tinged a rich rusty red from iron-fortified water that seeps through the living rock. Rock formations have formed shapes reminiscent of flowers, animals and toadstools, and some stalactites chime musically when tapped.

The chambers are connected by a labyrinth of narrow passages that have been given fanciful names: the Fairies' Alcove, the Great Hall, Hall of Draperies and the Organ Chamber (named after its stone tubes, which resemble the pipes of a huge organ). One passage opens rather alarmingly onto the edge of a 40-m (130-ft) abyss.

Above ground, a network of walking trails winds through the picturesque woodlands that surround the grotto.

⑮ Juan-les-Pins

📍F5 🚌 ℹ️Palais des Congres, 60 chemin des Sables; www.antibes juanlespins.com

To the east of Cannes is the hammerhead peninsula of Cap d'Antibes, a promontory of pines and coves where millionaires' mansions can be found. Just next door is one of the finest beaches in the area tucked in the west side of the cape in Golfe-Juan, where Napoleon came ashore from Elba in 1815. This is a 20th-century resort, promoted by American railroad heir Frank Jay Gould, who attracted high society in the 1920s and 1930s when writers F Scott Fitzgerald

and Ernest Hemingway stayed here. Today, in high season, it draws a young and lively crowd. The area at the junctions of boulevards Baudoin and Wilson is filled with bars, while action centres around the Eden Casino, the Palais des Congrés, and Pinède Gould pine grove, which gives shelter to the International Jazz à Juan Festival in July.

⑯ Antibes

📍F5 🚌🚉 ℹ️42 ave Robert Soleau; www. antibesjuanlespins.com

Originally the ancient Greek trading post of Antipolis, Antibes became heavily fortified over the centuries, notably by Vauban in the 17th century, who built the main port and Fort Carré, where Napoleon was allegedly temporarily imprisoned.

The old town is pleasant, with a picturesque market-place in cours Masséna. The town's high points include the 12th-century towers of the church and Grimaldi castle on the site of Antipolis. The Cathédrale Notre-Dame, which took over the town's watchtower as a belfry, has a wooden crucifix from 1447, a 16th-century Christ and a fine Louis Bréa altarpiece depicting the Virgin Mary.

The Château Grimaldi nearby houses the **Musée Picasso**, which displays over 50 drawings, paintings and ceramics created by the artist when he used the museum as a studio during 1946. The exceptional modern art collection housed here includes works painted by Nicolas de Staël in the last two years of

←

Antibes' ancient fortified walls, with views across the Mediterranean

his life, as well as pieces by Ernst, Modigliani, Léger and Miró. There are also sculptures on the terrace outside.

Further south, the **Musée d'Histoire et d'Archéologie** in the fortified Bastion St-André houses Greek and Etruscan finds, including a 3rd-century BC inscription to the spirit of Septentrion, a boy who danced at the Antipolis theatre.

Marineland leisure park, north of Antibes, includes a shark-filled aquarium and a range of marine animals such as polar bears and whales.

Musée Picasso

⊕⊗⊙ 🅰 Château Grimaldi, Place Mariejol 🆑 04 93 95 85 98 🅾 Tue–Sun 🛇 1 May, 1 Nov

Musée d'Histoire et d'Archéologie

⊕⊙ 🅰 Bastion St-André 🆑 04 93 95 85 98 🅾 Feb–Oct: Tue–Sun; Nov–Jan: Tue–Sat 🛇 1 May, 1 Nov

Marineland

⊕⊙⊙ 🅰 306 ave Mozart 🅾 Feb–Dec: daily 🔲 marineland.fr

⓱

Vallauris

🅰 F5 🚌 🛈 67 ave George Clemenceau & Golfe-Juan Vieux Port; www.vallauris-golfe-juan.fr

In summer, the wares of potters spill on to the avenues of this pottery capital. Picasso revitalized the town's ceramics industry, the history of which is traced in the **Musée de la Céramique**, which houses

ceramics that date from the end of the 19th century to the present day.

In a square just across from the museum, on rue Clément Bel, is Picasso's famous sculpture *L'Homme au Mouton* (1943).

Picasso's *La Guerre et la Paix* (1952), a striking work made up of 18 painted wooden panels, is installed around the curved walls and ceiling in the **Musée National Picasso**, housed in the Romanesque chapel of the Château de Vallauris.

Musée de la Céramique

⊕ 🅰 Pl de la Libération 🆑 04 93 64 71 83 🅾 Wed-Mon (Jul-Aug: daily) 🛇 1 Jan, 1 May, 1 & 11 Nov, 25 Dec

Musée National Picasso

⊕⊙ 🅰 Pl de la Libération 🆑 04 93 64 71 83 🅾 Wed-Mon (Jul-Aug: daily) 🛇 1 Jan, 1 May, 1 & 11 Nov, 25 Dec

CAVES OF PROVENCE

Exploring the underground world of Provence is a fascinating experience. The limestone bedrock of Provence is riddled with caves and grottoes carved over millions of years by underground streams.

GLITTERING CRYSTALS

Some caves, like the Grottes de St-Cézaire-sur-Siagne, are filled with glittering crystals reflected in mirror-calm pools. These are created by the slow drip of mineral-rich water seeping through the ancient rock and drying in elaborate formations.

FOSSILS, BONES AND PAINTINGS

Other Provençal caves reveal signs of humanity's deep past. In the Grotte de l'Observatoire in Monaco (p72), palaeontologists have found fragments of bone tools used by our ancient ancestors around 1,000,000 years ago. Caves in the Gorges du Verdon were used by Neanderthals around 70,000 years ago. From fossil evidence, we also know the same caves were used by giant cave bears, though probably not at the same time! Other caverns, like the Grotte Chauvet, show the remains of cave paintings by the first modern humans around 30,000 years ago.

↑ Alcove filled with crystals in the Grottes de St-Cézaire-sur-Siagne

⑱ Biot

AF4 🏛️🚌 **i**4 Chemin neuf;
www.biot-tourisme.com

The picturesque village of Biot, which has various themed walks (available at the tourist office), was the main pottery town in the region until Pablo Picasso revived the industry in Vallauris after World War II. Today, Biot is renowned for its bubble-flecked glassware. There are eight glassworks, including **La Verrerie de Biot**, where visitors can marvel at master craftsmen at work.

Biot was once the domain of the Knights Templar, and some fortifications remain, such as the Porte des Migraniers (grenadiers), a 1566 stone archway. The church has two fine 16th-century works: *L'Ecce Homo*, attributed to Canavesio, and *La Vierge au Rosaire*, attributed to Louis Bréa.

The **Musée National Fernand Léger** contains many of the artist's vibrant works.

CREATION OF BIOT GLASSWARE

Biot is the capital of glassblowing on the coast. Local soils provide sand for glassmaking, and typical Biot glass is sturdy, with tiny air bubbles (known as *verre à bulles*). The opening of Léger's museum led to an increased interest in all local crafts, and to the arrival of the Verrerie de Biot workshop in 1956. This revived old methods of making oil lamps, carafes and narrow-spouted *porrons*, from which a jet of liquid can be poured straight into the mouth.

La Verrerie de Biot

♿️🅿️🚻🎁 **A**5 chemin des Combes ⏰9:30am-6pm Mon-Sat, 10:30am-1:30pm & 2:30-6pm Sun 🚫1 & 15-27 Jan, 1 May 🌐verrerie biot.com

Musée National Fernand Léger

♿️🅿️🚻🎁 **A**316 chemin du Val-de-Pome ⏰10am-5pm Wed-Mon 🚫1 Jan, 1 May, 25 Dec 🌐musees-nationaux-alpesmaritimes.fr/fleger

⑲ Villeneuve-Loubet

AF4 🚌 **i**16 ave de la Mer; www.villeneuve-tourisme.com

This old village is dominated by a restored medieval castle built by Romée de Villeneuve. There is also a large church with a square belltower amid steeply sloping streets leading down to the new town.

It is also where the celebrated chef, Auguste Escoffier, (1846–1935) was born. The man who invented the *bombe Néro* and *pêche Melba* was *chef de cuisine* at the Grand Hotel, Monte-Carlo, before he was persuaded to become head chef at the Savoy in London. The **Musée Escoffier de l'Art Culinaire**, in the house of his birth, contains many showpieces in almond paste and icing sugar, and over 1,800 menus dating back to 1820. Each summer, the town celebrates Escoffier with a gastronomic festival.

Musée Escoffier de l'Art Culinaire

♿️🎁 **A**3 rue Auguste Escoffier ⏰Daily 🚫Nov-Dec, public hols 🌐fondation-escoffier.org

← Cobbled medieval street with shutters and lanterns in the charming village of Biot

↑ The town of Vence, set against the dramatic backdrop of the Alps

20

Vence

A F4 🚌 **𝒊 8 place du Grand-Jardin; www.vence-tourisme.fr**

Set on a rocky ridge, Vence is a delightful old cathedral town with a busy central market. Its natural beauty has long attracted artists and writers, including the English novelist and poet D H Lawrence, who died here in 1930.

The old town is entered by the Porte de Peyra (1441), beside the place du Frêne, named after a giant ash tree planted to commemorate the visits of King François I and Pope Paul III. The 16th-century castle of the lords of Villeneuve, seigneurs of Vence, houses the museum and the **Fondation Émile Hugues**, named after an illustrious former mayor.

The cathedral, one of the smallest in France, stands by the site of the forum of the Roman city of Vintium. Vence was a bishopric from the 4th to the 19th centuries. Its notable prelates included Saint Véran (d AD 492), and Bishop Godeau (1605–72). The 51 oak and pear choir stalls are carved with satirical figures. Marc Chagall designed the mosaic of *Moses in the Bulrushes* in the chapel (1979).

Perhaps the star attraction of Vence is the **Chapelle du Rosaire**, which was decorated by Henri Matisse (*p67*) in 1947–51. After undergoing surgery for cancer, the artist had been nursed back to health by a Domincan nun, Monique Bourgeois, who later entered a convent in Vence. Matisse bought a house in Vence in 1943 and, to thank Monique for her help, he agreed to help with the design and decoration of a new chapel being built by her convent. The chapel's bright blue roof, stained-glass windows and powerfully simple paintings were all conceived by the artist.

Fondation Émile Hugues
🏛️⊕ **A** Château de Villeneuve **📞** 04 93 24 24 23 **🕐** Tue–Sun **🔒** 1 Jan, 1 May, 25 Dec

Chapelle du Rosaire
⊕ **A** 466 Ave Henri Matisse **🕐** Tue & Thu–Fri, Mon & Wed pm only **🔒** Mid-Nov-mid-Dec, public hols **w** chapellematisse.com

EAT

Les Terraillers
Provençal wines accompany lobster bisque, truffles and foie gras at this fine-dining restaurant.

Q F4 A 11 rte Chemin Neuf, Biot w les terrailles.fr

€€€

La Litote
Inventive cooking in a charming setting with tables under lime trees.

Q F4 A 5 rue de l'Éveché, Vence 🔒 Tue & mid-Nov-mid-Dec w lalitote-vence.com

€€€

Les Bacchanales
Chef Christophe Dufau uses carefully chosen produce from Provence, Piedmont and Corsica in this stylish restaurant-cum-art gallery.

Q F4 A 247 ave de Provence, Vence w lesbacchanales.com

€€€

㉑

Cagnes-sur-Mer

⛰F4 🚍🚌 **ℹ6 blvd Maréchal Juin; www. cagnes-tourisme.com**

Picturesquely perched on its hilltop overlooking the sea, Haut-de-Cagnes is the uppermost and most appealing part of Cagnes-sur-Mer. It's a pleasing jumble of fine Renaissance houses, narrow lanes, steps and vaulted passages. Members of the Grimaldi royal family are entombed in the church of St-Pierre, and the fortress built by Rainier in 1309 still towers over the town. In 1620, Jean-Henri Grimaldi transformed the fortress into a handsome palace. It survived the ravages of the Revolution and occupation in 1815 by Piedmontese troops, who used its spectacular painted ceiling for target practice.

Within the dramatic battlements of the fortress is the **Château-Musée Grimaldi**, an eclectic complex of

museums where two levels of marble-columned galleries rise around a Renaissance courtyard filled with lush greenery and dappled sunlight.

On the ground floor, the Musée d'Olivier is devoted to the traditions of olive cultivation that are so central to Provençal history and culture. The Donation Suzy Solidor, on the first floor, includes portraits of the famed 1930s chanteuse by Jean Cocteau and Kisling, along with around 40 other works gifted to the museum by Solidor. A selection of works from the museum's permanent collection of modern Mediterranean art are on the first and second floors.

Below Haut-de-Cagnes, the former fishing village of Cros-de-Cagnes is the town's seaside annexe, with a small beach. There is a market here every Tuesday and Thursday morning, while Cagnes-Ville is the commercial centre.

East of the centre is Les Collettes, where artist Pierre-Auguste Renoir (1841–1919) built a home in 1907, hoping that the climate would relieve his rheumatism. He stayed here for the rest of his life,

and his home is now the **Musée Renoir**, where visitors can see 14 of his paintings, as well as works by his friends Bonnard and Dufy. Renoir's beloved olive groves are the setting for the bronze *Venus Victrix* (1915–16).

Château-Musée Grimaldi

♿⏰ 🏠Place du Château 🚌49 from Cagnes-sur-Mer railway station ⏰Times vary, check website 🌐cagnes-sur-mer.fr/culture/chateau-musee-grimaldi

Musée Renoir

♿⏰ 🏠19 Chemin des Collettes 🚌49 from Cagnes-sur-Mer railway station ⏰Wed-Mon 🌐cagnes-sur-mer.fr/culture/musee-renoir

---

㉒

Villefranche-sur-Mer

⛰G4 🚍🚌 **ℹJardin François Binon; www.tourisme-villefranche-sur-mer.com**

This unspoiled town overlooks a beautiful natural harbour, deep enough to be a naval port. The buildings here date

Did You Know?

The Rolling Stones recorded their album *Exile on Main Street* in a villa in Villefranche-sur-Mer.

back to the 17th century, though they now include the oceanographic observatory, the university and a national centre of marine research. The lively waterfront is lined with bars and cafés and the town has a market every Wednesday, Saturday and Sunday.

Chapelle St-Pierre, set on the quay, was once used for storing fishing nets. It was renovated in 1957, when Jean Cocteau added lavish frescoes showing scenes from the life of St Peter, intended as a tribute to the local fishermen. Steep lanes climb up from the quay, turning into tunnels beneath the tightly packed buildings. The vaulted rue Obscure has provided shelter from attack as recently as World War II. The Baroque Église St-Michel contains a 16th-century carving of St Rock and his dog as well as a 1790 organ.

Within the grounds of the 16th-century Citadelle de St-Elme are the chapel, open-air theatre and museums.

Chapelle St-Pierre

⊘ 🏠 1 ave Sadi Carnot
📞 04 93 76 90 70 🕐 Wed–Mon
🚫 Mid-Nov–mid-Dec, 25 Dec

23
Beaulieu-sur-Mer

🅰 F4 🚌 ℹ Pl Clémenceau; www.beaulieusurmer.fr

Hemmed in and protected by a rock face, this is one of the Riviera's warmest resorts in winter, with two beaches: the Baie des Fourmis and, by the port, Petite Afrique. The casino, formal gardens and the belle époque Rotunda, now a conference centre and museum, add to Beaulieu's old-fashioned air. Among its hotels is La Réserve, founded by James Gordon Bennett Jr, the owner of the *New York Herald* from 1866 until his death in 1924.

Beaulieu-sur-Mer is also home to the **Villa Grecque Kérylos**. Built by archaeologist Théodore Reinach to resemble an ancient Greek villa, the building took inspiration from Delos, Pompeii, Rome and Egypt, and took over six years to complete. Authentic techniques and precious materials were used to create lavish mosaics, frescoes and inlaid furniture. There are also numerous original Greek ornaments, and an antique sculpture gallery.

←

The pretty town of Villefranche-sur-Mer, set around a natural harbour

↑ Interior of the Villa Grecque Kérylos in Beaulieu-sur-Mer

Villa Grecque Kérylos

⊘ 🕐 🏠 Impasse Gustave Eiffel 🕐 Daily 🌐 villa kerylos.fr

24
Èze

🅰 G4 🚌 ℹ Pl Général de Gaulle; www.eze-tourisme.com

Èze, a dramatic eagle's nest *village perché*, is a cluster of ancient buildings on a peak some 429 m (1,407 ft) above the sea. Its warm climate allows tropical plants such as dates, bananas, orange and lemon trees to grow here. The **Jardin Exotique**, built around the ruins of a 14th-century castle, offers stunning views as far as Corsica.

Flower-bedecked, car-free narrow streets, shady squares and stone archways lead to an 18th-century church, which contains a bust of Christ made from olive wood that survived the terrible fires that raged close by in 1986.

Jardin Exotique

⊘ 🏠 Rue du Château
🕐 Daily 🚫 Christmas week
🌐 jardinexotique-eze.fr

25
Peillon

🅰 G4 🛈 4 carriera Centrale;
www.tourismepaca.fr

At a height of 373 m (1,225 ft), this pretty *village perché* is said by locals to mark the extremity of the inhabited world. Its streets are stepped and narrow, with houses that have scarcely changed since the Middle Ages. There is an attractive cobbled square with fine views, and the 18th-century parish church has an unusual octagonal lantern. But the most impressive sights of all are Giovanni Canavesio's frescoes in the Chapelle des Pénitents Blancs.

Peillon is ideally placed for pretty woodland walks, which will lead visitors to both Peille and La Turbie.

26
Trophée d'Auguste à La Turbie

🅰 G4 🚌 🛈 2 pl Detras;
www.ville-la-turbie.fr

There's an unforgettable view of Monaco and the coast from 480 m (1,575 ft) below the terraces of the grandiose Trophée d'Auguste, which crowns the hilltop village of La Turbie. The Romans built this huge triumphal rotonda, which can be seen from miles around, from white local stone in around 6 BC to mark the division between Italy and newly conquered Gaul.

Originally the Trophée stood on a square podium on which stood a circular colonnade topped by a stepped cone. Inscriptions on its base bear the names

↓ Remains of the imposing Trophée d'Auguste in La Turbie

> **The Romans built this huge triumphal rotonda, which can be seen from miles around, from white local stone in around 6 BC.**

of the 44 Ligurian tribes subjugated by the Emperor Augustus in 13 BC, and the original colonnade included niches that once housed statues of each of Augustus's victorious generals.

Stairs once led to every part of the structure, which was topped by a 6-m (20-ft) statue of the Emperor. When the Romans left, the original 50-m (164-ft) monument was gradually dismantled. Early Christian leaders like the 4th-century missionary St Honorat despised it as an object of pagan worship, and its masonry was pillaged to be reused in later buildings. What remained served as a fortress, and it was further demolished in the 17th century on the orders of Louis XIV, who feared it would fall to the invading Savoyards during their invasion of Provence in 1705.

Today, the **Musée du Trophée d'Auguste** documents the history of the building, with fragments of statuary, inscriptions, drawings, and a scale model that shows how it looked in its imperial heyday.

Huddled beneath this imposing relic, La Turbie is an appealing stop on a stretch of the Grande Corniche that crosses ravines and tunnels through mountains. Two medieval gateways lead to a village centre where narrow streets are splashed with purple bougainvillea.

The 18th-century Nice Baroque church Église St Michel Archange was built with stones plundered from the Trophée. Inside, there is an altar of multi-coloured marble and a 17th-century onyx and agate table, which was used

↑ Houses clustered together on the hillside in medieval Peille

for communion. The church also contains two paintings by Jean-Baptiste van Loo, a portrait of St Mark attributed to Paolo Veronese, and a Pietá from the Bréa School.

Musée du Trophée d'Auguste

🔄🔄🔄 🏠 18 ave Prince Albert Ier de Monaco ⏰ Tue–Sun 🌐 trophee-auguste.fr

27
Peille

🅰️ G4 🚌 ℹ️ 15 rue Centrale; www.peille.fr

Peille is a charming medieval village with a view from its war memorial across the Peillon Valley and as far as the Baie des Anges. Behind the village looms the massive Pic de Baudon, which rises to a height of 1,264 m (4,160 ft).

The town is filled with cobbled alleyways and covered passages. At the end of place A-Laugier, beyond a Gothic fountain, two arches beneath a house rest on a Romanesque pillar.

The Counts of Provence were lords of the castle, and the 12th-century church of Ste-Marie has a picture of Peille in the Middle Ages. There is also a fine 16th-century altarpiece by Honoré Bertone. The Hôtel de Ville is in the domed 18th-century former Chapelle de St-Sébastien, and there is a museum in rue de la Turbie.

28
Lucéram

🅰️ G4 🚌 ℹ️ Maison de Pays, Pl Adrien Barralis; www.luceram.fr

In the midst of this pretty, Italianate village is the tiled roof of the 15th-century Église Ste-Marguerite. The church contains art by Nice's Primitive masters, notably Louis Bréa, the artist of the 10-panelled altarpiece, who made Lucéram a centre for religious painting. Treasures include a silver statue of the Tarascon dragon and Ste Marguerite *(p146)*. Villagers decorate the streets with pine branches in December, and the church is the setting for a Christmas service, where shepherds, accompanied by flutes and tambourines, bring lambs and fruit as offerings.

EAT

Café de la Fontaine
This acclaimed bistro at the Hostellerie Jérome serves Provençal dishes such as lamb, seafood risotto, and rabbit with olives.

🅰️ G4 🏠 4 ave Général de Gaulle, La Turbie 🌐 hostelleriejerome.com

€€€

Restaurant L'Authentique
Elegant Niçois cooking, made using all local ingredients (including produce from the restaurant garden), is served alfresco here.

🅰️ G4 🏠 3 pl Auguste Arnulf, Peillon 🌐 auberge-madone-peillon.com

€€€

Boccafina
A village bar-restaurant with a quirky grotto setting offering beef daube, camembert gratiné, and home-made pizzas.

🅰️ G4 🏠 4 pl Adrien Barralis, Lucéram 🌐 boccafina.net

€€€

29
Roquebrune-Cap-Martin

🅰G4 🚃🚌 ℹ218 ave Aristide Briand; www.rcm-tourisme.com

Roquebrune is said to have the earliest feudal château in France, the sole example of the Carolingian style. **Château Grimaldi de Roquebrune** was built in the 10th century by Conrad I, Count of Ventimiglia, to ward off Saracen attack, and was remodelled by the Grimaldis (p72). Wealthy Englishman Sir William Ingram bought the château in 1911 and added a mock medieval *tour anglaise*.

In the early 1900s, Cap Martin was Provence's smartest resort, attracting the era's glitterati. Impératrice Eugénie, wife of Napoléon III, wintered here. In the 20th century, Coco Chanel, Winston Churchill, and Irish poet W B Yeats frequently visited, while the famous architect Le Corbusier tragically drowned off the cape in 1965.

Important prehistoric remains have been found in the area, some in caves such as the Grotte du Vallonet. Outside Roquebrune, on the Menton road, is the *olivier millénaire*, an olive tree thought to be at least 1,000 years old.

> 💬 INSIDER TIP
> ## Bags of style
>
> There are no border formalities between France and Italy, so visiting Ventimiglia's colourful Friday market is easy from Menton. Leather accessories are a good buy, but beware of fake designer brands.

Every August since 1467, in gratitude for being spared from the plague, Roquebrune's inhabitants have celebrated the Passion with a procession and concert.

Château Grimaldi de Roquebrune

◈ 🏠 Pl William Ingram ☎04 93 35 07 22 🕐Mon–Thu 🚫Nov–Dec, public hols

30
Menton

🅰G4 🚃🚌 ℹPalais de l'Europe, 8 ave Boyer; www.tourisme-menton.fr

Menton straddles the frontier between France and Italy, with only a road tunnel separating the town from the Italian resort of Ventimiglia. The beaches on the main waterfront Baie du

Did You Know?

Locals claim the first lemon groves in Menton were planted by Eve, after she was expelled from Eden.

Soleil are pebbly, but you'll find sandier stretches on the Baie de Garavan, east of the centre.

The town's mellow microclimate is perfect for growing citrus fruits, and the annual Fête du Citron, held for two weeks every February, is a colourful event in which sculptures created from vast heaps of the yellow fruit are paraded through the streets.

Menton has several fine sub-tropical gardens. Bougainvillea, palms, and other tropical plants flourish in the Jardin Botanique Exotique, in the grounds of Villa Val Rahmeh. Above the town is the Jardin

←

View from the Château Grimaldi de Roquebrune, over a jumble of rooftops

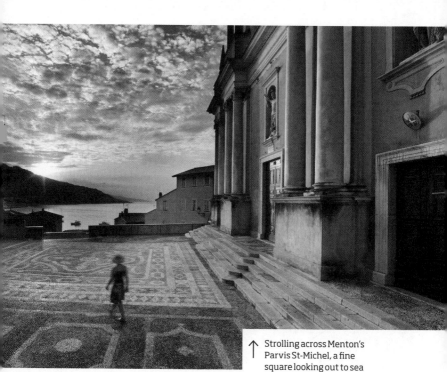

↑ Strolling across Menton's Parvis St-Michel, a fine square looking out to sea

des Colombières designed by artist and writer Ferdinand Bac (1859–1952). This private garden reputedly has France's oldest carob tree and can be visited in the summer by appointment.

The jetties offer good views of the old town, and steps lead to Parvis St-Michel, a fine square paved with the Grimaldi coat of arms, where summer concerts are held.

Menton's **Musée des Beaux-Arts**, was once the summer residence of the princes of Monaco. It features 13th- to 18th-century Italian, French and Flemish art, and 20th-century works by Utrillo, Dufy and Graham Sutherland.

Dedicated to the career of the multi-talented Jean Cocteau (1889–1963), the town's purpose-built **Musée Jean Cocteau** opened in 2011 to house 1,500 works by the author, artist and cinéaste, including sketches, paintings and clips from his famous cinematic productions.

Musée des Beaux-Arts
⊗ 🏠 Palais Carnolès, 3 ave de la Madone 📞 04 93 35 49 71
🕐 Wed-Mon 🚫 Public hols

Musée Jean Cocteau
⊗ 🏠 2 quai de Monléon
🕐 Wed-Mon 🚫 1 Jan, 1 May, 1 Nov & 25 Dec

The town's mellow microclimate is perfect for growing citrus fruits, and the annual Fête du Citron is a colourful event.

JEAN COCTEAU

Born near Paris in 1889, Cocteau spent much of his very public life around the Côte d'Azur. A man of powerful intellect and great energy, he became a member of the Académie Française in 1955. Among other talents, Cocteau was a dramatist (*La Machine Infernale*, 1934); the writer of *Les Enfants Terribles* (1929); and a surrealist film director. *Orphée* (1950) was partly shot against the barren landscape at Les Baux *(p148)*. He died in 1963, before his museum opened.

VAR AND ÎLES D'HYÈRES

The Var is a region of rolling lands, rocky hills, thick forests and swathes of vineyards. To the north, Provençal villages are thinly scattered by mountain streams, on hilltops and in valleys; to the south, a series of massifs slope down to the coast, making this stretch of the Côte d'Azur the most varied and delightful shore in France.

The A8 autoroute runs through the centre of the Var, dividing it roughly into two sections. To the south of this artery the influence of the sea is unmistakable. Toulon, the departmental capital, occupies a fine deep-water harbour that is home to the French Mediterranean fleet. Beyond it are the pleasant resorts of Bandol and Sanary, where Jacques Cousteau first put scuba-diving to the test. To the east are the sandy beaches beneath the great slab of the Massif des Maures. The Var's most famous resort, St-Tropez, facing north in the crook of a bay, lies in a glorious landscape of vineyards. Beyond it, just past Fréjus, the first Roman settlement in Gaul, the land turns blood red in the twinkling inlets and coves below the beautiful Corniche de l'Estérel, which heads east towards the Riviera. The more remote areas to the north of the autoroute have always provided a retreat from the bustling activity of the coast. This is where the Cistercians built their austere Abbaye du Thoronet. Today, visitors escape inland from the summer traffic around St-Tropez to the sparsely populated Haut Var, where towns seem to grow from tufa rock.

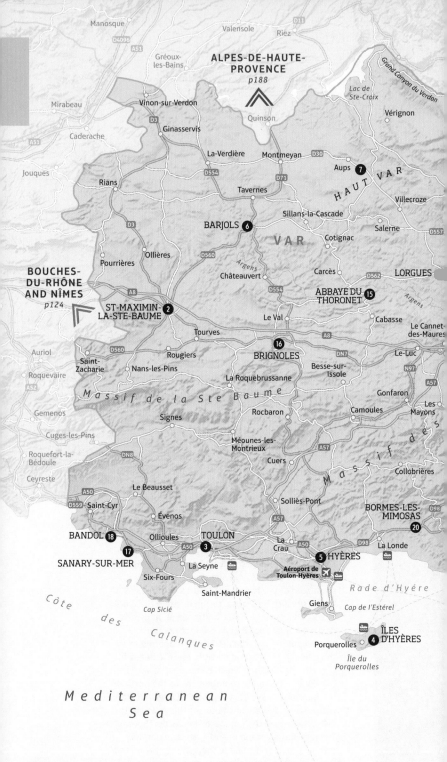

Manosque

Valensole

Riez

D11

ALPES-DE-HAUTE-
PROVENCE
p188

D4096

A51

Gréoux-
les-Bains

Vinon-sur-Verdon

Lac de
Ste-Croix

Grand Canyon du Verdon

Mirabeau

Caderache

Quinson

Vérignon

D3

Ginasservis

La-Verdière

Montmeyan

Aups

7

D30

HAUT VAR

Jouques

A51

Rians

Tavernes

Villecroze

D554

D71

BARJOLS

6

Sillans-la-Cascade

Salerne

D557

Pourrières

Ollières

VAR

Cotignac

D560

Argens

D3

BOUCHES-
DU-RHÔNE
AND NÎMES
p124

Châteauvert

Carcès

D562

LORGUES

A8

D554

ABBAYE DU
THORONET

15

Argens

ST-MAXIMIN-
LA-STE-BAUME

2

Le Val

Cabasse

Le Cannet-
des-Maures

Auriol

Saint-
Zacharie

D560

Tourves

A8

DN7

Le-Luc

N97

Rougiers

Nans-les-Pins

BRIGNOLES

16

Besse-sur-
Issole

A57

Roquevaire

La Roquebrussanne

Gonfaron

Les
Mayons

A52

M a s s i f   d e   l a   S t e   B a u m e

Gemenos

Signes

Rocbaron

Camoules

Cuges-les-Pins

Méounes-les-
Montrieux

M a s s i f   d e s

Roquefort-la-
Bédoule

DN8

Cuers

Collobrières

Ceyreste

Le Beausset

Solliès-Pont

A50

BORMES-LES-
MIMOSAS

20

D559

Saint-Cyr

Évenos

A57

D98

BANDOL

18

Ollioules

TOULON

La
Crau

La Londe

SANARY-SUR-MER

17

A50

3

A50

D98

La Seyne

5

HYÈRES

Six-Fours

Aéroport de
Toulon-Hyères

Saint-Mandrier

Giens

Rade d'Hyère

Cap Sicié

Cap de l'Estérel

C ô t e

Porquerolles

4

ÎLES
D'HYÈRES

d e s

Île du
Porquerolles

C a l a n q u e s

M e d i t e r r a n e a n
S e a

0 kilometres   10

0 miles   10

N

Sardinia

Corsica

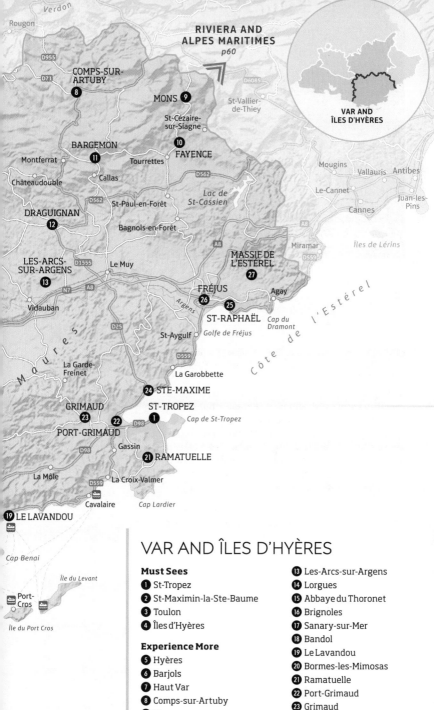

RIVIERA AND
ALPES MARITIMES
p60

↑ View of the rooftops of St-Tropez at sunset, seen from the Citadelle

❶

ST-TROPEZ

🅰 E5 ✈ Toulon-Hyeres, Nice 🚆 St-Raphael-Frejus
⛴ from Cannes and Nice 🇮 8 Quai Jean Jaurès; www.
saintropeztourisme.com

St-Tropez conjures up images of glamorous beach life, celebrity yachts and upmarket shopping, but there's more than frivolity and hedonism here. The ochre-painted walls and terracotta rooftops of the old town evoke a time before tourism. The many great artists who worked here are celebrated in a world-class art museum, while the imposing hilltop citadel is a reminder of a more turbulent past.

① ⊘

Musée de l'Annonciade

🏠 2 place Georges
Grammont ⏱ Mid-Jul-Oct:
10am-6pm daily; Nov-mid-July: 10am-6pm Wed-Mon
🗓 1-14 Feb, 15-30 Nov,
public holidays 🖥 saint-tropez.fr/fr/culture/musee-de-lannonciade

Painters of the Pointillism and Fauvism movements have pride of place in this gallery, which showcases works by some of the greatest artists of the 20th century. Wealthy art collector Georges Grammont funded the transformation of the 16th-century Chapelle de l'Annonciade by architect Louis Süe in the 1950s. The core of the collection comprises works by Paul Signac, the painter who first popularized St-Tropez when he moved here in 1892, and his Pointilliste followers (including Georges Seurat). Seek out paintings by the Les Nabis group, including Pierre Bonnard's *Nu Devant la Cheminée* (1919). Also look out for Signac's *L'Orage* (1895), with its bravura use of swirling brushwork to depict St-Tropez harbour. Matisse, Braque, Dufy and Delauney are among the many other artists whose work is on display.

DRINK

Les Caves du Roy
Rub shoulders with the rich and famous at this legendary, luxurious nightspot which turned 50 in 2017 and is still going strong.

🏠 27 ave Foch
🖥 lescavesduroy.com

Le Café
This is the perfect vantage point from which to watch a game of *pétanque* beneath the plane trees or to relax with a coffee after a morning browsing the market.

🏠 Traverse des Lices
83390 🖥 lecafe.fr

Bar du Port
Soft leather armchairs, polished wood and gleaming marble greet visitors at this landmark brasserie and bar.

🏠 9 quai Suffren
🖥 barduport.com

② Place des Lices

Locals still play pétanque beneath the plane trees on this pretty square as they have done for over a century, watched by spectators seated at the cafe tables which line each side. The Place des Lices is St-Tropez's social hub, and is at its liveliest on Tuesday and Saturday mornings, when it is transformed into a thronged marketplace where locals shop for fresh produce and visitors browse art and antiques stalls.

③ Église de Notre Dame de l'Assomption

🏠 Rue de l'Église ⏰ Times vary, check website 🌐 paroisse-saint-tropez.com

A garishly painted bust of Saint Torpes, the Christian martyr after whom St-Tropez is named, is the pride of this church, built in faux-Baroque style in the late 18th century. According to legend, Torpes was a Roman gladiator and an early convert to Christianity who was beheaded as a heretic

on the orders of the Emperor Nero. His headless corpse was put in a boat with a dog and a cockerel, which were expected to devour and desecrate the corpse. Miraculously, it washed up unmolested here in AD 68. The saint's bust is paraded through the streets on 16 May during the traditional *bravades*, an annual religious festival.

④ 🚻 🚫 Musée de la Citadelle

🏠 Citadelle de Saint-Tropez 📞 04 94 97 59 43 ⏰ 10am–5:30pm daily 🚫 Public holidays

Peacocks patrol the wooded precincts of the sturdy Citadelle de St-Tropez, the early 17th-century fortress that squats on the hilltop east of the harbour. It's worth making your way to its multi-angled ramparts just for the view of the coast. Within, you can discover the maritime history of the area and learn about the lives of some of the port's most famous citizens, such as Admiral Pierre-André de Suffren, a hero of France's 18th-century wars with Britain.

ST-TROPEZ'S BEACHES

St-Tropez's famed beaches stretch for 9 km (5.6 miles) in a long, golden crescent along the Baie de Pampelonne, starting 5 km (3 miles) south of St-Tropez. Lined with posh beach clubs and bar restaurants, Pampelonne attracts up to 30,000 visitors a day, but finding a space on its sands can be costly. For a quick dip, you'll find smaller beaches with free access north of the old town centre at Plage la Glaye and Plage de la Fontanette. Those seeking an all-over tan can find "clothing optional" stretches at Plage Tahiti.

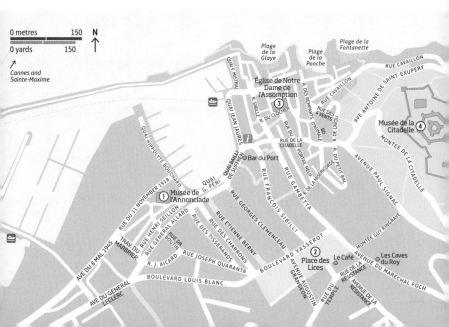

A SHORT WALK
ST-TROPEZ

Distance 1 km (half a mile) **Time** 15 minutes

Clustered around the old port and nearby beaches, the centre of St-Tropez, partly rebuilt in its original style after World War II, is full of pretty pastel-coloured old fishermen's houses. In the port itself, traditional fishing boats are still to be seen moored side by side with sleek luxury cruisers. Behind the port-side cafés of the quai Jean-Jaurès, the narrow, bustling streets are packed with boutiques and restaurants.

La Fontanette beach leads to a coastal walk with views over Ste-Maxime.

*The **Tour Vieille** separates the Port de Pêche from La Glaye beach next door.*

*The **Ponche Quarter** is a comparatively quiet and unspoiled area of St-Tropez.*

↑ The 15th-century Tour du Portalet, part of the city's original defences

Tour Vieille

Place de la Ponche

Tour du Portalet

LA GLAYE

RUE DE LA PONCHE

STA

PLACE DE L'HÔTEL DE VILLE

QUAI FRÉDÉRIC MISTRAL

RUE SIBILLE

Môle Jean Réveille

QUAI   JEA

Did You Know?

St-Tropez first attracted the jet set after Brigitte Bardot filmed *And God Created Woman* here in 1956.

*The attractively painted houses and packed cafés lining the **quai Jean-Jaurès** have enticed visitors and inspired artists for over a century.*

↑ Ochre-coloured rooftops of the Old Town, seen from the Citadelle

*The **Église Notre-Dame de l'Assomption** is known for its prized bust of St Torpès, the patron saint of St-Tropez.*

RUE FONTANETTE

RUE DES PÊCHEURS

ES REMPARTS

RUE D'AUMAVE

RUE DE LA CITADELLE

RUE DU CLOCHER

RUE DE L'ÉGLISE

RUE VICTOR LAUGIER

URÉS

QUAI SUFFREN

Statue of Pierre André de Suffren

⬤ FINISH

0 metres 50
0 yards 50

N ↑

↑ Statue of Admiral Pierre André de Suffren on the quay

ST-MAXIMIN-LA-STE-BAUME

🅰D5 🏠Place de l'Hôtel de Ville 🕐Basilica: 9am–7:30pm daily (except during services) 🌐lesamisdelabasilique.fr

Surrounded by hills and vineyards, St-Maximin-la-Ste-Baume is dominated by Provence's finest example of Gothic architecture, the basilica Ste-Marie-Madeleine and its attached former monastery.

According to Provençal tradition, Ste-Marie-Madeleine was built on the site of the tombs of St Mary Magdalene and of St Maximin, the legendary first bishop of Aix. The saints' remains, hidden from the Saracens (p55), were rediscovered in 1279. The basilica appears unfinished from the outside (there is no belfry) but within, the sense of balance is stunning. So too are the treasures, notably a 16th-century altarpiece depicting the Passion of Christ, and a renowned 17th-century organ. Mary Magdalene's remains are in a reliquary in the crypt.

The adjoining Royal Monastery, so called because the French kings were its priors, was abandoned by Dominican friars in 1957. It is now a popular hotel-restaurant.

↑ Exterior of the 14th-century apse at St-Marie-Madeleine

Organ

Antoine Ronzen's wooden retable (1517–1520) and the surrounding panels include the first picture of the Papal Palace in Avignon (p158).

This bronze gilt reliquary (1860) holds the skull of St Mary Magdalene. Although pilgrim popes and princes took away other parts of her body, the majority of her relics can still be found here.

Timeline

C.1130
△ Ramon Berenguer, Count of Provence, establishes the town of St-Maximin under his governance

1279
▽ The town becomes a popular pilgrimage site when Charles II, Count of Provence, rediscovers the tombs of St Mary Magdalene and St Maximin

1295
Charles II founds a cathedral on the site of the tombs, and control of the monastery is granted to the Dominican order

1316
The cathedral is consecrated, and marble tombs from the Roman era are placed in the newly completed crypt

1532
▽ Work on the cathedral is abandoned, leaving the building incomplete and lacking a finished frontage or belltowers

→
Cloisters overlooking the courtyard of the monastery, now a hotel

St-Maximin-la-Ste-Baume's town hall was formerly the pilgrims' hostelry.

Discovered along the Roman Aurelian Way (see p125), this 1st-century milestone is now on display at the entrance to the cloisters.

Former refectory

↑ Illustration of Ste-Marie-Madeleine and its attached monastery

↑ The magnificent high altar, set in the apse of Ste-Marie-Madeleine

↑ Toulon's impressive natural harbour and urban sprawl

③

TOULON

🅐D6 ✈Toulon-Hyères 24 km (15 miles) E 🚆Gare SNCF, blvd de Tessé 🚌Gare Routière, blvd de Tessé ⛴Ferries to/from Corsia, Sardinia, Majorca 🛈12 place Louis Blanc; www.toulontourisme.com

Toulon has a rough-edged charm that is quite at odds with the coastal resorts to its east and west and the tranquil villages of the Var hinterland. Sited on a superb natural harbour, it is steeped in maritime history and has for centuries been home to France's Mediterranean fleet. Badly damaged during World War II, and a byword for urban deprivation in following decades, it has transformed itself in the 21st century to become a vibrant, rejuvenated city that remains true to its roots and makes an interesting contrast to the chicer stretches of Provence's coastline. For foodies, it offers a menu that stretches from authentic seafood to imaginative Mediterranean-fusion.

①

Darse Vielle

You'll still see smartly uniformed matelots taking a break from their duties (aboard the frigates of France's Mediterranean fleet) in the cafés and bars along the Darse Vielle, a small sheltered harbour built to protect ships from the elements in 1604–10. For centuries, these quaysides were the beating heart of Toulon, and up until the end of the 19th century, the port employed more than 10,000 dock workers. The traditional fishing boats known as *pointus* still moor here, but these days dockers, fishermen and sailors are usually outnumbered by crowds of strolling visitors who have just disembarked from the giant cruise ships which make Toulon a regular port of call.

② 🗺 Ⓜ 🛍

Musée National de la Marine

🅐Place Monsenergue 🚌15 🕙10am–6pm Wed–Mon 🌐musee-marine.fr

Colossal statues of Mars and Bellona, god and goddess of war, flank the grand gateway that leads into Toulon's former royal naval shipyard. Built in the 17th century, the arsenal where France's galleys and galleons were built stretched for more than 240 ha (595 acres) and aimed to make France a major Mediterranean sea power.

Now a museum, the arsenal gatehouse shows exhibits spanning centuries of French maritime history, from early models like that of the 17th-century galley Dauphine to 21st-century nuclear submarines, aircraft carriers and other warships. Wooden figureheads carved by Louis XIV's naval sculptor Pierre Puget (1620–94) and antique navigational instruments provide context to the big ships on display. A special exhibition focuses on the French Navy's darkest hour, the scuttling of the pride of its fleet at Toulon in November 1942.

③ 🏛

Cathédrale Ste-Marie-de-la-Seds

📍 55 place de la Cathédrale
🕐 7:30am–noon & 2:30–7pm daily ☎ For cathedral services 🌐 diocese-frejus-toulon.com

Works by Pierre Puget and Jean-Baptiste Van Loo (1684–1745) are among the main attractions of the city's 11th-century cathedral, which lurks behind a clumsy 17th-century Classical façade that belies its early medieval roots. Puget's nephew and disciple Christophe Veyrier (1637–1689) contributed the alabaster reredos in the chapel to the south of the spectacular Baroque high altar.

↑ Interior of the 11th-century Cathédrale Ste-Marie-de-la-Seds

④

Musée d'Art de Toulon

📍 113 blvd Général Leclerc
🕐 Until end 2019

Founded in the latter half of the 19th century, this museum grew in the 1970s into an outstanding collection of more than 1,000 works by cutting-edge 20th century artists like Yves Klein, Christo, and other American and European Minimalists, Nouveau-Realists and Conceptualists. It also houses a collection of more than 400 photographs by Henri Cartier-Bresson and other pioneers of photography. The museum is due to reopen in late 2019 following a two-year renovation programme.

💬 INSIDER TIP
Toulon beaches

To find sandy stretches beyond Toulon and enjoy a budget journey across its sheltered bay (the Petit Rade), hop on a water-bus from the ferry terminal at Quai Cronstadt to beaches at Les Sablettes, La Seyne and St Mandrier.

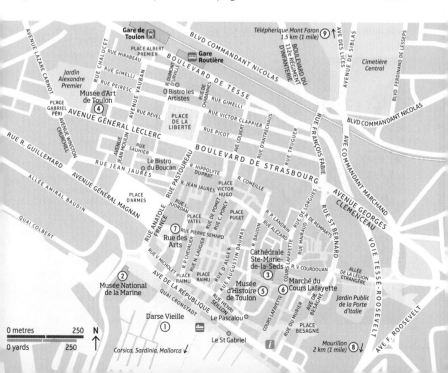

⑤

Musée d'Histoire de Toulon

🏠 10 rue Saint Andrieu
📞 04 94 62 11 07 🚌 15
🕐 3-6pm Mon-Sat

The star of this quaint museum is the young Napoleon Bonaparte, whose first triumph came when he rallied French revolutionary forces to drive the British from Toulon in 1793. Maps, models, sketches and prints offer glimpses into multiple aspects of the city's history. The collection also includes works by the prolific sculptor Pierre Puget, who was in charge of decorating Toulon's port and its grand public buildings during the reign of Louis XIV.

⑥

Marché du Cours Lafayette

🏠 Cours Lafayette 🚌 15
🕐 7:30am-12:30pm Tue-Sun

Cours Lafayette, next to the Cathédrale Ste-Marie-de-la-Seds, is the venue for this lively market where locals shop for colourful fresh produce and household goods. Alongside stalls selling everyday necessities, visitors will discover vendors of antiques and curios, souvenirs and arts and crafts. The market bustles with life every morning, but is at its busiest and most interesting on Saturdays and Sundays, when it spills over into the neighbouring petit cours, place Paul Comte, place Louis Blanc and rue de Lorgues.

⑦

Rue des Arts

🏠 Rue Pierre Sémard
🌐 ruedesarts.fr

This formerly run-down district in the heart of the old town has been reborn as a chic artists' and artisans' quarter, filled with designer studios and small galleries, showcasing the work of adventurous young local creative talents. Trendy shops and lively café-bars line the area's tree-shaded squares, where an array of street musicians provide a lively soundtrack.

EAT

Le St Gabriel
Grilled octopus is the signature dish at this bright modern brasserie by the harbour.

🏠 334 ave de la République 📞 04 94 09 32 82

€€€

O Bistro les Artistes
The emphasis here is on clean, sharp flavours and fresh local produce, with a menu that features dishes like salmon carpaccio, steak tartare and foie gras.

🏠 10 rue Dumont Durville 🌐 obistrodes artistes.com

€€€

Le Bistrot du Boucan
This vibrant restaurant offers a menu that ranges from favourites like seared duck breast to light dishes such as gravlax with blinis, all beautifully presented.

🏠 223 rue Jean Jaurès 🌐 lebistrodu boucan.com

€€€

Le Pascalou
Not far from Cours Lafayette, this restaurant serves delicious family-style seafood dishes.

🏠 3 pl à l'Huile 📞 04 94 62 87 02

€€€

← Artichokes on sale at the Marché du Cours Lafayette

← Café on a narrow street in Toulon's old town

where you can buy a range of refreshments and soak up the view.

Also at the top of the mountain is the **Mémorial du Débarquement de Provence**, a memorial to the 1944 Allied landings in Toulon. A fascinating multi-media exhibition illustrates the landings by Free French troops and their US allies that began the liberation of Provence.

Memorial du Débarquement de Provence

⊘ 🅐 Mont Faron 🕒10am–12:30pm & 1:15–5:15pm Wed-Mon (Apr-Sep: to 7:15pm) 🚫2nd fortnight in Dec 🅦 cheminsdememoire. gouv.fr.

⑧ Mourillon

Toulon's seaside quarter is an attractive jumble of colourful old houses rising from a long stretch of sand and pebbles, around 2 km (1.5 miles) southeast of the city centre. It's a pleasant spot for a day at the beach or a seafood lunch, and also worth the trip for the **Musée des Arts Asiatiques**, an exotic collection dedicated to Asian sacred and decorative art, where visitors will find delicate paintings on silk depicting scenes from the life of the Buddha, temple carvings from Tibet and beautiful porcelain used in age-old Japanese tea ceremonies. Many were brought home by French mariners, while almost 500 pieces in jade and metal from China, Japan, Tibet and India were donated in 1961 by the journalist and collector Hippolyte Fauverge de French.

Musée des Arts Asiatiques

⊘ 🅐Villa Jules Verne, 169 littoral Frédéric Mistral 📞04 94 36 83 10 🚌3 🕒Noon–6pm daily

⑨ ⊘ 🖵 Téléphérique Mont Faron

🅐Blvd Amiral Vence 🚌40 🕒10am–5:30pm daily (Mar: to 6pm; May, Jun & Sep: to 7pm; Jul-Aug: to 7:45pm) 🚫Dec 🅦telepherique-faron.fr

It's worth taking the giddy cable car ride from street level to the summit of Mont Faron, 584 m (1,916 ft) above sea level, just for the stupendous view which allows you to appreciate fully the magnificent, sheltered natural harbour that is the city's great natural asset. There is an excellent restaurant right at the top of the mountain

↑ Spectacular view of Toulon from the Téléphérique Mont Faron

---

HARBOUR BOAT TOUR

For an insight into how Toulon became one of the world's greatest naval bases, take a boat tour of the harbour, where grey-painted leviathans like the aircraft carrier Charles de Gaulle, pride of the French navy, can be seen looming above pleasure craft and fishing boats. One-hour cruises with Bateliers de la Côte d'Azur leave from Quai Cronstadt, next to the ferry terminal *(www.bateliersdelacotedazur.com).*

④
ÎLES D'HYÈRES

🅐E6 ✈Toulon-Hyères 🚗🚌🚊From Hyères ℹRotonde du Park Hotel, 16 ave de Belgique; www.hyeres-tourisme.com

Not for nothing are the Îles d'Hyères also known as the "Îles d'Or" or "Golden Isles". Each of these three tiny islets, which lie 10 km (6 miles) off the Var coast, has its own charms. They have a chequered history thanks to their strategic position; occupiers have included Greeks, Romans, Saracens and pirates.

Porquerolles

Porquerolles, the largest of the trio, is a car-free paradise of sandy beaches, pine-scented woods and olive groves, with a network of easy-going trails to explore on foot or with a rented bike.

The newest jewel in its crown is the Fondation Carmignac, opened in 2018, where a collection of radical contemporary and modern art can be explored in a former villa and an underground labyrinth of galleries where visitors walk barefoot. Above ground, giant masks and boulders are scattered around the wooded estate. The permanent collection includes works by Basquiat, Lichtenstein, Warhol and other 20th and 21st-century giants.

> A marine national park extends to the seabed, where brightly coloured rainbow wrasse swim and octopuses lurk among the rocks.

Port-Cros

Port-Cros is a delight for nature lovers. Around it, a marine national park extends to the sea-bed, where brightly coloured rainbow wrasse swim and octopuses lurk among the rocks. An underwater trail leads snorkellers around the island's shores. On land, the Route des Crêtes leads through pine and arbutus woods to the island's highest point. The prosaic walls and barracks of the 18th-century Fort du Moulin overlook the harbour.

Le Levant

To visit Le Levant, visitors must either be naked or in uniform. Most of the island is a French naval base, and so is off-limits to civilians. The other 10% is occupied by Heliopolis, Europe's first naturist resort.

Beach on Porquerolles; diver on a marine trail in Port-Cros (inset) ↓

JACQUES-YVES COUSTEAU

Godfather of scuba diving, Jacques-Yves Cousteau (1910–97) dedicated his career to undersea exploration and to raising awareness of the plight of the oceans. He patented the first successful self-contained underwater breathing apparatus, the Aqua-Lung in 1946. He also directed the 1956 documentary film version of his book *The Silent World,* which won a Palme d'Or at the Cannes Film Festival.

Pretty, flower-filled back streets in the town of Hyères ↑

EXPERIENCE MORE

⑤

Hyères

🅰D6 ✈Toulon-Hyères
🚇🚌🚢 *i* Rotonde du Park Hotel, 16 ave de Belgique; www.hyeres-tourisme.com

The town of Hyères is one of the most agreeable on the Côte d'Azur, and the oldest of the south of France winter resorts. Hyères lies at the centre of well-cultivated land that provides fresh fruit and vegetables all year. It has three leisure ports, 25 km (16 miles) of sandy beach and a peninsula facing the Îles d'Hyères.

A palm-growing industry was established here in 1867, soon becoming the largest in Europe. The industry is still important and thousands of palms line the boulevards of the new town.

Hyères' main church is St-Louis in Place de la République. Romanesque and Provençal Gothic, it was completed in 1248. From place Massillon, rue St-Paul leads past the 11th-century Église St-Paul, full of 17th-century ex-votos. The road continues to the ruined 12th-century Château St-Bernard, which has good views.

A must-see is the stunning **Villa de Noailles** (1924), high above the pedestrianized old town. A great attraction for 20th-century artists, the villa was where Man Ray filmed *Les Mystères du Château du Dé*; it has also hosted the likes of Dalí, Miró and Picasso.

Villa de Noailles
🏠 Montée de Noailles 📞 04 98 08 01 98 🕐 2–7pm Wed–Thu & Sat–Sun, 4–8pm Fri 🚫 Public holidays

↑ Fontaine du Monument aux Morts
  in Place Victor Hugo, Barjols

6
Barjols

A D5 🚌 🛈 Blvd Grisolle;
www.barjols.fr

Once renowned for its busy
tanneries, Barjols now lies
peacefully among woods and
fast-flowing streams. In 1983,
after almost 400 years, the
leather industry folded. The
abandoned factories have
now become artisans' studios.

Two traditional Provençal
instruments, the three-holed
flute (galoubet) and the narrow
drums (tambourins), were still
made in Barjols until recently.
These instruments resound
each January at the annual
fête of St Marcel, the town's
patron saint.

St Marcel's relics can be
seen in the 11th-century
church of Notre-Dame-de-
l'Assomption. A mixture of
Romanesque, Byzantine and
Gothic architectural styles,
the church also contains a
beautiful organ dating from
1656. There are good views of
the surrounding countryside
from the bell tower.

Of the many stone fountains
dotted around the town, the
most famous is the mossy
Champignon in place Capitaine
Vincens. It stands under what
is reputed to be the largest
plane tree in Provence.
Between the church and the
old tanneries are the restored

buildings of the old quartier
du Réal. Exotic porticoes, particularly on the Renaissance
Hôtel de Pontevès, add spice
to otherwise drab streets.

7
Haut Var

A E4 ✈ Toulon-Hyères,
Nice 🚆 Les Arcs 🚌 Aups
🛈 Pl Martin Bidoure, Aups;
www.aups-tourisme.com

The most remote and
unspoiled lands of the Var are
situated between Barjols and
Comps-sur-Artuby, up towards
the Gorges du Verdon (p192).
Much of the land here has
been taken over by the military.

Aups, set among undulating
hills on the plateau edge, is
the region's centre. Epicureans
may be drawn by the local
honey and olive oil, or by the
truffle market each Thursday
morning in winter. It is an
attractive town with a grand
old square and castle ruins.
The 15th-century St-Pancrace
church has a Renaissance
doorway. Also worth a visit
is the excellent **Musée Simon
Segal**, which is housed in a
former Ursuline convent.

The museum contains works
by Segal and Paris painters,
as well as local scenes.

About 5 km (3 miles)
northwest on the D9 is the
village of Moissac-Bellevue.
Many of its buildings date
from the 16th and 17th
centuries and its church was
mentioned in a papal edict
of 1225. South from Aups is
Villecroze, set against the
dramatic backdrop of the
Grottes Troglodytiques.
These are natural caves on
three levels, which local lords
in the 16th century turned
into dwellings. The arcaded
streets and the keep of the
feudal castle give the town a
medieval flavour. A short drive
from Villecroze leads up to
Tourtour, a smaller, prettier
and more popular village.
Renowned French express-
ionist painter Bernard Buffet
lived his last days here. Two of
his creations – large, metal-
built insect sculptures – are
still displayed in the village.

The valley town of Salernes
lies in the opposite direction,
10 km (6 miles) west on the
D51. Smoke pumps from the
kilns of its 15 ceramic factories.
Salernes is one of the best-
known Provençal tile-making
centres, noted for tomettes –
hexagonal terracotta floor-tiles.

→ Gushing cascades at the
  Grottes Troglodytiques
  waterfall, near Villecroze

18th-century paintings, artifacts, tapestries and furniture. The garden, by Le Nôtre, is publicly owned.

Musée Simon Segal
🏠 Rue Albert Premier 📞 04 94 70 01 95 🕐 Jun-Sep: Wed-Mon

Grottes Troglodytiques
♿ 🏠 Villecroze 📞 04 94 67 50 00 🕐 Times vary, call ahead

Château d'Entrecasteaux
♿♿ 🏠 83570 Entrecasteaux 🕐 Easter-mid-Jun: Sun & public hols; mid-Jun-Sep: Sun-Fri 🌐 chateau-entrecasteaux.com

↑ Chapel of St-André, overlooking the Artuby Gorges

Cotignac, west of Salernes, is an echo of Villecroze, with a cave-pocked cliff behind it. Behind the *mairie* (town hall), a river springs from the rocks, and beyond is an open-air theatre. The intriguing **Château d'Entrecasteaux** lies 15 km (9 miles) east of Cotignac. The 17th-century castle is filled with 17th- to

€1,000

The price that can be paid for 1 kg (2.2 lbs) of truffles or the "black gold" of the Var.

8
Comps-sur-Artuby

🅰 E4 🚌 ℹ 2 ave Lazare Carnot, Draguignan; 04 98 10 51 05

The eastern approach to the Gorges du Verdon (*p192*) passes through Comps-sur-Artuby. The village nestles at the foot of a rock topped by the 13th-century chapel of St-André, which has been restored. From the church there are grand views of the Artuby Gorges.

To the east lies Bargème, a village of steep streets with a population of 86. At 1,094 m (3,589 ft) it is the highest community in the Var. The village is closed to traffic.

Dominating Bargème is a large, well preserved 14th-century castle. There is also the 13th-century Romanesque Église St-Nicolas with a carved, wooden altarpiece depicting Saint Sebastian.

9
Mons

🅰 F4 🚌 ℹ Pl St Sébastien; 04 94 76 39 54

Situated on a rock-spur, Mons, with its tiny lanes and overhanging arches, has an almost magical appeal. The Place St-Sébastien looks out across the coast, with views from Italy to Toulon.

Originally a Celtic-Ligurian settlement, its Château-Vieux quarter dates from the 10th century, but was mainly built by Genoese who repopulated the village after the plague in the 14th century. The first families came from Figounia; their legacy is the local dialect, *figoun*, which survives thanks to the isolated position of the village. Nearby is the *roche taillée*, a Roman aqueduct carved from solid rock.

10
Fayence

🅰E3 💬 ℹ️ Pl Léon Roux;
www.paysdefayence.com

The hillside town of Fayence is the largest between Grasse and Draguignan and is an international centre for local crafts as well as gliding. Dominated by a wrought-iron clock tower, it still has a few remains of its 14th-century defences, including a Saracen-style gate.

The Église St-Jean-Baptiste was built in the 18th century with a Baroque marble altar (1757) crafted by a local mason, Dominique Fossatti. Its terrace offers a sweeping view over the town's glider airfield.

On the hillside opposite, in the community of Tourettes, there is a striking château. Part modelled on the Cadet school in St Petersburg, it was built in 1824 for General Alexandre Fabre, who once worked as a military engineer for Tsar Alexander I of Russia. He originally intended to make the building a public museum, but failed to finish the task and so it remains private.

There are a number of attractive villages nearby. Among the best are Callian and Montauroux to the east, and Seillans, 5 km (3 miles) to the west, where the German-born painter Max Ernst (1891–1976) chose to spend his last years. The prestigious Musique en Pays de Fayence festival in September brings string quartets who perform in the charming local churches.

The adjoining library houses a lavishly illuminated 14th-century manuscript of the *Roman de la Rose,* considered to be the most important book of courtly love in France.

11
Bargemon

🅰E3 🚉 Les Arcs 💬
ℹ️ Ave Pasteur; www.ot-bargemon.fr

This medieval village, fortified in AD 950, has three 12th-century gates and a tower from the mid-16th century. The village is laid out around a number of squares with fountains, shaded by plane trees.

The angels' heads on the high altar of the 15th-century church, St-Étienne, now the Musée-Galerie Honoré Camos, are attributed to the school of Pierre Puget, like those in the Chapelle Notre-Dame-de-Montaigu. The chapel contains an oak-wood carving of the Virgin brought here in 1635. The Fossil and Mineral Museum on rue de la Résistance displays over 3,000 pieces.

12
Draguignan

🅰D4 💬 ℹ️ 2 ave Lazare Carnott; www.tourisme-dracenie.com

During the day, the former capital of the Var *département* has the busy air of a small market town. At night, however, the only sign of life are groups of young people in the place des Herbes. Baron Haussmann, planner of modern Paris, laid out Draguignan's 19th-century boulevards. At the end of his plane-tree-lined allées d'Azémar, there is a Rodin bust of the prime minister

Georges Clémenceau (1841–1929) who represented Draguignan for 25 years.

The pedestrianized old town has a 24-m (79-ft) clockless clock tower, built in 1663, on the site of the original keep, and there is a good view from its wrought-iron campanile. The Église St-Michel contains a statue of St Hermentaire. In the 5th century he slew a dragon, giving the town its name.

Draguignan has two good local museums. The **Musée des Arts et Traditions Provençales** deals with the region's social and economic history. It occupies buildings that date back to the 17th century. Regional country life is shown using reconstructed kitchens and barns.

The **Musée Municipal d'Art et d'Histoire** shows local and regional archaeology as well as collections of ceramics and furniture. The adjoining library (by appointment only) houses a lavishly illuminated 14th-century manuscript of the *Roman de la Rose*, considered to be the most important book of courtly love in France.

Northwest of the town on the D955 is the enormous prehistoric dolmen Pierre de la Fée, or Fairy Stone.

↑ Neat hedges in the formal garden at the Château de Villeneuve, Les Arcs-sur-Argens

Musée des Arts et Traditions Provençales
◉◉ ◨ 75 pl Georges Brassens **(** 04 94 47 05 72 ◉ Tue–Sat ⊠ 1 May, 25 Dec

Musée Municipal d'Art et d'Histoire
9 rue de la République **(** 04 98 10 26 85 ⊠ For restoration until the end of 2019

13

Les-Arcs-sur-Argens

🅰 D4 🚋🚌 ℹ Place du Général de Gaulle; www.tourisme-dracenie.com

Wine centre for the Côtes de Provence, Les Arcs has a medieval quarter, Le Parage, set around the 13th-century Château de Villeneuve. The Église St-Jean-Baptiste (1850), contains a screen by Louis Bréa (1501).

To the east of Les Arcs is the 11th-century Abbaye de Ste-Roseline, named after Roseline de Villeneuve, daughter of the Baron of Arcs. Legend has it that when her father stopped her taking food to the poor, the food turned into roses. She entered the abbey in 1300, later becoming its abbess. The **Chapelle Ste-Roseline** contains the body of the saint in a glass shrine, as well as a Chagall mosaic.

Chapelle Ste-Roseline
🏠 RD 91, Les Arcs-sur-Argens **(** 04 94 73 37 30 ◉ Tue–Sun pm ⊠ Mid-Dec–Jan, pub hols

PIERRE DE LA FÉE

The massive stone slab that crowns this 2.5-m- (8-ft-) high dolmen is 6 m (20 ft) long and estimated to weigh 60 tonnes. It was built around 2,500–2,000 BC, and is the only true prehistoric dolmen in Provence. Rock carvings suggest the region was first inhabited about a million years ago.

←

Looking out over the rooftops of Bargemon to the green hills beyond

↑ Austere cloisters within the Cistercian Abbaye du Thoronet

14

Lorgues

🅰E5 🚌 ⓘ 12 rue du 8 mai; www.lorgues-tourisme.fr

Near oak and pine woodland, Lorgues is surrounded by vineyards and olive groves. Its old town was fortified in the 12th century. Two 14th-century gates and city wall remains can be seen, along with 18th-century municipal buildings and monuments.

In the centre of town is the stately Collégiale St-Martin, consecrated in 1788. Its organ, dating from 1857, is the finest example of the work of the Augustin Zeiger factory, Lyon. A marble Virgin and Child (1694) here is attributed to the school of Pierre Puget.

15 🌀 🖎 🛍

Abbaye du Thoronet

🅰E5 🏠 83340 Le Thoronet 🅲 04 94 60 43 90 🅞 Daily 🅺 1 Jan, 1 May, 1 & 11 Nov

Founded in 1146, Le Thoronet was the first Cistercian building in Provence. It occupies a

remote site in deep woodland. Along with the Romanesque abbeys of Sénanque (p170) and Silvacane (p152), it forms one of the three "Cistercian sisters" of Provence.

The cool geometry of the church, cloister, dormitory and chapter house reflects the austerity of Cistercian principles. Only the bell tower breaks with the order's strict building regulations: instead of wood, it is made of stone, to enable it to withstand the strong Provençal winds.

Dilapidated by the 1400s, the abbey was abandoned in 1791. Its restoration, like that of many medieval Provençal buildings, was instigated by Prosper Mérimée, Napoleon III's Inspector of Historic Monuments, who visited in 1834. Just beside the abbey

Did You Know?

Every year in June, the fishermen of Sanary-sur-Mer prepare a bouillabaisse for up to 3,000 people.

is the modern Monastère de Bethléem, home to Cistercian nuns.

16

Brignoles

🅰D6 🚌 ⓘ Carrefour de l'Europe; www.la-provence-verte.net

Bauxite mines have stained the Brignoles countryside red: over a million tonnes of metal are mined here annually. The medieval town remains above it all, quiet and empty for most of the year. An unexpected delight is the **Musée du Pays Brignolais** in a 12th-century castle that was built as a summer retreat for the Counts of Provence. The eclectic collection includes La Gayole marble sarcophagus, which is carved with both pagan and Christian images; a boat made of cement designed by J Lambot (1814–87), who gave the world reinforced concrete; and a collection of votive offerings. St Louis, bishop of Toulouse and patron of Brignoles, was born in a palace beside the Église St-Sauveur in 1274.

Musée du Pays Brignolais

🌀🌀 🏠 2 place des Comtes de Provence 🅞 Apr-Sep: Wed-Sun; Oct-Mar: Wed-Sat 🅺 1 Jan, Easter, 1 May, 1 Nov 🆆 museebrignolais.com

17

Sanary-sur-Mer

🅰D6 🚊 Ollioules-Sanary 🚌 ⓘ Maison du Tourisme, 1 quai du Levant; www.sanary-tourisme.com

In the agreeable, clear blue waters of Sanary-sur-Mer, the diver Jacques Cousteau's

→

Boats at dusk in the yachting harbour at Bandol

experiments to develop the modern aqua-lung took place (p115). Diving and fishing (mainly for tuna and swordfish) are still popular pursuits in this delightful resort, where rows of pink and white houses line the bay. Its name derives loosely from St-Nazaire; the lovely local 19th-century church took the saint's name. Dating from about 1300, the landmark medieval tower in the town still contains the cannon that saw off an Anglo-Sardinian fleet in 1707. It is now part of a hotel.

Sanary-sur-Mer has enticed visitors for many years. Once the home of the British writer Aldous Huxley (1894–1963), it was a haven between the wars for innumerable other authors. Bertolt Brecht (1898–1956) and Thomas Mann (1875–1955) fled here from Nazi Germany. To the east of Sanary, the coast becomes dramatic and rocky. By the peninsula's extremity at the Cap Sicié is the Notre-Dame-du-Mai chapel, built in the 17th century and now a pilgrimage destination full of votive offerings. Its stepped approach offers a wonderful panorama over the coast and surrounding hills.

CÔTES DE PROVENCE VINEYARDS

The slopes of the Côtes de Provence wine-growing region stretch from the Haut Var to the coast, and produce luscious red, white and above all rosé wines, around 80 per cent of the region's vintages. Cinsaut, Carignan, Mourvèdre, Grenache and Tibouren are the main grape varieties grown. To sample some of the 800 regional wines, visit the Maison des Vins Côtes de Provence at Les Arcs (www.maison-des-vins.fr).

Outside the town, the **Parc Animalier & Exotique Sanary-Bandol** is home to wildlife including monkeys, small cats and some rare and tropical plants.

Parc Animalier & Exotique Sanary-Bandol

⊘⊘ ⊙ 🏠 131 ave Pont d'Aran, Sanary-sur-Mer ⊙ Mar-Oct: 9:30am–6pm daily (Apr–Sep: to 7pm); Nov-Feb: 9:30am–5:30pm Wed, Sat & Sun 🛇 Public hols 🆆 zoaparc.com

18

Bandol

🅰 D6 🚉 ℹ Allée Alfred Vivien 🆆 bandoltourisme.fr

Tucked away in a bay, this cheerful resort has a tree-lined promenade (with plenty of shops and restaurants), a casino and a yachting harbour. The shelter of encircling hills provides excellent grape-growing conditions. Indeed, Bandol has produced superb wines since 600 BC.

Did You Know?

In 2000, the Mayor of Le Lavandou passed a by-law making it illegal to die in the town.

19

Le Lavandou

🅐E6 🚌 🚂 ℹ️ Quai Gabriel Péri; www.ot-lelavandou.fr

An embarkation port for the nearby Îles d'Hyères, Le Lavandou is a fishing village now almost entirely given over to tourism. This is due to its 12 beaches, each with a different coloured sand. It is a centre for watersports and offers moorings for luxury yachts. Full of bars, nightclubs and restaurants, Le Lavandou is a favourite of younger, less well-heeled visitors.

The village takes its name not from the lavender fields in the hills, but from a *lavoir* (wash-house) depicted in a painting of the town in 1736 by Charles Ginoux. During the 19th century, when it was no more than a fishing village,

Le Lavandou was popular with artists. The most famous was Ernest Reyer (1823–1909), a composer and music critic after whom the main square is named. From this square there is a view over the Îles du Levant and Port-Cros.

Much of nearby Brégançon is in the hands of the military, and the French president has a summer residence there.

19

Bormes-les-Mimosas

🅐E6 🚌Hyères ℹ️1 place Gambetta; www.bormesles mimosas.com

Bormes is a medieval hill village on the edge of the Dom Forest, bathed in the scent of oleander and eucalyptus, with a flower-lined walk around its castle. "Les Mimosas" was added to its name in 1968, a century after the plant was first introduced from Mexico. A pretty and popular village, Bormes serves a marina of more than 800 berths. Plummeting streets such as Rompi-Cuou lead to lively cafés and coastal views.

A statue of St Francis di Paola stands in front of the 16th-century Chapelle

STAY

Domaine du Mirage
This classy hotel has some fabulous sea views and a lovely palm-shaded swimming pool.

🅐E6 🏠38 rue de la Vue des Îles, Bormes-les-Mimosas 🕸domaine dumirage.com

€€€

Hôtel le Suffren
A pleasant hotel with balconies overlooking the marina and canals of Port-Grimaud.

🅐E5 🏠16 pl du Marché, 83310 Port-Grimaud 🕸hotel-suffren.com

€€€

Hôtel Baptistin
Set right next to the sea in Le Lavandou, every room in this small modern hotel has a balcony.

🅐E6 🏠Quai Baptistin Pins, 83980 Le Lavandou 🕸hotel-baptistin.com

€€€

St-François, commemorating the saint's timely arrival during a plague outbreak in 1481. The 18th-century church of St-Trophyme has restored 18th-century frescoes. The works of local painter Jean-Charles Cazin (1841–1901) are well represented in the **Musée d'Arts et d'Histoire**.

Musée d'Arts et d'Histoire
🏠 103 rue Carnot 📞 04 94 71 56 60 🕐 Tue–Sun (Oct–Apr: Tue–Sat)

21
Ramatuelle

🅰 E6 🚌 ℹ️ Pl de l'Ormeau; www.ramatuelle-tourisme.com

Surrounded by vineyards, and dotted with fig trees, this attractive hilltop village was called "God's Gift" (Rahmatu 'llah) by the Saracens who left behind a gate, now restored. It is one of three particularly quaint villages on the St-Tropez peninsula (with Grimaud and Gassin). Gérard Philipe (1922–59), the leading young French actor during the 1950s, is buried here. Theatre and jazz festivals take place here annually.

↑ Visible from afar, the pretty village of Grimaud spreading down the hillside among the trees

Nearby, Les Moulins de Paillas (322 m, 1,056 ft), offers a fine panorama, as does Cap Camarat, with its lighthouse, at the tip of the peninsula, 5 km (3 miles) east of Ramatuelle.

22
Port-Grimaud

🅰 E5 🚌 ℹ️ Les Terrasses, rue de l'Amarrage; www.grimaud-provence.com

This beautiful port village was dreamed up entirely by the renowned Alsace architect François Spoerry (1912–98). In 1962 he bought up the marshy delta lands of the River Giscle west of the Golfe St-Tropez. Four years later, work began on a mini-Venice of 2,500 canal-side houses with moorings covering 90 ha (222 acres).

There are now three "zones", a marina and a beach. Its church, St-François-d'Assise, in the place de l'Église, contains some stained glass by Victor Vasarély (1908–97), and offers a sweeping view of the port from the top of its tower.

← Soft dawn light illuminating the rugged coastline of Le Lavandou

The port is traffic-free and the *coche d'eau* offers a water-taxi service. Port-Grimaud has about one million visitors a year.

23
Grimaud

🅰 E4 🚌 ℹ️ 679 route nationale; www.grimaud-provence.com

The medieval, fortified, traffic-free *village perché* of Grimaud dates back to the Gallo-Roman days. During the 11th century, its steep summit allowed Grimaud to dominate the Gulf of St-Tropez (also known as the Golfe de Grimaud) and control access to the town from the North and Maures mountains. Grimaud has no connection to the ubiquitous Grimaldi family; it can instead be associated with the much older Grimaldo dynasty. The 11th century castle of Grimaud was ruined in the Wars of Religion (p56). The view of the coast made it an ideal vantage point from which to watch for invasion.

The rue des Templiers is the town's oldest street, lined with arcades designed to be battened down in case of attack. Legend has it that the Knights Templar stayed here.

Golden sunlight over the port of Ste-Maxime in the bay of St-Tropez ↑

24

Ste-Maxime

🅰E5 🚏St-Tropez, St-Raphaël 🛈Promenade Aymeric Simon-Lorière; 08 26 20 83 83

Facing St-Tropez across the Gulf, Ste-Maxime is protected by hills. Visitors come year-round – attracted by the resort's watersports, nightlife, beaches and casino – but numbers peak in the summer.

Ste-Maxime was once protected by the monks of Lérins, who named the port after their patron saint and put up the defensive Tour Carrée des Dames which is now the **Musée de la Tour Carrée**.

Musée de la Tour Carrée

♿ 🏠Place Mireille de Germond 📞04 94 96 70 30 🕒Wed–Sun (pm only) 🚫1 Jan, Feb, 1 May, 25 Dec

25

St-Raphaël

🅰F5 🚉🚍 🛈99 quai Albert Premier; www.saintraphael.com

This staid family resort dates to Roman times when rich families came to stay near where the modern seafront casino now stands. Napoleon put the town on the map when he landed here in 1799 on his return from Egypt, and 15 years later when he left St-Raphaël for exile on Elba.

Popularity grew when the Parisian satirical novelist Jean-Baptiste Karr (1808–90) publicized the town's delights. In the old part is the 12th-century church of St-Raphaël and the **Musée Archéologique**, which contains Greek amphorae and other important finds.

Musée Archéologique

🏠Place de la Vieille Église 📞04 94 19 25 75 🕒2–5pm Tue–Fri, 10am–12:30pm Sat 🚫Public hols 🌐musee-saintraphael.com

26

Fréjus

🅰F5 🚉St Raphaël 🚍 🛈249 rue Jean-Jaurès; www.frejus.fr

Visibly wealthy in history, Fréjus is one of the highlights of the coast. The oldest Roman city in Gaul, it was founded by Julius Caesar in 49 BC and greatly expanded by Augustus. Lying on the Aurelian way – a huge road built in the reign of Augustus from Rome to Arles – it covered 40 ha (100 acres), had a population of 30–40,000 and, as a port, was second in importance only to Marseille.

Although substantial sections of the Roman city were decimated by the Saracens in the 10th century, a few parts of their walls remain, including a tower of the western Porte des Gaules. The opposite eastern entrance, the Porte de Rome, marks one end of a 40-km (25-mile) aqueduct.

→ The imposing 12th-century Cathédrale St-Léonce in Fréjus

Just to the north of here lie the remains of the semi-circular, 1st-century theatre, where performances are still held. The praetorium or Plateforme – military head-quarters that formed the eastern citadel – lie to the south. North of the Porte des Gaules, on the road to Brignoles, stands the large 1st–2nd-century **Arènes de Fréjus**, built to hold 12,000 spectators, now used for music and dance.

The spectacular **Cathédrale St-Léonce et Cloître** houses a Musée Archéologique with finds from all around Fréjus. The Chapelle Notre-Dame, decorated by Cocteau, and Musée d'Histoire Locale are also well worth a visit.

South of the town is the Butte St-Antoine citadel, which once overlooked the harbour. The canal linking the harbour to the sea began silting up in the 10th century; by the 1700s it was entirely filled in, forming a new land mass that later became Fréjus-Plage. A little over 2 km (1 mile) from the town's centre, this modern resort stretches along a sandy beach towards the town of St-Raphaël.

Arènes de Fréjus

⊛ 🄰296 rue Henri Vadon
📞04 94 51 34 31 🄾Apr-Sep: Tue-Sun; Oct-Mar: Tue-Sat
🄿Public hols

Cathédrale St-Léonce et Cloître

⊛⊛🄰 🄰58 rue du Cardinal Fleury 🄾Cathedral: daily; Cloisters: Tue-Sun (Jun-Sep: daily) 🄿Public hols
🅆cloitre-frejus.fr

27

Massif de l'Estérel

🄰F5 🅇Nice 🄰🚌Agay, St-Raphaël 🄸Quai Albert Premier, St-Raphaël; 04 94 19 52 52

The Estérel, a mountainous volcanic mass, is a wilderness compared with the bustling coast. Although it rises to no more than 620 m (2,050 ft), and a succession of fires have destroyed its forests, its innate ruggedness and the dramatic colours of its porphyry rocks remain intact.

Until the mid-1800s, it was a popular refuge for highwaymen and escaped convicts from the Bagne prison in Toulon. Indeed, after being fêted on arrival in St Raphaël, Napoleon and his coach were robbed of all their valuables on the Estérel while on their way to Paris.

The north side of the massif is bounded by the DN7 which runs through the Estérel Gap. To reach Mont Vinaigre, take the road to the Malpey ranger station, and walk the final 45 minutes to the highest point on the massif, where there is a fine panorama from the Alps to the Massif des Maures.

On the seaward side of the massif, the D1089 from St-Raphaël twists along the top of startlingly red cliffs to Agay.

Round the bay is Pointe de Baumette where there is a memorial to French writer and World War II aviator, Antoine de St-Exupéry.

At La Napoule is the 14th-century **Château de la Napoule**, refurbished by American sculptor Henry Clews (1876–1937), who left his work scattered about the estate. The château is now an art centre, the Clews Center for the Arts.

Château de la Napoule

⊛⊛🄰🄰 🄰1 blvd Henry Clews, Mandelieu-La Napoule 🄾Mar-Oct: 10am-6pm daily; Nov-Feb: 2-5pm Mon-Fri
🅆chateau-lanapoule.com

Did You Know?

The scrubland on the Massif de l'Estérel is blanketed with iris flowers in spring.

BOUCHES-DU-RHÔNE AND NÎMES

This southwestern corner of Provence has a feel that's unique in the region. It is the land of Van Gogh, brightly patterned materials and beaches of shifting sands. Many inland towns reflect the region's Greek and Roman past. The Greeks first settled in France in around 600 BC and founded Marseille, now a cosmopolitan cultural centre and the country's second largest city. The Romans, who arrived after them, built the theatre at Arles and the amphi-theatre at Nîmes, and left the remains of Classical houses at the archaeological site of Glanum. They also built the huge aqueduct Pont du Gard, a great feat of engineering, which runs beween a spring at Uzès to a water tower at Nîmes.

Bloodthirsty warriors ruled in the Middle Ages from an extraordinary eyrie in Les Baux-de-Provence. This former fief was paradoxically famous as a Court of Love during the 13th century. In the 15th century, Good King René held his court in the castle of Tarascon and in Aix-en-Provence, the ancient capital of Provence. Aix's university, founded by René's father, Louis II of Aujou, in 1409, is still the hub of this lively student town.

BOUCHES-DU-RHÔNE AND NÎMES

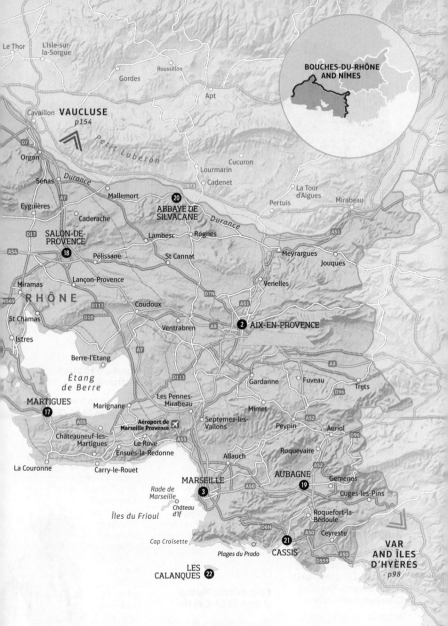

Le Thor
L'Isle-sur-la-Sorgue
Gordes
Roussillon
Apt

Cavaillon
VAUCLUSE
p154

Petit Luberon

Orgon
Cucuron
Lourmarin
Cadenet
La Tour d'Aigues
Mirabeau
Sénas
Durance
Mallemort
Eyguières
Pertuis
Caderache
Mallemort
ABBAYE DE SILVACANE 20
Rognes
Lambesc
SALON-DE-PROVENCE 18
Pélissane
St Cannat
Meyrargues
Jouques
Lançon-Provence
Miramas
RHÔNE
Coudoux
Venelles
St Chamas
Ventrabren
2 **AIX-EN-PROVENCE**
Istres
Berre-l'Etang
Étang de Berre
Gardanne
Fuveau
Trets
MARTIGUES 17
Marignane
Les Pennes-Mirabeau
Mimet
Châteauneuf-les-Martigues
Aéroport de Marseille Provence
Septemes-les-Vallons
Peypin
Auriol
Le Rove
Ensuès-la-Redonne
La Couronne
Allauch
Roquevaire
Carry-le-Rouet
MARSEILLE 3
AUBAGNE 19
Gemenos
Rade de Marseille
Cuges-les-Pins
Château d'If
Îles du Frioul
Roquefort-la-Bédoule
Cap Croisette
Ceyreste
VAR AND ÎLES D'HYÈRES *p98*
Plages du Prado
21 **CASSIS**
LES CALANQUES 22

*M e d i t e r r a n e a n
S e a*

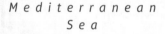

0 kilometres 10
0 miles 10

N

❶

NÎMES

🅰A4 ✈Nîmes-Arles-Carmargue 🚉🚌Pl de l'ONU
ℹ6 rue Auguste; www.ot-nimes.fr

The Romans left their mark on Nîmes more firmly than on any other city in Provence. In the 21st century, their vast amphitheatre, Les Arènes, is still the cultural hub of a city of broad boulevards and airy squares, dotted with architectural relics of the Roman era. The city is also famous for developing denim (de Nîmes), the tough material used for blue jeans and traditionally worn by Camargue cowboys.

❶ 🖊 Ⓜ 🛍

Les Arènes (L'Amphithéâtre)

🅰Blvd des Arènes 📞04 66 21 82 56 🕘9:30am–5pm daily 🗓Ferias (fairs) & performance days 🌐arenes-nimes.com

At 130 m (427 ft) by 100 m (328 ft) and with seating for 24,000, Nîmes's amphitheatre is only slightly smaller than the arena at Arles (p134). It was built as a venue for gladiatorial combat, but after Rome's collapse in AD 476 it became a fortress, a knights' headquarters, and eventually a slum, housing 2,000 people. Restored in the 19th century, it is thought to be one of the best preserved of all Roman amphitheatres. Today, it is used for rock concerts rather than for gladiatorial contests.

❷

Cathédrale Notre-Dame et St-Castor

🅰Pl aux Herbes 📞04 66 67 27 72 🕘Times vary, call ahead

Nîmes's cathedral dates from the 11th century but was extensively rebuilt in the 19th century. The west front has a partly Romanesque frieze with scenes from the Old Testament.

❸ Ⓜ

Musée d'Histoire Naturelle

🅰13 blvd Amiral Courbet 📞04 66 76 73 45 🕘10am–6pm Tue–Sun 🗓1 May, 1 Nov

Set around a cloister and 17th-century chapel, this museum covers three themes: the prehistoric period, ethnography and zoology. Visitors can see collections on birds and mammals, botany, geology, mineralogy, palaeontology and even prehistoric archaeology.

→

Bronze sculpture of matador Nimeño II, outside Les Arènes

 ④

Maison Carrée

🏛 Pl de la Maison Carrée
📞 04 66 21 82 56 🕐 10am–
1pm & 2–4:30pm daily
🌐 arenesnimes.com

The Maison Carrée ("square house") is the world's best preserved Roman temple. Built by Marcus Agrippa, it is

←
Exterior of Les Arènes, Nîmes's well preserved Roman amphitheatre

Hellenic with Corinthian columns around the main hall. A multimedia film – *Nemausus, the birth of Nîmes* – is shown inside the temple.

---

⑤ 🖼

Les Jardins de la Fontaine

🏛 Quai de la Fontaine 📞 04 66 21 82 56 (Tour Magne)
🕐 9am–5pm daily

The city's main park is named after an underground spring harnessed in the 18th century. The park's 2nd-century Temple of Diana is today in ruins.

Another highlight of the park is the octagonal Tour Magne. Dating from 15 BC, it is the earliest surviving Roman building in France. Visitors can climb the tower's 140 steps for spectacular views.

⑥ 🖼

Carré d'Art (Musée d'Art Contemporain)

🏛 Pl de la Maison Carrée
🕐 10am–6pm Tue–Sun
🌐 carreartmusee.com

On the opposite side of the square from the Maison Carrée, this modern, light-flooded art complex opened in 1993 and was designed by Norman Foster.

---

⑦ 🖼

Musée des Beaux-Arts

🏛 Rue Cité Foulc 📞 04 66 28 18 32 🕐 10am–6pm Tue–Sun 🕐 1 May, 1 Nov

A diverse collection in the Fine Art Museum includes paintings by Boucher, Rubens and Watteau. The ground floor displays a large Roman mosaic, *The Marriage of Admetus*, found in 1883 in Nîmes's former covered market.

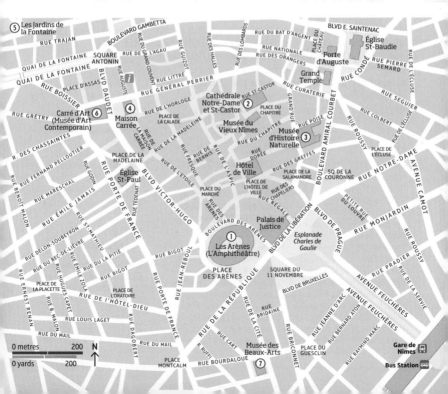

↑ Visitors roam the markets at Aix-en-Provence's bustling Place Richelme

②

AIX-EN-PROVENCE

🅰C5 🚉Ave Victor Hugo 🚌Ave de l'Europe ℹ300 ave Giuseppe Verdi; www.aixenprovencetourism.com

Provence's former capital is an international students' town, with one of the region's most cosmopolitan streets of restaurants and bars, rue de la Verrerie. The university was founded by Louis II of Anjou in 1409 and flourished under his son, Good King René. Another wave of prosperity transformed the city in the 17th century, when the mansion-lined cours Mirabeau was built. Aix's fountains were added in the 18th century.

① Old Town

North of the cours Mirabeau, between the Cathédrale St-Sauveur and the place d'Albertas, lies the town's old quarter. Sights include the Musée du Palais de l'Archevêché, housed in the former Bishop's palace, and the 17th-century Hôtel de Ville. Built around a courtyard by French architect Pierre Pavillon, it stands in a square now used as a flower market. Nearby is the 16th-century clock tower.

② Cathédrale St-Sauveur

🅰34 pl des Martyrs de la Résistance ☎04 42 23 45 65 ⏰Times vary, call ahead

The cathedral at the top of the old town creaks with history. The main door has solid walnut panels sculpted by Jean Guiramand (1504). On the right there is a fine 4th–5th-century baptistry, with a Renaissance cupola standing on 2nd-century Corinthian columns. The jewel of the church is the triptych of *The Burning Bush* (1476) by Nicolas Froment.

③ Musée du Vieil Aix (Musée Estienne de Saint-Jean)

🅰17 rue Gaston de Saporta ☎04 42 91 89 78 ⏰Wed-Mon

Gain insight into Aix's fascinating heritage and traditions in the town's history museum, housed in a former aristocratic townhouse. The eclectic collection includes a 19th-century *crèche parlante* (puppet show) and figures from the Corpus Christi parade that was first celebrated during the medieval reign of King René.

④ Musée Granet

🅰Pl St-Jean de Malte ⏰Tue-Sun 🗓1 Jan, 1 May, 25 Dec 🌐museegranet aixenprovence.fr

The city's main museum sits in a 17th-century former priory of the Knights of Malta.

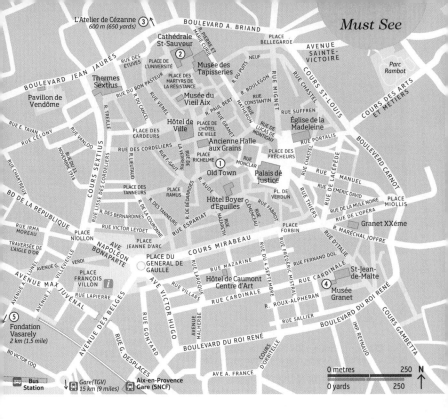

François Granet (1775–1849), a local artist, bequeathed his collection of French, Italian and Flemish paintings to Aix, including Ingres' *Portrait of Granet* and *Jupiter and Thetis*. There is also a room devoted to Granet's own paintings. The museum also features works by other Provençal painters, such as Van Gogh and Pablo Picasso, as well as eight canvases by Paul Cézanne, plus artifacts from Roman Aix.

⑤ 🖾 🅼 🛍

Fondation Vasarely

🏠 1 ave Marcel Pagnol
🕐 Daily 🚫 1 Jan, 24–26 Dec
🔲 fondationvasarely.org

Op Art master Victor Vasarely's peculiar hexagonal complex of steel cubes, adorned by black and white circles, houses a permanent collection of his monumental works and a calendar of temporary exhibitions, concerts and conferences starring local, national and international talents. The building was fully refurbished in 2018.

⑥ 🖾 🅼 🖵

L'Atelier de Cézanne

🏠 9 ave Paul Cézanne
🕐 Mar–Oct: daily; Nov–Feb: Mon–Sat 🚫 1 May, 25 Dec
🔲 cezanneen-provence. com

Ten minutes' walk uphill from the Cathédrale St Sauveur is the house of renowned artist Paul Cézanne *(p36)*, seen by many as the father of modern art (although he was jeered at in his hometown during his lifetime). The studio is much as he left it when he died in 1906. Not far from here you can see the scenic Montagne Ste-Victoire, a favourite subject of the painter.

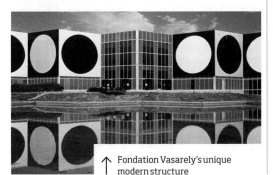

↑ Fondation Vasarely's unique modern structure

3

MARSEILLE

🅰 C5 ✈ 25 km (15 miles) NW Marseille 🚃🚌 Pl Victor
ℹ 11 la Canebière; www.marseille-tourisme.com

Marseille, founded more than 2,500 years ago, may be France's oldest city, but it's busily re-inventing itself as a vibrant 21st-century community around its bustling waterfront. It's dotted with stunning examples of modern architecture – from Le Corbusier's Cité Radieuse, opened in 1952, to Norman Foster's literally dazzling Miroir Ombrière at the rejuvenated Vieux Port – as well as other powerhouses of the city's cultural renaissance.

①

La Vieille Charité

🅰 2 rue de la Vieille Charité
Ⓜ Joliette 🕙 10am-6pm
Tue-Sun 🌐 vieille-charite-marseille.com

With its serene arcades and courtyards, this 17th-century almshouse is one of the finest buildings in the old town and is worth visiting for its architecture alone. Begun in 1671, the building was designed by Pierre Puget, court architect to Louis XIV, and was originally intended to house rural migrants. It now houses the Musee d'Archéologie Méditerranéenne, a rich collection of ancient Egyptian artifacts. Those with more

contemporary tastes can also enjoy a changing schedule of exhibitions by 20th and 21st century artists.

②

Cathédrale de la Major

🅰 Place de la Major 🚌 60
🕙 10am-5:30pm Wed-Mon
(Apr-Sep: to 6:30pm)
🌐 marseille.catholique.fr

The pompous, colossal Neo-Byzantine cathedral, completed in 1893, is a landmark on the west side of the old town. Bishops of Marseille are interred in its crypt. Next to it is the 11th-century Ancienne Cathédrale, with a 1073 reliquary altar.

③

Musée des Civilisations de l'Europe et de la Méditerranée (MUCEM)

🅰 7 promenade Robert Laffont 🚌 82, 60, 49
🕙 Times vary, check website 🌐 mucem.org

Art from all around the shores of the Mediterranean and from every era since Neolithic times to the present day is on show in a striking Post-Modern building, and in the adjacent Fort St-Jean. These buildings are connected by a roof-level bridge suspended over the sea over the sea.

↑ Visitors relax by the waterfront outside the MUCEM

← Marseille's stunning harbour port and impressive city skyline

piece of religious architecture. Between Notre-Dame and the port, it was founded in the 5th century and belonged to one of the most powerful religious foundations in Provence. Its patron, the hermit St Victor, was martyred in the 3rd century, and within is his cave, crypts and sarcophagi.

which houses a collection of works by Provençal artists and by French, Italian and Flemish old masters.

⑥ Musée d'Histoire de Marseille

🏠 2 rue Henri Barbusse 🚍 83, 55 Ⓜ Vieux Port ⏰ 10am–6pm Tue–Sun (Mid-May–mid-Sep: to 7pm) 🚫 1 May, 1 & 11 Nov 🌐 musee-histoire-marseille-voie-historique

Visitors to this museum follow remnants of a paved Roman road through the Jardin des Vestiges, site of Marseille's oldest port. The most fascinating exhibits are the hulls of ancient Greek and Roman vessels retrieved from the seabed, and sarcophagi unearthed at nearby archaeological sites.

⑤ Palais Longchamp

🏠 Blvd de Montrichet 🚍 81 Ⓜ Cinq avenues Longchamp 🚊 T2 Longchamp ⏰ 10am–6pm Tue–Sun 🌐 marseille.fr

This 19th-century palace, surrounded by green gardens and gushing fountains, is home to the Musée des Beaux-Arts,

④ Abbaye de St-Victor

🏠 Place St-Victor 🚍 55, 60, 61, 80, 82, 83 Ⓜ Vieux Port ⏰ 4am–6pm Mon-Fri 🌐 saintvictor.net

The fortress-like basilica of St Victor is Marseille's finest

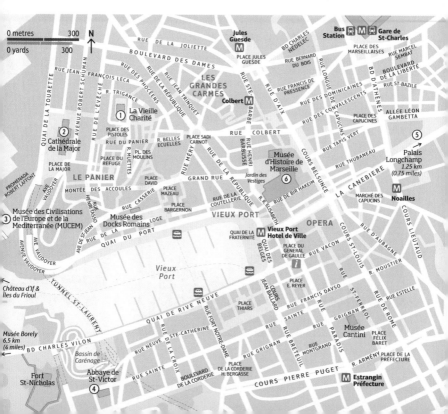

EXPERIENCE **Bouches-du-Rhône and Nîmes**

④
ARLES

🅰B4 ✈Nîmes-Ales-Camargue 🚍AveP Talabot 🚌AveP Talabot
ℹBlvd des Lices; www.arlestourisme.com

Like a miniature version of Rome, charming Arles spreads out around a massive arena and remnants of its Roman heyday are scattered all around its narrow streets. It's even better known for its connection with Vincent Van Gogh, who, inspired by its bright light and rich colours, enjoyed the most creative period of his tragically short life here. On the east bank of the Rhône, it's also the gateway to the unique wetlands of the Camargue (p140), with its flamingos and distinctive herds of black cattle and white horses. Most guided tours and safaris into the wilds of the delta start here.

①

Les Arènes

🅰Rond-point des Arènes
🕐9am-6pm daily 🎫Events
🌐arenes-arles.com

The largest Roman building in Gaul is as impressive now as when it was built around 90 AD, with seats for 20,000 spectators to watch chariot races and bloody gladiatorial battles. Today, it is used for concerts and other spectacles. The top tier of seating provides an excellent panoramic view of Arles. Just to the southwest of the amphitheatre is the elegant Théâtre Antique, another beautifully preserved Roman-era stadium with 2,000 seats.

②

Cryptoportiques

🅰Hôtel de Ville, place de la République 🕐10am-6pm Wed-Mon 🚫Tue and public holidays 🌐patrimoine. ville-arles.fr

Beneath the site of the Roman Forum, these huge, horseshoe-shaped underground galleries – up to 10 m (33 ft) wide and ventilated by air shafts – were probably used as granaries. Constructed in the 1st century AD, then buried beneath later church buildings, they were left forgotten and inaccessible until archaeologists began the task of re-opening them in 1935.

Les Thermes de Constantin are all that remains of Constantin's Palace, built in the 4th century AD.

← ④ *Fondation Vincent Van Gogh Arles (50 m; 55 yards)*

← ⑥ *Musée Départementale de l'Arles Antique (1 km; half a mile)*

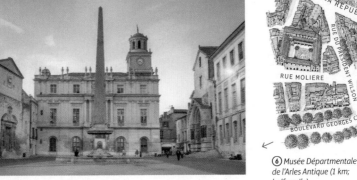

↑ Sunset over the Roman obelisk in place de la République

↑ Exterior of the impressive Les Arènes

← Aerial illustration of the historic centre of Arles

One of Provence's most impressive monuments, Les Arènes was the largest Roman building in Gaul.

Did You Know?

An Advantage Pass allows you to visit all the major sights in Arles for a bargain price.

Église Notre-Dame-de-la-Major is dedicated to Saint George, patron saint of the Camargue gardians (cowboys).

Once a fortress, the stones of the Théâtre Antique were later used for other buildings.

The cloister of Église St-Trophime features some exquisite examples of Romanesque carving.

⑤ Luma Foundation
(500 m; 550 yards) →

⑦ Les Alyscamps
(300 m; 330 yards) ↘

A Roman obelisk with fountains at its base stands in the place de la République. It came from the Roman circus across the Rhône.

↑ Garden at the Fondation Vincent Van Gogh Arles; museum exterior *(inset)*

aims to put Van Gogh's work in context and highlights the artist's influence on his contemporaries and successive generations of painters.

---

③ 🖊️ 🎨 🛍️

Musée Reattu

🏠 10 rue du Grand-Prieuré
🕐 10am–5pm Tue–Sun (Mar–Oct: to 6pm)
🌐 museereattu.arles.fr

The work of local artist Jacques Réattu (1760–1833) and his contemporaries form the basis of this collection. A Picasso donation and a photographic display are among the other 20th-century pieces exhibited.

---

④ 🖊️ 🎨 🛍️

Fondation Vincent Van Gogh Arles

🏠 35 rue du Dr Fanton
🕐 11am–6pm Tue–Sun (Apr–Sep: to 7pm) 🔒 Between exhibitions, check website
🌐 fondation-vincentvan gogh-arles.org

Housed in a 15th-century mansion, the Hôtel Léautaud de Donines, this foundation

⑤ 🖊️ 🎨 🍴 🍷 🖥️ 🛍️

Luma Foundation

🏠 45 chemin des Minimes
🕐 11am–6pm Tues–Sun
🌐 luma-arles.org

Soaring above the old town like a starship ready for lift-off, Frank Gehry's gleaming metallic landmark opened in summer 2018, endowing Arles with a brand-new venue for world-class contemporary art and performance. The Luma Foundation, led by Swiss art collector Maja Hoffmann, forms a 20-acre complex of

↑ Extraordinary metallic exterior of the Luma Foundation

galleries, theatres, studios and workshops dedicated to producing new and adventurous work in photography and conceptual art. The collection is split between Gehry's new building and six former factory and warehouse spaces. It also hosts events and exhibitions during the annual Rencontres d'Arles Festival of Photography.

---

⑥

Musée Départmentale de l'Arles Antique

🏠 Presqu'île du Cirque Romain ⏰ 10am–6pm Wed-Mon 🚫 Public holidays 🌐 arles-antique.cg13.fr

A marble statue of the Emperor Augustus, a statue of Venus and a massive altar dedicated to Apollo are among the highlights of this museum's collection of Roman sculptures, which date from pre-Christian times to the period that followed the Christian conversion of the Empire in AD 312. A new wing opened in 2013 to house the Arles Rhône 3, a fantastically well-preserved Roman 31-m-(102-ft-) long flat-bottomed wooden river barge that was retrieved from the bed of the Rhône.

⑦

Les Alyscamps

🏠 Ave des Alyscamps ⏰ 9am–6pm daily

Christ is claimed to have appeared to early Christians who met in secret at this vast necropolis, which was one of the largest and most famous cemeteries in the western world. An avenue of marble sarcophagi marks the site where many of the city's dignitaries were buried. Superstitious pagan Roman shunned the place at night, making it an ideal rendezvous for clandestine Christian worshippers under their early teacher, St Trophime. Later, Christians were often honoured by burial next to the tomb of Genesius, a beheaded Christian martyr.

⑧

Église St-Trophime

🏠 Place de la République ⏰ 10am–6pm Wed-Mon 🌐 patrimoine.ville-arles.fr

This is one of the Provence's great Romanesque churches. The portal and cloisters are decorated with biblical scenes.

St Trophime, thought to be the first bishop of Arles in the early 3rd century, appears with St Peter and St John on the carved northeast pillar.

⑨

Les Thermes de Constantin

🏠 Rue du Grand-Prieuré ⏰ 10am–6pm Wed-Mon 🌐 patrimoine.ville-arles.fr

Built by the Roman emperor Constantine in 306 AD, these once vast public baths were partially restored at the end of the 19th century. The three remaining original buildings attest to the ingenuity of Roman engineering.

📷 **PICTURE PERFECT**
Footsteps of Van Gogh

Visit the atmospheric place du Forum in the evening for a snap of the Restaurant-Cafe Van Gogh, still painted just as it was when it inspired his *Café Terrace at Night* (1888).

↑ Carved figures of St John *(left)* and St Peter *(right)* at Église St-Trophime

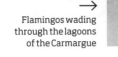

→

Flamingos wading through the lagoons of the Camargue

5

CAMARGUE

🅰 A5-B5 🌐 Bouches-du-Rhône ✈ Nîmes, Marseille
🚉🚌 Arles 🌐 parc-camargue.fr

The mighty Rhône meets the Mediterranean in the Camargue, a delta of reedbeds, wetlands and marshland pastures where half-wild white horses and black cattle roam. At its heart is the vast Étang de Vaccarès, part of a network of channels and lagoons edged by a seemingly endless arc of beaches, such as the Plage de Beauduc.

①

St-Gilles-du-Gard

🛈 1 place F Mistral; www.tourisme.saint-gilles.fr

Perched on the northern edge of the delta, the small town of St-Gilles-du-Gard is the 12th-century gateway to the Camargue. It's noted for its many festivals devoted to local music, culture, produce (including fruit from its famed apricot and peach orchards) and black bulls. In the heart of the old town, the Abbaye de St-Gilles is a UNESCO-listed *étape* on the Saint-Jacques de Compostelle pilgrimage route. The lovely carved façade is all that remains of the original building, which was founded by Raymond IV, Count of Toulouse in the 12th century.

②

Saintes Maries-de-la-Mer

🛈 5 avenue Van Gogh; www.saintesmaries.com

Miles of long sandy beaches stretch either side of this easy-going seaside village, which is full of restaurants serving local produce, and shops selling colourful Camargue ceramics and textiles.

The 9th-century Église de Notre-Dame-de-la-Mer, with its black Madonna, is the focus of a huge and colourful gypsy festival in May. Parades, horse races, and flamenco dances celebrate the village's three patron saints, Mary Magdalene, Mary Jacobe (sister of the Virgin) and Mary Salome (mother of the apostles James and John). According to local legend, all three washed up here in AD 40 and first brought Christianity to Provence.

③ 🚶 🚲

Parc Ornithologique du Pont-de-Gau

📍 RD570, pont-de-Gau
🕙 10am-6pm daily
🚫 Weekends in Jan & 1 May
🌐 parcornithologique.com

Wooden walkways and viewing platforms let visitors get close to flocks of wading flamingos, herons and many other waterfowl in this 24-ha

↑ Visitors on the roof of Église Notre-Dame-de-la-Mer

Visit in the evening to admire and photograph the Provençal coast's most spectacular sunsets.

④ 🚲 🏛

Musée de la Camargue

🏠Mas pont de Rousty, D570, Arles ⏰Oct-Mar: 10am-12:30pm & 1-5pm daily; Apr-Sep: 9am-12:30pm & 1-6pm daily 🚫Weekends in Jan & 1 May 🌐museedela camargue.com

The customs and lifestyles of the Camargue are the focus of this museum, housed in the huge barn of a traditional Provençal *mas* or farmhouse. Displays, including video footage and slide shows, provide an excellent intro-duction to the people, environment and wildlife of the wetlands. Among the many subjects covered are the lives of the Camargue cowboys, and the history of the *grand* and *petit* Rhône rivers which once flowed far to the east of Nîmes. Many

↑ Spectacular sunset over the wetlands of the Camargue

of the displays are focused on the story of Frédéric Mistral, a local man who won the Nobel Prize for literature in 1904.

A signposted 4-km (2-mile) walking trail leads out from the museum to the Marré de la Grand Mare, and back again in a pleasant circular route. An observation tower at the end of the walk affords great views over the surrounding countryside.

Did You Know?

The salt pans in the southeast corner of the Camargue produce 800,000 tonnes of salt a year.

(60-acre) expanse of lagoons, pastures and reedbeds. Aviaries dotted around the marshland house unusual birds that are very usually difficult to spot in the wild.

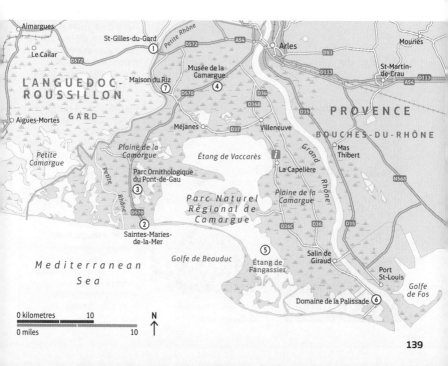

STAY

L'Auberge Cavalière du Pont des Bannes

Stay in luxury rooms in these lovely waterside farmhouse-style villas. Perks include swimming pools, a spa, riding stables and an excellent restaurant.

📍Rte d'Arles, Les Saintes Maries-de-la-Mer 🔗auberge cavaliere.com

€€€

Mas Saint Germain

Accommodation in spacious self-catering gîtes and guesthouse rooms among Camargue fields and pastureland.

📍Villeneuve-Camargue, Arles 13200 🔗massaint germain.com

€€€

---

⑤

Étang de Fangassier

📍Rte d'Arles, 13129 Salin de Giraud ⏰For guided tours only 📅Oct-Mar 🔗guides-nature.com

The Étang de Fangassier is home to France's only breeding colony of flamingos. Between 10,000 and 15,000 pink-plumaged pairs raise their young on and around a lagoon island that was used for salt production until 2008. The flamingos feed on shrimp and other tiny creatures that thrive in the lagoon, and during the breeding season you can hear the birds from hundreds of metres away.

---

⑥

Domaine de la Palissade

📍13129 Salin de Giraud ⏰9am–5pm Wed–Sun (Mar–Oct: daily) 📅Dec–Jan, 1 May, 11 Nov 🔗palissade.fr

This lovely, richly bio-diverse estate is one of the last expanses of the delta to survive untouched by the land reclamation projects, drainage channels and saltpans that have gradually altered the face of the Camargue over centuries. It comprises a dozen different habitats, each home to colourful wild-flowers and butterflies. Rare birds such as bitterns, terns, avocets and other waders nest and roost here. Vast expanses of dunes and marshland can be explored on foot or on a half-wild white Camarguais horse, with guided tours lasting from 30 minutes to 3 hours.

Start your expedition at the nature centre, which provides free maps of the three walking tours on the estate, and binoculars to hire.

---

⑦

Maison du Riz

📍Mas de la Vigne, Chemin de Figares, 13123 Albaron ⏰Apr–Oct: 9:30am–12:30pm & 2–7pm daily 📅Nov–Mar 🔗maison duriz.com

Generations of the Roziere family have grown rice at their farm in the heart of the Camargue wetlands, and their mission is to bring this agricultural tradition to life. Visit in spring and early summer to help with planting the fields, or in September and October to take part in the harvest. To immerse yourself fully in the life of the farm, you can stay in one of the farm's five self-catering gîtes, and buy gourmet rice products from the shop there.

> 💬 INSIDER TIP
> **Mosquitoes**
>
> Don't forget to pack mosquito repellent if venturing off the beaten track – Camargue mosquitoes are noto-riously bloodthirsty.

↑ Salt flats of the Étang de Fangassier

BIRDS AND BEASTS OF CAMARGUE

The Camargue's extensive areas of salt marshes, lakes, pastures and sand dunes – covering a vast 1,400 sq km (540 sq miles) – provide shelter and nutrients to a varied array of wildlife. Native horses and black bulls roam the green pastures; migrating seabirds and wildfowl shelter in the wetlands.

CAMARGUE BIRDS

The Camargue is a paradise for birders, particularly in spring when migrant birds visit on their journey north. This is the only French breeding site of the slender-billed gull, and the red-crested pochard, rarely seen in Europe, also breeds here.

HORSES

The half-wild, free-roaming white horses of the Camargue *(below)* are a primitive breed. Descended from wild horses that roamed Provence in prehistoric times, they are dark brown at birth and gradually turn white between four and seven years of age.

GREATER FLAMINGOS

The icons of the Camarague, wild flamingos stalk the delta's shallow lagoons. The Camargue is home to more than 20,000 of these fabulous pink birds, but multiple threats, such as climate change, pollution and illegal hunting, place their future at risk.

CAMARGUE BULLS

Raised on ranches called *manades* and herded by *gardians*, Camargue bulls are bred for the *course Camarguaise*, a type of bloodless variant on the bullfight. Under the name *raço di biòu*, the meat of Camargue bulls has AOC status and features in many local dishes.

CAMARGUE GARDIANS

The native white horses and black bulls of the Camargue have been herded, branded and tended to by the region's cowboys, or *gardians* since the 16th century. There are around 2,500 active *gardians* working across the region – of whom around 10 per cent are women – but social and economic pressures are taking their toll on the profession and making it harder to maintain.

6

AIGUES-MORTES

A5 ✈ 30 km (15 miles) W Montpellier ⊟ Rte de Nîmes ⊟ Tour de Constance ⓘ Pl St-Louis; www.ot.aigues

A sturdy sentinel set among the salt marshes of the Camargue, Aigues-Mortes ("dead waters" in Provençal) looks much as it must have done when it was completed in around 1300. Then, however, the Rhône had not yet deposited the silt which now landlocks the town, and canals transported the vast blocks used to make its walls from quarries in Beaucaire. Only the Hundred Years' War saw the town's ramparts breached: now its gates are always open to the besieging armies of admiring visitors.

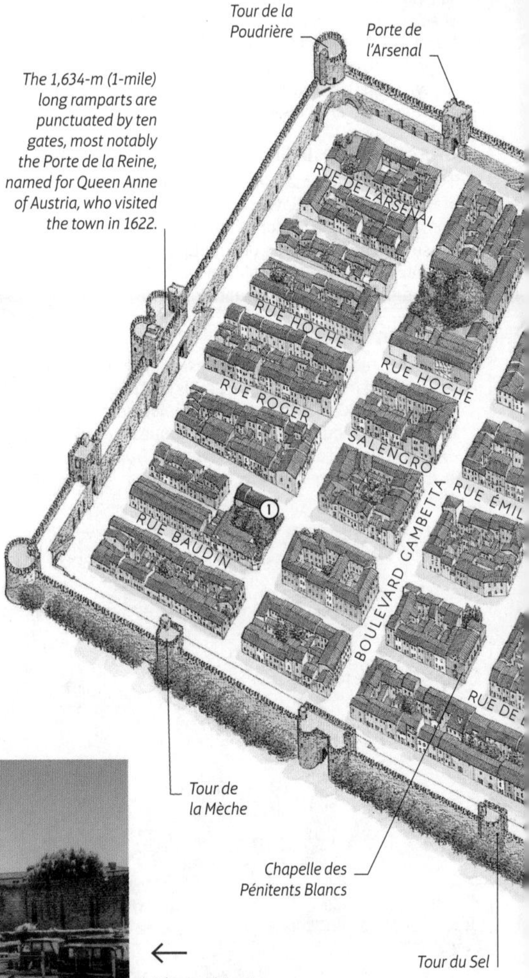

① Chapels of the Grey and White Penitents

Founded around 1400, the Chapelle des Pénitents Gris is still used by the "grey penitents", a Catholic monastic order founded in 1400. Named for their grey cowls, they walk with the white-cowled Pénitents Blancs in the annual Palm Sunday procession. Built in 1668, the Chapelle des Pénitents Blancs has an outstanding mural depicting the descent of the Holy Spirit.

② The Towers

The Tour de Constance, at the southeast corner, often held religious prisoners such as the Knights Templar, condemned as heretics by Philip the Fair in the early 14th century. The Tour des Bourguignons was used to keep the salt-pickled

The 1,634-m (1-mile) long ramparts are punctuated by ten gates, most notably the Porte de la Reine, named for Queen Anne of Austria, who visited the town in 1622.

Tour de la Poudrière

Porte de l'Arsenal

RUE DE L'ARSENAL

RUE HOCHE

RUE HOCHE

RUE ROGER

SALENGRO

RUE ÉMIL

BOULEVARD GAMBETTA

RUE BAUDIN

RUE DE

Tour de la Mèche

Chapelle des Pénitents Blancs

Tour du Sel

← Aigues-Morte harbour, seen next to the Tour de Constance

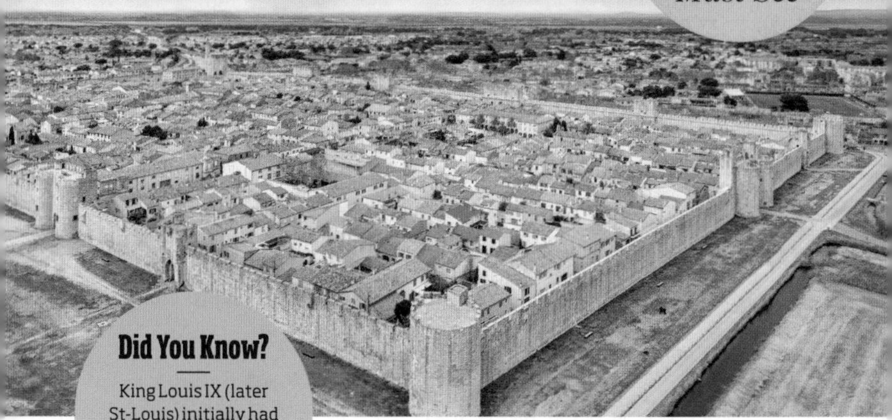

Did You Know?

King Louis IX (later St-Louis) initially had to bribe people to settle in the inhospitable salt marshes.

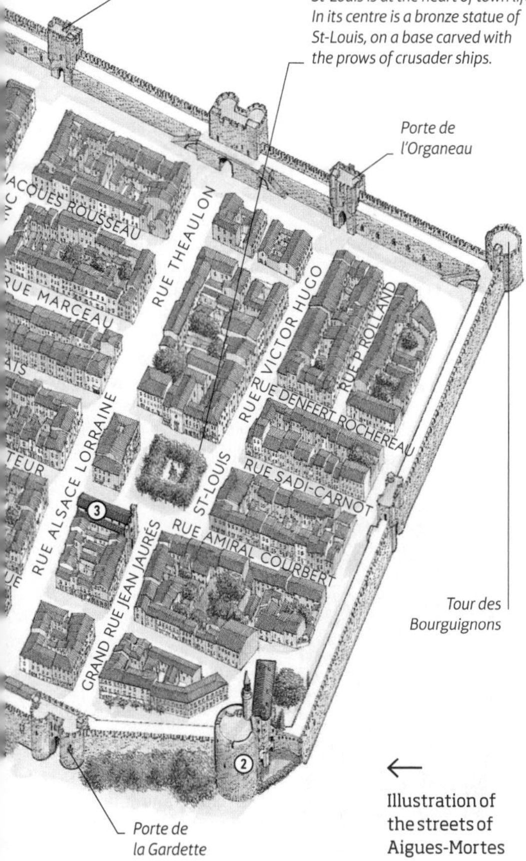

The beautifully preserved medieval city of Aigue-Mortes ↑

corpses of hundreds of Burgundian troops slain when Gascon troops seized the town, and The Tour de la Mèche or "wick tower" held a constant flame used to light cannon fuses. The Tour de la Poudrière at the northeast corner of the fortifications was the arsenal, where weapons and gunpowder were stored, while the Tour du Sel was used to store the salt that was the town's most highly valued commodity.

③
Notre-Dame des Sablons

The Gothic church of "Our Lady of the Sands", was built in the mid-12th century, before the construction of Aigues-Mortes' rectangle of ramparts. Although it pre-dates most of the town's buildings, it lay derelict for almost a century following the collapse of its bell-tower in 1634 and was extensively rebuilt between 1738 and 1744. In the 1960s much of the elaborate 19th-century decoration was removed to return the building to a plainer style more in keeping with its medieval heritage. The interior is beautifully lit by luminously colourful stained-glass windows created in 1991 by Nîmes-born artist Claude Viallat (b. 1936).

Porte de la Marine

Porte des Galions

Lined with cafés, leafy Place St-Louis is at the heart of town life. In its centre is a bronze statue of St-Louis, on a base carved with the prows of crusader ships.

Porte de l'Organeau

Tour des Bourguignons

← Illustration of the streets of Aigues-Mortes

Porte de la Gardette

EXPERIENCE MORE

7

Barbentane

🅰B4 🚉Avignon, Tarascon
🚌 ⓘ3 rue des Pénitents;
www.barbentane.fr

Members of Avignon's Papal court liked to build summer houses in Barbentane, beside the Rhône, 10 km (6 miles) south of the city. One such building, opposite the 13th- to 15th-century Notre-Dame-de-Grace, was the handsome Maison des Chevaliers, which was owned by the Marquises of Barbentane. Only the 40-m (130-ft) Tour Anglica remains of the town's 14th-century castle. Just outside the medieval quarter is the Château de Barbentane,

---

💬 HIDDEN GEM
Massif de la Montagnette

Just outside Barbentane, the peaceful wilderness of the vast Massif de la Montagnette makes for a great weekend escape. Here, gentle hills cloaked in pine, olive groves and almond trees are criss-crossed by a network of walking, cycling and riding trails.

---

a finely decorated Italianate mansion, built in 1674 by the Barbentane aristocracy who still own and reside in it.

Also in the town is the 16th- to 17th-century Moulin de Mogador, which was an oil mill and now hosts dinners.

8

Abbaye de St-Michel de Frigolet

🅰B4 🕐8am-6pm daily;
check website for tours and
group visits 🌐frigolet.com

The abbey is situated south of St-Michel de Frigolet, in the La Montagnette countryside. A cloister and small church date from the 12th century, but in 1858 a Premonstratensian abbey was founded, and one of the most richly decorated churches of that period was built. The whole interior is colourfully painted in rich tones of red and green, with golden stars on the ceiling and bright saints on the pillars. The small 12th-century Église St-Michel is on the Abbey road, near the entrance.

After a brief period of exile in Belgium at the beginning of the 20th century, the monks returned to Frigolet. The word *frigolet* is Provençal for thyme.

> The whole interior is colourfully painted in rich tones of red and green, with golden stars on the ceiling and bright saints on the pillars.

9

Beaucaire

🅰B4 🚉Tarascon 🚌
ⓘ8 rue Victor Hugo; www.
beaucaire.fr

The bullring in Beaucaire occupies the site of one of the largest fairs in Europe. Held every July for the past seven centuries, it attracted up to a quarter of a million people. A smaller version of the fair takes place today, with a procession on 21 July.

It was inaugurated by Raymond VI in 1217, who enlarged the **Château de Beaucaire**. This was later used by the French kings to watch over their Provençal neighbours across the river. It was partly dismantled on the orders of Cardinal Richelieu but the triangular keep and enough of the walls remain to indicate its impressive scale. There is a Romanesque chapel within the walls, and various medieval spectacles take place here, including frequent displays of falconry.

The Abbaye de St-Roman is situated 5 km (3 miles) from Beaucaire. Dating from the 5th century, it is the only troglodyte monastery in Europe.

Château de Beaucaire
🕔 📍Place Raimond VII
📞04 66 59 90 07 🕐Wed-Sun

←

Rich colours and detail in the interior of the Abbaye de St Michel de Frigolet

PONT DU GARD

The Pont du Gard is a triumph of Roman engineering. Begun around 19 BC, the three-tiered aqueduct is made of huge limestone blocks, some of them weighing up to six tonnes. Amazingly, no mortar was used in its construction. Blocks of masonry that supported scaffolding during the construction of the aqueduct can still be seen jutting from its mighty arches.

The Pont du Gard's water channel, covered by stone slabs, was in its uppermost tier, and it is thought that it may have been supplying the citizens of Nîmes with water as recently as the 6th century AD. Until the early 20th century the Pont du Gard was used as a road bridge, but since being declared a UNESCO World Heritage Site its location has been cleared of more recent constructions and it appears once again as it did in Roman times.

Did You Know?

The Pont du Gard could carry 20 million litres (4 million gallons) of water each day.

WATER TRANSPORT SYSTEM

The Pont du Gard was part of a vast system of underground channels and bridges that included the Pont de Bornègre, where the aqueduct emerged from an underground tunnel to cross a triple-arched bridge, and the Pont de la Lône, an overhead arcade carrying the water channel for some 400 m (1,320 ft). The Pont Roupt, a huge bridge that was more than 255 m (840 ft) long (of which 37 arches survive), was also part of this water system. It At Sernhac, downstream from the Pont du Gard, you can explore two tunnels, each about 60 m (197 ft) long, which carried the stream onwards towards Nîmes.

↑ Water tunnels at Sernhac, part of the water transport system fed by the Pont du Gard

The triple-tiered arched design ensures the heavy water load is supported.

Water channel, covered by stone slabs

Protruding stones for supporting scaffolding during construction

Skilfully designed cutwaters have ensured the bridge has resisted many violent floods.

↑ The beautifully preserved Roman Pont du Gard

Beautiful remains of the vast medieval abbey church of St-Gilles-du-Gard ↑

10

St-Gilles-du-Gard

A4 Nîmes 1 place Frédéric Mistral; www.tourisme.saint-gilles.fr

Known as the "Gateway to the Camargue", St-Gilles is famous for its Abbaye de St-Gilles. The building was damaged in 1562 during the Wars of Religion, and all that remains are the west façade, chancel and crypt. The carved façade is the most beautiful in all Provence. It includes the first sculpture of the Passion in Christendom, from the late 12th century.

Founded by Raymond VI of Toulouse, the abbey church was the Knights of St John's first priory in Europe. It soon became one of the key destinations on the pilgrimage route to Santiago de Compostela in Spain, and a port of embarkation for the Crusades. The crypt houses the tomb of Saint Gilles, a hermit who arrived by raft from Greece.

The belltower of the original abbey contains *La Vis*, a spiral staircase which is a masterpiece of stonemasonry.

LEGEND OF THE TARASQUE

According to legend, the tarasque - a man-eating monster with a lion's head and mane, a snake's tail, the claws of a bear and a turtle-like shell - terrorized Tarascon until it was killed by St Martha. An effigy of the beast is paraded though the streets during the last weekend in June in an annual celebration that has taken place since the 15th century

---

11

Tarascon

B4 62 rue des Halles; www.tarascon.fr

The gleaming white vision of the **Château Royal de Provence** is one of the landmarks of the Rhône. Little is left of the glittering court of Good King René who finished the building his father, Louis II of Anjou, began early in the 15th century *(p50)*. Following René's death in 1480, Provence fell to France, and the castle became a prison until 1926. A drawbridge leads to the poultry yard and garrison quarters. Beside it rises the impressive main castle, centred on a courtyard from where two spiral staircases lead to royal apartments in its sturdy towers. Prisoners' graffiti and some painted ceiling panels remain, but the only adornment is a handful of borrowed 17th-century tapestries which depict the deeds of Roman general Scipio (237–183 BC).

The Collégiale Ste-Marthe nearby has a tomb in the crypt to the monster-taming St Martha *(p46)*, who rescued the inhabitants from the Tarasque, a man-eating monster, which gave the town its name.

In the old town is the 16th-century Cloître des Cordeliers where exhibitions are held. On the rue des Halles is the 17th-century town hall, with a carved façade and balcony.

The traditional life of the area and its hand-printed fabrics is seen in the **Musée Souleïado**. The ancient textile industry was revived in 1938, under the name *Souleïado*, meaning "the sun passing through the clouds" in Provençal. The museum has a huge collection of woodblocks, many of them still used for the company's colourful prints.

The **Musée d'Art et d'Histoire**, housed in the Couvent des Cordeliers, covers the history of the Fête de la Tarasque, and also holds temporary art exhibitions.

→ Enjoying a break under the trees in Place Fevier, St Rémy

Château Royal de Provence

⊛⊛⊚ 🏠 Blvd du Roi René ⏰ Daily 🚫 1 Jan, 1 May, 1 & 11 Nov, 25 Dec 🌐 chateau.tarascon.fr

Musée Souleïado

⊛⊛ 🏠 39 rue Charles Deméry 📞 04 90 91 08 80 ⏰ Mon-Sat 🚫 1 Jan, 1 & 11 Nov, 25 Dec

Musée d'Art et d'Histoire

🏠 Pl Frédéric Mistral 📞 04 90 91 38 71 ⏰ May & Oct-Jan: Mon-Fri; Jun-Sep: Tue-Fri & Sat pm

---

⑫ St-Rémy-de-Provence

🅰B4 🚌 Avignon ℹ️ Pl Jean-Jaurès; www.saintremy-de-provence.com

St-Rémy is ideal for exploring the Alpilles countryside where the plants for its traditional *herboristeries*, or herb shops grow. The **Musée des Arômes et du Parfum**, in Graveson, displays the tools of perfumery.

One of the town's most attractive 15th–16th-century mansions is now a museum. The **Musée des Alpilles** has a fine ethnographic collection. The well-known 16th-century physician and astrologer, Nostradamus, was born in a house in the outer wall of the avenue Hoche, in the old quarter of St-Rémy.

40,000

The number of 18th-century woodblocks that are kept at the Musée Souleïado.

The **Musée Estrine Centre**, in the 18th-century Hôtel Estrine, houses modern and contemporary art. Temporary exhibits pay tribute to Van Gogh's relationship with St-Rémy. In May 1889, after he had mutilated his ear, Van Gogh arrived at the **Cloître et Cliniques de St-Paul de Mausole**, which is situated between the town and Glanum. The grounds and the 12th-century monastery house a museum and culture centre in which an entire wing is dedicated to the painter's stay. You can visit a reconstruction of Van Gogh's room and the field that he painted 15 times.

Just behind the clinic is Le Mas de la Pyramide, a farmstead half-built into the rock, which was once a Roman quarry. The remains of the earliest Greek houses in Provence, from the 4th-century BC, are in **Site Archéologique de Glanum** (*p44*), a Greco-Roman town at the head of a valley in the Alpilles. Along the roadside stands a triumphal arch from 10 BC, celebrating Caesar's conquest of the Greeks and Gaul, and a mausoleum dating from about 30 BC.

Musée des Arômes et du Parfum

⊚ 🏠 Ancien chemin d'Arles, Graveson-en-Provence ⏰ Daily 🚫 1 Jan, 1 May, 25 Dec 🌐 museedesaromes.com

Musée des Alpilles

⊛ 🏠 Place Charles Favier 📞 04 90 92 68 24 ⏰ Tue-Sun (Oct-Apr: Tue-Sat pm only)

Musée Estrine Centre

⊛ 🏠 8 rue Lucien Estrine ⏰ Tue-Sun (Mar & Nov: pm only) 🚫 Dec-Feb 🌐 musee-estrine.fr

Cloître et Cliniques de St-Paul de Mausole

⊛ 🏠 Chemin St-Paul ⏰ Mar-Dec: daily 🚫 Public hols 🌐 saintpauldemausole.fr

Site Archéologique de Glanum

⊛⊛⊚ 🏠 Ave Vincent Van Gogh ⏰ Daily (Oct-Mar: Tue-Sun) 🚫 1 Jan, 1 May, 1 & 11 Nov, 25 Dec 🌐 site-glanum.fr

13

Les Alpilles

🅰 B4 🚉 Arles, Tarascon, Salon-de-Provence 🚌 Les Baux-de-Provence, St-Rémy-de-Provence, Eyguières, Eygalières 🅸 St-Rémy-de-Provence; 04 90 92 05 22

St-Rémy-de-Provence is on the western side of the limestone massif of Les Alpilles, a 24-km (15-mile) chain between the Rhône and Durance rivers. A high point is La Caume, at 387 m (1,270 ft), which can be reached from St-Rémy, just beyond Glanum.

East of St-Rémy, the road to Cavaillon runs along the north side of the massif, with a right turn to Eygalières. The painter Mario Prassinos (1916–85) lived here. Just beyond the village is the 12th-century Chapelle St-Sixte.

The road continues towards Orgon where there are views across the Durance Valley and the Luberon. Orgon skirts the massif on the eastern side. A right turn leads past the ruins of Castelas de Roquemartine and Eyguières, a pleasant village with a Romanesque church. It is a two-hour walk to

Les Opiés, a 493-m (1,617-ft) hill crowned by a tower. This forms part of the GR6 which crosses the chain to Les Baux, one of the best walking routes in Provence. From Castelas de Roquemartine the road heads back west towards Les Baux.

The countryside of Les Alpilles is filled with olive trees and vast green fields with the spectacular Montmajour abbey visible in the distance from the D17, en route to Les Baux-de-Provence.

14

Les Baux-de-Provence

🅰 B4 🚌 🅸 La Maison du Roy; www.lesbauxde provence.com

The attractive and popular town of Les Baux-de-Provence sits on a spur of the Alpilles (*bau* in Provençal means escarpment). The majestic fortified **Château des Baux** offers breathtaking views of the surrounding region from Aix to Arles and across to the Camargue (*p138*). The most dramatic fortress site in the region, it is extremely popular, welcoming nearly two million

> **Did You Know?**
> ———
> Giant catfish of up to 130 kg (285 lb) in weight lurk in the Rhône, south of Arles.

visitors every year, so avoid midsummer, or go early in the morning to avoid the crowds. The pedestrianized town has a car park beside the Porte Mage gate. When the Lords of Baux built their fine citadel here in the 10th century, they claimed one of the three wise men, King Balthazar, as an ancestor and took the star of Bethlehem as their emblem. These fierce warriors originated the troubadour Courts of Love, and wooed noble ladies with poetry and songs. This became the medieval convention known as courtly love and paved the way for a literary tradition.

The citadel ruins lie on the heights of the escarpment. Their entrance is via the 14th-century Tour-du-Brau. A plateau extends to the end of the escarpment, where there is a monument to the French farmer and poet Charloun Rieu (1846–1924).

In the town centre there are two other museums of local interest. At the **Fondation Louis Jou**, medieval books are housed in a beautifully restored Renaissance home of Spanish typographer and engraver Louis Jou, after whom the museum is named, along with a collection of prints and drawings by Dürer, Goya and Jou. At the **Musée des Santons**, located in the town's 16th-century old town hall, a traditional Provençal crib scene has

← The dramatic walls of the Château des Baux rise up above the landscape

↑ The modest 1814 Moulin de Daudet lies near Fontvielle

> **When the Lords of Baux built their fine citadel here in the 10th century, they claimed one of the wise men, King Balthazar, as an ancestor.**

been created, representing the nativity at Les Baux. Exquisite handmade clay *santons*, or figurines representing saints and local figures, show the evolution of Provençal costume.

Next door to the imposing 12th-century Église St-Vincent is the Chapelle des Pénitents Blancs, decorated in 1974 by renowned local artist Yves Brayer.

Located on the D27 road to the north of Les Baux, and within walking distance of the main car park in Les Baux, is the Val d'Enfer, or the Valley of Hell. This jagged gorge, said to be inhabited by witches and spirits, may have inspired some of Dante's poetry. It is also the site where bauxite was discovered in 1821 by the geologist Berthier, who named it after the town.

It was in this large quarry that the Cathédrale d'Images, or the **Carrières de Lumières** as it is presently known, was established. The imaginative slide show is projected not only onto the white limestone walls of the natural theatre, but also onto the floor and ceiling, creating a dramatic three dimensional effect. The 35-minute show is renewed each year. Accompanied by captivating music, it makes for a truly extraordinary audio-visual experience.

Château des Baux

🛇😊🏛 🕘9am–6pm daily 🅦chateau-baux-provence.com

Fondation Louis Jou

🛇 🅐Hôtel Brion, grande rue 🅒0490543417 🕘By appointment only

Musée des Santons

🅐La Maison du Roy 🅒0490 543439 🕘10am–5pm daily

Carrières de Lumières

🛇😊🏛 🅐Route de Maillane 🕘9:30am–7pm daily 🅦carrieres-lumieres.com

⑮

Fontvieille

🅰B4 🚉🚌 🅘Ave des Moulins; www.fontvieille-provence.fr

Fontvieille is an agreeable country town in the flat fruit and vegetable lands of the irrigated Baux Valley. There is a market here every Monday and Friday. Halfway between Arles and Les Alpilles, the town makes an excellent centre from which to explore the area. Until the French Revolution in 1789, the town's history was bound up with the Abbaye de Montmajour. The oratories that stand at the four corners of the small town were erected in 1721 to celebrate the end of the plague.

To the south on the D33 is the Moulin de Daudet and the remarkable remains of a Roman aqueduct at Barbegal.

16 🎫

Abbaye de Montmajour

🅰 B4 **🏁 Route de Fontvieille** **📞 04 90 54 64 17** **🕐 Daily (Oct-Mar: Tue-Sun)** **📅 1 Jan, 1 May, 1 & 11 Nov, 25 Dec**

Standing out like Noah's ark on Mount Ararat, situated 5 km (3 miles) northwest of Arles, this Benedictine abbey was built in the 10th century. At the time, the site was an island refuge in marshland. The handful of monks in residence spent all their spare time draining this area of marshland between the Alpilles chain and the Rhône.

The abbey is an imposing place, though all the Baroque buildings were destroyed by fire in 1726 and were never restored. The original church is said to have been founded by Saint Trophime as a sanctuary from the Romans. It grew rich in the Middle Ages when thousands of pilgrims arrived at Easter to purchase pardons. After 1791, the abbey was broken up by two successive owners who

bought it from the state. The abbey was largely restored in the 19th century.

The Église Notre-Dame is one of the largest Romanesque buildings in Provence. Below, the 12th-century crypt has been built into the sloping hill. The cloister has double pillars ornamented with beasts, and lies in the shadows of the 26-m (85-ft) tower, built in the 1360s. It is worth climbing the 124 steps to the tower platform to see the stunning view across to the sea.

Also carved into the hillside is the atmospheric Chapelle de St-Pierre. It was established at the same time as the abbey and is a primitive place of worship. There are a number of tombs in the abbey grounds, but the principal burial area is the 12th-century Chapelle Ste-Croix. It lies not far to the east and is built in the shape of a Greek cross.

17

Martigues

🅰 B5 **🚗🚌** **ℹ Rond-Point de l'Hôtel de Ville; www.martigues-tourisme.com**

The Étang de Berre, situated between Marseille and the Camargue, has the largest petroleum refinery industry in

France, which dominates the landscape. However, on the inland side of the Canal de Caronte is the former fishing port and artists' colony of Martigues, which still attracts a holiday crowd.

Martigues lies on both banks of the canal and on the island of Brescon, where the Pont San Sébastien is a popular place for artists to set up their easels. Félix Ziem (1821–1911) was the most ardent admirer of the canals, bridges and docks of this "little Venice"; his paintings, as well as works by a variety of contemporary artists, can be viewed in the **Musée Ziem**.

→ Imposing tower at the abbey of St Pierre at Montmajour

Musée Ziem

🏛 Blvd du 14 Juillet 🕐 Wed-Sun pm (Jul-Aug: Wed-Mon)

18

Salon-de-Provence

🗺 B4 🚌 ℹ 249 pl Morgan; www.visitsalonde provence.com

Known for its olives (the olive oil industry here was established in the 1400s) and soap, Salon-de-Provence is dominated by the castellated **Château de l'Empéri**, which overlooks the Crau plain. Standing on its rocky base, the chateau was once home to the archbishops of Arles, and it now contains the Musée de l'Empéri, which has a large collection of militaria dating from the time of Louis XIV up to World War I. Near the

château is the 13th-century Église de St-Michel and in the north of the old town stands the Gothic St-Laurent, where the French physician and astrologer Nostradamus, Salon's most famous citizen, is buried. Here, in his adopted home, he wrote *Les Centuries*, his book of predictions, published in 1555. It was banned by the Vatican, as it foretold the diminishing power of the papacy. However, his renown was widespread and in 1560 he became Charles IX's physician.

Salon is the host of a two-week classical music festival, which takes place from late July to August, with concerts in the château, Église de St-Michel, Abbaye de Sainte-Croix and the town's theatre.

From the Place Croustillat, you can admire the Tour de l'Horloge clock tower and the mushroom-shaped, moss-covered Fontaine Moussue.

Château de l'Empéri

⊚ 🏛 Montée du Puech 📞 04 90 44 72 80 🕐 Tue–Sun pm 🚫 1 Jan, 1 May, 1 Nov, 24-25 & 31 Dec

↑ Rainbow-coloured houses overlooking the harbour at Martigues

---

GAME FISHING FROM MARTIGUES

Straddling the channel that links the Étang de Berre with the open sea, Martigues is famous among anglers hoping to hook prized trophy fish like marlin, tuna and even shark. But game fishers are aware of conservation issues. Many release their catch after winning their battles, and ethical "no-kill" skippers no longer return to Martigues with their catch dangling from the rigging. These days, the trophies are selfies and video footage, even though chartering a boat and skipper costs around €1,200 per day (€220 for those willing to share a boat with other anglers).

Colourful and busy, the harbourfront at Cassis is a great place to stroll

19

Aubagne

C5 🚌 8 cours Barthelémy; www.tourisme-paysdaubagne.fr

Marcel Pagnol's life and work is the main attraction of this simple market town. A plaque at No. 16 cours Barthélemy marks the birthplace of the much-loved Provençal writer and film-maker. The town also has a tradition of making ceramics and *santons* (figurines). The town's tableaux can be seen in the Petit Monde de Marcel Pagnol display on the Esplanade de Gaulle, about 300 m from the tourist office.

Just outside the town is the headquarters of the French Foreign Legion, moved here from Algeria in 1962. The headquarters is home to the **Musée de la Légion Étrangère** with memorabilia on display from a variety of campaigns ranging from Mexico to IndoChina.

Musée de la Légion Étrangère

Chemin de la Thuilière 10am-12pm & 2-6pm Tue-Sun musee.legion-etrangere.com

20

Abbaye de Silvacane

C4 RD 561 Daily (Oct-May: Tue-Sun) 1 Jan, 1 May, 25 Dec abbaye-silvacane.com

Like her two Cistercian sister abbeys, Sénanque and Le Thoronet, Silvacane is a harmonious 12th-century monastery tucked away in the countryside. A bus from Aix-en-Provence travels regularly to Roque-d'Anthéron, the nearest village.

The abbey was founded on the site of a Benedictine monastery, in a clearing of a "forest of reeds" *(silva canorum)*. It adheres to the austere Cistercian style, with no decoration. The church, with nave, two aisles and a high, vaulted transept, is solid, bare and echoing. The cloisters, arcaded like a pigeon loft, are 13th century, and the refectory dates from the 14th century. Shortly after the refectory was built, all the monks left and the church served the parish. After the Revolution, it was sold as state property and became a farm until transformed back into an abbey.

21

Cassis

C6 🚌 Quai des Moulins; www.ot-cassis.com

A favourite summer resort of artists such as Derain, Dufy and Matisse, Cassis is a delightful port, tucked into limestone hills. The Romans admired it, too, and built villas here, and when Marseille prospered during the 17th century a number of mansions were erected. It was also a busy fishing centre in the 19th century, and is still

PAINTERS INSPIRED BY CASSIS

Cassis, its landscapes, rich hues and brilliant light, inspired painters such as André Derain, Raoul Dufy and Henri Matisse, all three of whom painted scenes from the village in the early 20th century. It also lured artists from as far away as Scotland, including Colourists who visited in the 1920s.

known for its seafood. The local delicacy is sea urchins, enjoyed with a glass of Cassis's reputed AOC white wine.

The **Musée Municipal Méditerranéen** has items dating back to the Greeks, some rescued from the seabed. It shows Cassis to have been a substantial trading port until World War II. Other items include paintings by Félix Ziem and other early 20th-century artists who were equally drawn to Cassis.

There are three good beaches nearby, notably the Plage de la Grande Mer. The red cliffs of Cap Canaille, between Cassis and La Ciotat offer a 4-hour walk (one-way) along Route des Crêtes.

Musée Municipal Méditerranéen d'Art et Traditions Populaires
🕒 🏛Place Baragnon 📞04 42 01 88 66 🕐Wed-Sat

㉒

Les Calanques
🅰C6 🚆🚍🚌Cassis, Marseille 🌐calanques-parcnational.fr

Between Marseille and Cassis, the coast is broken up by calanques – fjord-like inlets lying between vertical white cliffs. Deep under the blue waters, they offer safe natural harbours and fascinating aquatic life, with glorious views from the high clifftops. The precipitous cliff face provide a challenge for keen climbers. The Parc National des Calanques is the only national park in Europe to include land, marine and semi-urban areas. Opened in 2012, it is home to over 200 protected animal, plant and marine species.

From Cassis, it is possible to walk to the nearest *calanque*, Port-Miou. Beyond it lies Port-Pin, with occasional pine trees and a shady beach, but the most scenic is En-Vau, which has a sandy beach and needle-like rocks rising from the sea. Walking paths often close in summer, due to the risk of fire. On the western side, the Sormiou and Morgiou inlets can be reached by road.

In 1991, the entrance to a cave was found 100 m (350 ft) under the sea at Sormiou. It is decorated with pictures of prehistoric animals resembling the ancient cave paintings at Lascaux in the Dordogne. Bear in mind when visiting the area that the main car parks serving Les Calanques beaches are notorious for theft.

EAT

La Villa Madie
Enjoy idyllic sea views and spectacular seafood at this fine-dining restaurant.

🅰C6 🏠Ave Revestel, Cassis 📞04 96 18 00 00 🕐Mon-Tue, Jan-mid-Feb

€€€

Fleurs de Thym
An attractive and affordable bistro with a seafood-heavy menu and a pretty outdoor terrace.

🅰C6 🏠5 rue Lamartine, Cassis 📞04 42 01 23 03 🕐Sun-Mon

€€€

L'Hemisphere
Family-run seafood bistro on the quayside, serving squid with pimento and roast cod.

🅰B5 🏠6 quai Lucien Toulmond, Martigues 📞04 42 80 63 23 🕐Tue

€€€

Breathtaking Calanque En-Vau, with its turquoise waters and dramatic cliffs ↑

VAUCLUSE

The jewel of Vaucluse is the fortified riverside city of Avignon, home to the popes during their "Babylonian exile" from 1309–77, and now host to one of the greatest music and theatre festivals in France. The popes' castle at Châteauneuf-du-Pape is now a ruin, but the village still produces stupendous wines. The Rhône valley wine region is justly renowned, and its vineyards spread as far northeast as the slopes of the towering giant of Provence, Mont Ventoux.

The Roman legacy in Vaucluse is also remarkable. It is glimpsed in the great theatre and triumphal arch in Orange, and in the ruins of Vaison-la-Romaine which were preserved by successive civilizations. Carpentras was also a Roman town, but its claim to fame is its possession of France's oldest synagogue. The story of the Jews, who were given papal protection in Vaucluse, is one of many religious histories which can be traced through the region. Another is the Baron of Oppède's brutal crusade against the Vaudois heretics in 1545, when many villages were destroyed.

Near Oppède, at Lacoste, a path leads to the château of France's notorious libertine Marquis de Sade. Perhaps a more elevated writer was Petrarch, who also made Fontaine-de-Vaucluse his home.

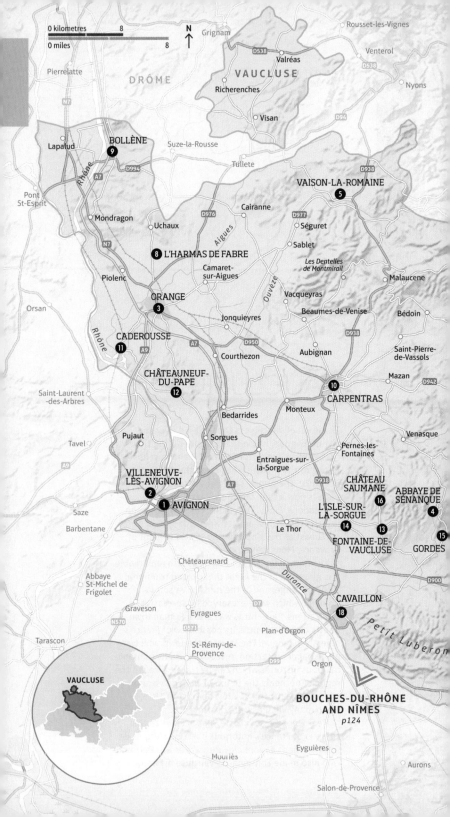

VAUCLUSE

Must Sees
1 Avignon
2 Villeneuve-lès-Avignon
3 Orange
4 Abbaye de Sénanque
5 Vaison-la-Romaine
6 Mont Ventoux
7 Le Colorado Provençal

Experience More
8 L'Harmas de Fabre
9 Bollène
10 Carpentras
11 Caderousse
12 Châteauneuf-du-Pape
13 Fontaine-de-Vaucluse
14 L'Isle-sur-la-Sorgue
15 Gordes
16 Château Saumane
17 Roussillon
18 Cavaillon
19 Cadenet
20 Apt
21 Ansouis
22 Pertuis
23 La Tour d'Aigues

① AVIGNON

A B4 ✈ 8 km (5 miles) Avignon-Caumont 🚉🚌 Blvd St-Roch; Gare TGV (pl de l'Europe, Courtine) 🛈 42 cours Jean-Jaurès; www.avignon-tourisme.com

With its beautifully preserved medieval centre set along the Rhône and surrounding the magnificent Palais des Papes, Avignon attracts millions of visitors, so its main sights bustle for much of the year, especially during the summer Avignon Festival. To experience the city like a local, venture a couple of blocks from the focal place du Palais and place de l'Horloge to discover lively open-air markets and café terraces.

① Palais des Papes

A Place du Palais ⏰ 9:30am-5:45pm daily 🌐 palais-des-papes.com

The white stone walls of this 14th-century palace complex soar above Avignon's historic heart, a reminder of the power and wealth of the seven French popes who lived here after

Pope Clement V moved the papacy from Rome to Avignon (p55). Pope Benedict XII was responsible for the sober, Cistercian architecture of the Palais Vieux; his successor, Clement VI, added the Palais Neuf in Gothic style, creating a flamboyant ensemble of turrets and hefty stone walls.

Entrance to this miniature Vatican is by means of the Porte des Champeaux, beneath the twin pencil-shaped turrets of the Palais Neuf. Inside, highlights include La Chambre du Pape, the Grande Chapelle, and the main courtyard, La Cour d'Honneur, which makes a grand central setting for the summer festival.

② Place de l'Horloge

Café tables clutter Avignon's main square, overlooked by

 ↑ Wooden horses prancing round on the carousel in Place de l'Horloge

←

Café tables spilling out
onto place Crillon, shaded
by plane trees

museum in 1976, and houses
Avignon's medieval collection,
which includes works by
Simone Martini and Botticelli,
as well as works from the
Avignon School.

Les Halles

🏠 Place Pie 🕐 6am–4:30pm
Tue–Fri & 6am–2pm Sat & Sun
🌐 avignon-leshalles.com

Savvy locals shop for fine
produce at this state-of-the-
art covered market. There
are stalls where you can stand
and sip a coffee or a glass of
fizz, and booths where you
can sit down to a seafood
platter. The outer wall, facing
place Pie, is an amazing
vertical garden.

Must See

AVIGNON FESTIVAL

France's greatest
theatre event is really
two festivals. The offi-
cial one takes over the
Palais des Papes Cour
d'Honneur and other
venues for both modern
and classical drama.
However, it is the
unofficial "off" festival
that enlivens the town,
with street performers
and up to 400 shows a
day, from dance to
burlesque comedy.

the Gothic clock tower that
gives it its name. Built on the
site of the city's ancient forum,
the square is home to the
19th-century town hall and
opera house. During the
Avignon festival, the square
becomes a stage for lively
street performers. At other
times of the year, the main
attraction is the traditional
belle époque carousel, where
colourful wooden horses
provide some excellent photo
opportunities for families
with children.

Musée du Petit Palais

🏠 Palais des Archevêques,
Place du Palais 🕐 10am–
1pm & 2–6pm Wed–Mon
🌐 petit-palais.org

Set around an arcaded
courtyard, the "little palace",
built in 1318, was modified in
1474 to suit Michelangelo's
patron Cardinal Rovere, later
Pope Julius II. It became a

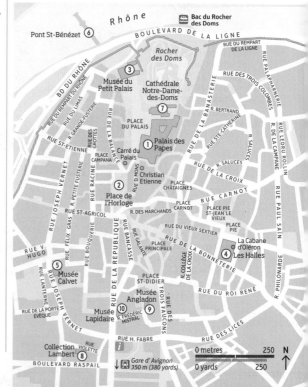

EAT

Christian Etienne

This Michelin-starred restaurant has a good-value lunch menu, while dinner features costlier items like oysters and lobster.

⌂ 10 rue du Mons
ⓦ christian.etienne.fr

€€€

La Vieille Fontaine

The menu here is dazzlingly eclectic, with options like Brittany scallops with truffles, shrimp ceviche with coriander and garden cherries, and cold garden pea soup.

⌂ Hotel d'Europe, 12 place Crillon
ⓦ heurope.com

€€€

La Cabane d'Oléron

Tucked away in a corner of Avignon's extraordinary covered market, this eatery has a handful of tables and a surprisingly affordable connoisseur's choice of fruits de mer.

⌂ Rue de l'Olivier, Les Halles ☎ 0698 29 10 88

€€€

Carré du Palais

The two-course menu at this restaurant and wine bar in a historic building on place de Palais is a bargain. The six-course tasting menu is more indulgent, and the wine list is long and ever-changing.

⌂ 1 place du Palais
ⓦ carredupalais.fr

€€€

---

⑤ 🖼️

Musée Calvet

⌂ 65 rue Joseph Vernet
⌚ 10am–1pm & 2–6pm Wed–Mon ⓦ musee-calvet.org

Works by Soutine, Manet and Dufy are highlights of the Victor Martin collection of 19th and 20th century art in this gracious 18th-century townhouse, which also houses fine art, faïences and bronzes, and a new collection of ancient Egyptian art.

---

⑥

Pont St-Bénézet

⌂ Blvd de la Ligne
⌚ 9:30am–5:45pm daily

Angelic voices heard by a shepherd boy inspired the building of the first bridge here in 1185. Its arches were so often washed away by floods that in the early 17th century the townsfolk gave up rebuilding them, so it now ends abruptly in the middle of the river. Just four of the original 22 arches remain, as well as the gatehouse at the Avignon end of the bridge, and the Tour Philippe-le-Bel, the western terminus in Villeneuve-lès-Avignon that once connected Avignon's papal enclave with the rest of France (p164).

---

⑦

Cathédrale Notre-Dame-des-Doms

⌂ Pl du Palais ⌚ Daily
ⓦ metropole.diocese-avignon.fr

Founded in the 12th century and rebuilt several times since then, Avignon's cathedral stands next to The Palais des Papes. A larger-than-life golden Madonna, poised atop its tower since the 19th century, seems to bless Avignon and its citizens. Inside, the altar of the original 6th-century church stands in the Chapelle St-Roch. Next to the cathedral, the

1177–1185
▽ Pont St-Bénézet is
built (for the first time)

1947
▽ The first Avignon
festival is held at the
Palais des Papes

43 BC
▲ Avignon flourishes
as it becomes a
Roman colony

1309–52
▲ Pope Clement V
moves the papacy
from Rome to Avignon;
Palais Vieux and Petit
Palais are built to hold
the papal court

gardens of the Rocher des Doms offer a pleasant escape from busy city streets.

⑧ 🚲 Ⓜ 💻 🏛

Collection Lambert

🏠 5 rue Violette ⏰ 11am–7pm Tue–Sun (Jul–Aug: daily) 🌐 collectionlambert.fr

The Collection Lambert is located in an 18th-century mansion, next to the School of Art, and houses an outstanding collection of contemporary art on loan for 20 years from gallery-owner Yvon Lambert. Paintings date from the 1960s and include all the major art movements since then. Highlights include ground-breaking works by Jean-Michel Basquiat, Louise Bourgeois, Carl Andre, Anselm Kiefer and Cy Twombly. The museum also runs creative courses for children.

⑨ 🚲 Ⓜ

Musée Angladon

🏠 5 rue Laboureur ⏰ 1–6pm Tue–Sat (Apr–Sep: also Sun) 🌐 collectionlambert.fr

This dazzling hi-tech museum cleverly combines modern science with the intimacy of a private home. It displays an outstanding private collection of art dating from the 18th to the 20th centuries, including works by Degas, Van Gogh, Picasso, Modigliani and other greats. Temporary exhibitions feature contemporary guest stars like David Hockney.

⑩ 🚲

Musée Lapidaire

🏠 27 rue de la République ⏰ Tue–Sun 🚫 1 Jan, 1 May, 🌐 musee-lapidaire.org

Once a 17th-century Baroque Jesuit college, this museum houses a fascinating selection of Celtic-Ligurian, Egyptian, Gallic and Roman artifacts, including a 2nd-century Tarasque monster (*see p148*). In the summer, the museum holds temporary exhibitions relating to the collection.

←

The remaining arches of Pont St-Bénézet over the Rhône

A SHORT WALK
AVIGNON

Distance 2 km (1 miles) **Nearest station**
Gare d'Avignon Centre **Time** 30 minutes

Bordered to the north and west by the Rhône,
the medieval city of Avignon is the chief city
of Vaucluse and the gateway to Provence.
Its walls cover nearly 5 km (3 miles) and are
punctuated by 39 towers and seven gates.
Within the walls thrives a culturally rich city
with its own opera house, university, several
foreign language schools and numerous
theatre companies.

*Chapelle St-Nicolas was
named after the patron
saint of bargemen and is a
16th-century building on a
13th-century base. Entrance
is via Tour du Châtelet.*

*The **Pont St-Bénézet**
was begun in 1177 by
shepherd boy Bénézet.
The bridge is the subject
of the famous rhyme
Sur le Pont d'Avignon.*

The historic
**Porte du
Rhône**

START

FINISH

RUE FERRU

*You can access the
14th-century **ramparts**
from the entrance
to the Pont St-Bénézet.*

Did You Know?

The Palais des Papes is
the biggest Gothic
palace in the world.

RUE DE LIMAS

RUE GRANDE FUSTERIE

RUE DES GROTTES

RUE DE LA BALANCE

RUE ST-ETIENNE

RUE PETITE FUSTERIE

RUE RACINE

PLACE DE L'HORLOGE

↑ Visitors stroll past the
carousel in Avignon's
Place de l'Horloge

Place de l'Horloge, the main
square, was laid out in the
15th century. Many of today's
buildings date from the
19th century.

*The façade of the **Hôtel
des Monnaies**, the
former mint, built in
1619, bears the arms of
Cardinal Borghese.*

Musée du Petit Palais, *the former episcopal offices, houses a museum of medieval and Renaissance Italian paintings and French works by the Avignon School, including the 1457 Vierge de Pitié.*

↑ Golden Madonna on the top of Cathédrale Notre-Dame des Doms

BD DE LA LIGNE

ROCHES DES DOMS

The hillside gardens of **Rocher des Doms**, *behind Notre-Dame-des-Doms, are the site of Avignon's earliest settlement.*

PLACE DU PALAIS

Popes ruling in the 14th century built the grand, fortress-like **Palais des Papes** *(p160). The Chambre du Pape, in particular, is exquisitely decorated.*

RUE VICE LEGAT

RUE PEYROLLERIE

↑ Dining in front of the impressive Palais des Papes, dramatically lit at night

Église St-Pierre *was built during the 14th to early 16th centuries. The doors on its west façade were carved in 1551 by Antoine Valard. Inside the church is a fine 15th-century pulpit.*

0 metres 100
0 yards 100

N ↑

VILLENEUVE-LÈS-AVIGNON

🅰 B4 ✈ 8 km (5 miles) Avignon-Provence 🚉🚌 Ave de la Gare
ℹ Place Charles David; www.tourisme-villeneuvelezavignon.fr

This tranquil town on the west bank of the Rhône is within sight of Avignon (p160), but even in high season it seems a world away from the tourism-thronged streets of its high-profile big sister.

With some lovely places to stay and a central square lined with budget-friendly eateries, Villeneuve-lès-Avignon is a fabulous base for exploring Avignon, and has some important sights that make it a destination in its own right.

The connecting bridge between Avignon and Villeneuve-lès-Avignon, Pont St-Bénézet, was at one time guarded by the Tour Philippe-le-Bel, built in 1307. Its rooftop terrace, 176 steps up, gives a fine panorama of the papal city. Even better is the view from the two giant 40-m (130-ft) round towers at the entrance to the impressive 14th-century Fort St-André, which originally enclosed a small town, monastery and church.

Between these two bastions lie the Église-Collégiale Notre-Dame and the Musée Pierre de Luxembourg, both spectacular 14th-century buildings containing prize collections of medieval and Renaissance art.

Another major sight is the Chartreuse du Val-de-Bénédiction, a vast former monastery with some lovely gardens.

For a stroll in the countryside and views of Villeneuve-lès-Avignon and the Avignon skyline, head for the Île de la Barthelasse. This long, narrow island in the Rhône is said to be Europe's largest river island, and stretches of its shoreline are listed as special zones of ecological interest.

INSIDER TIP
Evening kayak

Take a moonlit kayak and float down the Rhône beneath the famous arches of the Pont St-Bénézet for a truly unforgettable nocturnal experience.

1 Imposing towers dominating the entrance to the impressive 14th-century Fort St-André.

2 *Coronation of the Virgin* (1454) by Enguerrand Quarton, in the Musée Pierre de Luxembourg.

3 View of Fort St-André and Villeneuve-lès-Avignon from the top of Tour Philippe-le-Bel.

←
Rooftops of Villeneuve-lès-Avignon, seen from the Fort St André

TOP 4
SIGHTS IN VILLENEUVE-LÈS-AVIGNON

Tour Philippe-le-Bel
⌖ Rue Montée de la Tour
This 14th-century tower guarded the west end of the Pont St-Bénézet.

Fort St-André
⌖ Rue Montée du Fort
w fort-saint-andre.fr
A vast fortress that once contained a village and monastic community.

Chartreuse du Val-de-Bénédiction
⌖ 58 rue de la République
w chartreuse.org
A former monastery with elegant gardens.

Musée Pierre de Luxembourg
⌖ 3 rue de la République
Treasures of medieval art are housed here.

❸

ORANGE

🅰 B3 ✈ Avignon 37 km (23 miles) S Vaucluse 🚌 Ave Frédéric Mistral 🚌 Blvd Daladier 🅸 5 cours Aristide Briand; www.orange-tourisme.fr

The revered vineyards of the Côtes du Rhône surround Orange, part of a lush patchwork of fields, orchards and olive groves. Olives, fragrant honey and truffles find their way to stalls in the lively market on place Georges Clemenceau, but its big attractions are two of the finest Roman monuments in Europe, the Théâtre d'Antique d'Orange (p168) and the Arc de Triomphe.

①

Parc de la Colline St-Eutrope

🅰 148 allée du Dr Rassat

There's a bird's eye view of Orange's vast Roman theatre from the top of the Colline St-Eutrope, and a sweeping panorama of the surrounding countryside stretching all the way to the heights of Mont Ventoux. The scanty remnants of a 17th-century castle, built by Prince Maurice of Nassau and later blown up on the orders of Louis XIV, can be seen on its summit. The leafy park also has plenty of places for a picnic.

②

Musée d'Art et d'Histoire d'Orange

🅰 1 rue Madeleine Roch
🕐 9:45am–12:30pm & 1:30–4:30pm daily ⓦ theatre-antique.com

The exhibits found in the courtyard and ground floor of this museum reflect the history of Orange. They include more than 400 marble fragments which, when assembled, proved to be plans of the area, based on three surveys dating from AD 77. Also on display are portraits of members of the Royal House of Orange and paintings by the British artist, Sir Frank Brangwyn (1867–1956). One room demonstrates how printed fabrics were made in 18th-century Orange.

③

Arc de Triomphe

🅰 Ave de l'Arc de Triomphe

Originally dedicated to the victories of Julius Caesar and the Roman II Augusta legion, this triple triumphal arch was redesigned in the reign of the

Did You Know?

The Dutch dynasty of Nassau inherited Orange in 1544 and ruled until 1713.

← Orange's monumental Arc de Triomphe, one of its star attractions

Emperor Tiberius to celebrate victories in Germany and at sea. Look out for the ropes and anchors that form a recurrent decorative theme, and for the defeated Gauls and Teutons that are shown chained and naked on the elaborately carved east face.

Almost 20 m (65 ft) in height, the monument was later built into the city's defensive ramparts, and so escaped the fate of many of Orange's Roman buildings, which were demolished during the Middle Ages so that their stone could be re-used. However, it was not left completely unscathed: the visible pockmarks that cover the arch are believed to have been made by medieval cross-bowmen practising their aim.

The arch is the oldest surviving example of a design that would later be used in Rome for the Arch of Septimius Severus and the Arch of Constantine. It is now listed as a UNESCO World Heritage Site.

CHORÉGIES D'ORANGE

On sultry summer evenings, the perfect acoustics of Orange's Roman theatre provide a superb setting for France's oldest music festival, which celebrated its 150th anniversary in 2019. The seven-week festival takes place between mid-June and early August each year and its programme of opera and choral music features some of the world's greatest voices and classical ensembles. To enjoy it for free, take a picnic to the lower slopes of Colline St-Eutrope, immediately above the Théâtre Antique.

④
Ancienne Cathédrale de Notre-Dame

🏠 4–8 rue du Renoyer
🕐 Daily

Orange's cathedral, with its crumbling Romanesque portal, has had a turbulent history. Built in the 12th century, it was damaged during the 16th-century Wars of Religion, then restored between 1584 and 1599. It was again damaged during the Revolution, when for some years it served as a "Temple to Reason and the Supreme Being" as part of the Revolution's attempt to replace Christianity. It was returned to the Catholic church in 1795, but ceased to be the seat of the Bishopric of Orange in 1801.

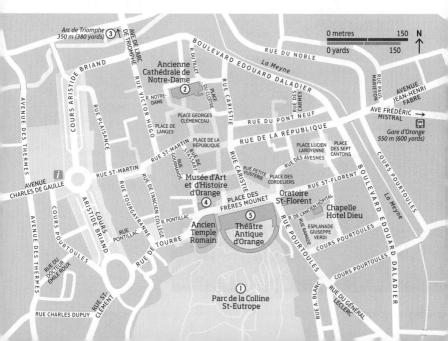

⑤ 🗝️ 🎭 🖥️ 🏛️

THÉÂTRE ANTIQUE ET MUSÉE D'ORANGE

📍1 rue Madeleine Roch 📞04 90 51 17 60 🕐Jan–Feb & Nov–Dec: 9:30am–4:30pm daily; Mar & Oct: 9:30am–5:30pm daily; Apr, May & Sep: 9am–6pm daily; Jun–Aug: 9am–7pm daily 🚫1 Jan, 25 Dec 🌐theatre-antique.com

Orange's Roman theatre, a UNESCO World Heritage site, is one of the best preserved in Europe. It still retains its original stage wall, the only Roman stage wall to remain intact, and it continues to be a popular venue for concerts and performances.

The highlight of the Parc de la Colline St-Eutrope (p166), this theatre was built at the start of the Christian era. Its stage wall was designed to ensure perfect acoustics, while its hollow stage doors amplified the voices of actors who stood in front of them. The *cavea*, or tiered semicircle, originally held up to 7,000 spectators. From the 16th to 19th centuries, the theatre was filled with squalid housing, traces of which can still be seen.

Today, crowds of up to 9,000 are packed into the theatre for rock concerts, operas and ballets. A new roof covers the stage, and a fascinating multimedia presentation of great moments in the theatre's history is shown in four grottoes behind the tiers of the amphitheatre. Some parts of the theatre may be closed for restoration, so check the website before you visit.

Did You Know?

The productions performed here in Roman times were totally free to attend and open to all.

Still visible on the exterior walls are corbels which held the huge velum-bearing masts.

A canvas awning, known as a velum, protected the theatregoers from sun or rain.

↑ Reconstruction showing how the theatre looked in Roman times

← National Music Day concert at the Théâtre Antique in Orange

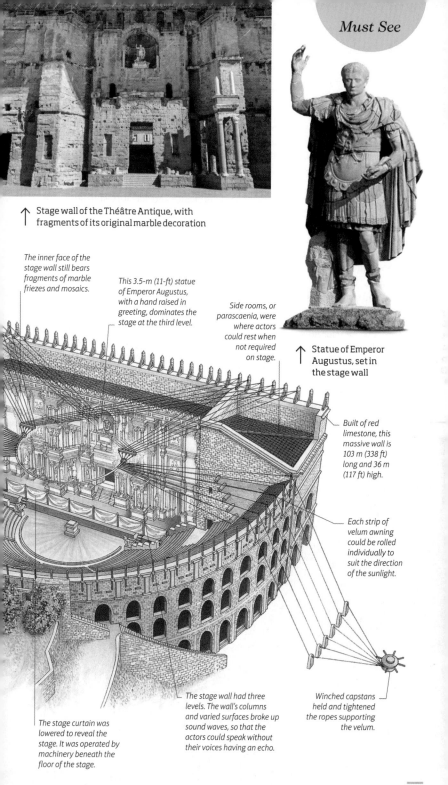

↑ Stage wall of the Théâtre Antique, with fragments of its original marble decoration

The inner face of the stage wall still bears fragments of marble friezes and mosaics.

This 3.5-m (11-ft) statue of Emperor Augustus, with a hand raised in greeting, dominates the stage at the third level.

Side rooms, or parascaenia, were where actors could rest when not required on stage.

↑ Statue of Emperor Augustus, set in the stage wall

Built of red limestone, this massive wall is 103 m (338 ft) long and 36 m (117 ft) high.

Each strip of velum awning could be rolled individually to suit the direction of the sunlight.

The stage curtain was lowered to reveal the stage. It was operated by machinery beneath the floor of the stage.

The stage wall had three levels. The wall's columns and varied surfaces broke up sound waves, so that the actors could speak without their voices having an echo.

Winched capstans held and tightened the ropes supporting the velum.

4 ⬡ ⬡ ⬡

ABBAYE DE SÉNANQUE

EXPERIENCE Vaucluse

🄰 C4 🄳 D117, Gordes 🚌 Gordes 🕐 9am–11:30am Mon–Sat, or for guided tours (in French, check website for times) 🅦 senanque.fr

Swathes of purple lavender surround this serene 12th-century Cistercian abbey, built of pale grey stone and roofed with limestone slabs. This is one of three Romanesque monasteries in Provence and, like its Cistercian siblings at Silvacane *(p152)* and Le Thoronet *(p118)*, its austere architecture reflects the simple ideals of the order. It was founded in 1148 by an abbot and 12 monks, who came to this isolated plateau to pray and contemplate. The monks today continue this legacy, dedicating their lives to prayer and to maintaining the abbey and its land.

Lavender Gardens

When the acres of immaculately groomed lavender fields that surround the Abbaye de Sénanque are in full flower in July, they are loud with the humming of bees gathering lavender pollen, which in turn gives a distinctive perfume to their honey. The Cistercians built a system of channels to carry water from the nearby Senancole to irrigate their gardens, turning the native garrigue into cultivable land. Nevertheless, lavender is one of the few crops that is hardy enough to flourish in this harsh climate terrain. The monks harvest the lavender to make honey, soap, perfume, nougat and essential oils, all of which are available to buy in the Abbey's boutique.

HISTORY OF THE ABBEY

Although initially founded on simple ideals, Sénanque grew wealthy in medieval times. Its monks yielded to earthly temptations and the abbey was sacked by the Protestant Vaudois in 1544. Plague struck in 1580, and by the 17th century only two monks remained in the tumbledown abbey. The abbey was restored in 1854, and since 1988 it has once again been home to a small monastic community.

The Abbey cloisters, adorned with exquisite carvings of vines and foliage ↑

→

Austere church interior, stripped bare in 1544 by Protestants

Abbey Church

Building work on the beautifully proportioned abbey church began in 1160, 12 years after the foundation of the abbey, and one of its four altars dates from that time. Beneath an octagonal dome, the barrel-vaulted nave is five bays long, with three stone steps connecting nave and transept. A modest tombstone in the transept marks the tomb of the 13th-century Lord of Venasque, the Abbey's former patron.

Cloister, Scriptorium and Chapterhouse

Delicate carvings of flowers, leaves and vines adorn the dove-grey limestone columns which support the arcades around Sénanque's square central cloister, which forms the core of abbey. These superb works of craftsmanship date from between 1180 and 1220.

On the north side of the cloister is the scriptorium, the only room which was permitted to be heated under the order's austere regime. This enabled the monks to read and write in relative comfort. It is no longer in use for this purpose. Next to it is the chapterhouse, lined with stone seats where monks gathered to hear the abbot read from the Bible, or from the Rule of St Bernard, founder of the Cistercian order.

←

Vibrant lavender fields surrounding the Abbey

⑤

VAISON-LA-ROMAINE

Ⓐ B3 **✈** Aéroport Avignon Provence 60 km (37 m) **🚌** From Orange Gare SNCF
Ⓦ vaison-ventoux-tourisme.com

Straddling a steep-sided gorge of the river Ouvèze, Vaison-la-Romaine
is a picturesque town boasting a magnificent array of Roman relics.
The modern town sits beside two Roman sites, the Puymin and Villasse
quarters, opposite the medieval Haute Ville on the other side of the river.

Founded by the Celtic Vocontti tribe, the town
was named Vasio Vocontiorum after the Roman
conquest, and for four centuries it flourished
until the collapse of the empire, when the
original site was abandoned for the walled
Haute Ville and its castle. The Roman city
was excavated between 1907 and 1955.

Roman Remains

The biggest of the two Roman sites, the
Puymin quarter, contained the courthouse,
temples, shops and noble townhouses. The
star attraction is the extraordinary Théâtre
Antique. Carved out of the living rock by Gallo-
Roman craftsmen, this 1st-century AD theatre is
a dazzling display of Roman building skill, with
34 semi-circular rows of stone benches seating
up to 7,000 spectators.

The Villasse quarter, the second Roman
site, is home to the remains of an array of villas
and shops, some featuring elegant mosaic
floors. The site is dotted with copies of original
statues that are now kept in the excellent
Musée Théo Desplans.

EAT

Moulin à Huile
Set in a former oil mill, this restaurant has a pretty terrace for alfresco dining. Truffles are a menu highlight here when in season.

🏠 1 quai Maréchalé Foch
🕐 Wed 🌐 lemoulin ahuile84.fr

€€€

Bistro du 'O
Exceptional food made with local produce and served with carefully selected wines.

🏠 Rue Gaston Gevaudan
🕐 Sun & Mon
🌐 bistroduo.fr

€€€

← Vaison's medieval Haute Ville and the Pont Romain, a 2,000-year-old bridge

Haute Ville

Vaison's 2,000-year-old Roman bridge connects the north bank with the upper town on the south bank. The pretty old quarter, with its 17th-century townhouses, courtyards and fountains, is ringed by ramparts and entered through a massive 14th-century gateway. At the highest point stands the dramatic castle, built in 1194 by the Count of Toulouse.

← Ancient Roman statue among the ruins

↑ Excavation of the Puymin quarter of the Roman city

MONT VENTOUX

🗺 C3 ✈ Avignon 48 km (30 miles) SW of Vaucluse 𝑖 Avenue de la Promenade, 84390
Sault en Provence 🅆 ventoux-en-provence.com

Swept by the mistral winds that blow down the Rhône valley, the "Giant of Provence" looms high above the hills, fertile plains and vineyards that surround it. Snow-capped in winter, its treeless limestone summit also gleams white in the summer.

Soaring 1,912 m (6,242 ft) into the blue sky of Provence, Mont Ventoux is all the more impressive because it stands lonely and aloof above the foothills that surround it. It has awed and inspired artists and adventurers for centuries, from the Renaissance poet Petrarch (1304–74) who made the first recorded ascent to the top in 1336, to competitive road cyclists, for whom the mountain is one of the most gruelling climbs in the world, frequently featuring in the legendary Tour de France race. Keen walkers can make it to the summit in around five hours on well-marked roads starting from Sault, on the east side of the mountain, Bedoin to the south and Malaucene on the southern slopes.

But you don't need to be super-fit to enjoy the panorama from the peak, where a viewing table helps you make out the misty ranges of the Cevennes and the Luberon in the distance, and the peak of Ste-Victoire. The lower slopes are idyllic places in which to ramble through oak and beech woodlands and wildflower meadows. At higher levels, conifers rise to the treeline, around 1,000 m (3280 ft), and give way to slopes where alpine poppy and trumpet gentian add colour in early summer.

Did You Know?

Mont Ventoux is popular with unpowered gravity racers. The current speed record is 85.612 mph.

↑ Sun setting over the summit of Mont Ventoux, with a road winding its way up to the top

1 A skiier on the slopes at Mont Serein (also called Mont Ventoux-Nord), below the summit of Mont Ventoux.

2 A Zygaena moth settles on a wildflower on the lower slopes of the mountain.

3 Cyclists tackle the ascent to the mountain's summit in one of the many competitive races that take place in the summer.

TOP 3 MOUNTAIN ACTIVITIES

Guided Walks
Start before dawn from Malaucene to follow in Petrarch's footsteps, and watch the sun rise from the summit. Walks with an experienced guide also start from Bedoin and Sault.

Winter Sports
Ski and snowboard at Mont Serein (Mont Ventoux-Nord), 5 km (3 miles) below the summit, where there are 20 pistes and 7 lifts. Ski season starts just before Christmas and lasts until late March.

Watch Cycle Racing
Vantage points are hard to find when the mountain is a stage in the Tour de France but you can watch super-fit cyclists battling for supremacy in a packed calendar of races on the mountain's slopes every summer.

1 ⟳ ⟲

LE COLORADO PROVENÇAL

🏠 Maison du Colorado, 84400 Rustrel ⏰ Feb-Jun & Sep-Dec: 10am-4pm daily; Jul-Aug: 8am-7pm daily 🌐 colorado-provencal.com

The weird landscapes of the old ochre quarries around Rustrel, with their crimson, orange and yellow gulches and pinnacles, immediately trigger the imagination of sci-fi and western movie fans, but sweet-smelling herbs and pines and the sound of shrilling cicadas remind you that this incredible place is still in Provence.

You wouldn't be surprised to encounter Han Solo or Dr Who among the other-wordly scenery of Le Colorado Provençal, a former ochre quarry. Walking trails wind through 30 hectares (74 acres) of man-made spires, ravines and canyons that change colour from pale yellow to deep crimson. The main walking circuit is an easy-going walk that takes around four hours. You'll find shady picnic spots along the way, but don't forget to bring plenty of water with you.

Between the 1880s and 1950s the ochre quarry here employed almost all the population of the nearby village of Rustrel. With its ochre-tinted pink and yellow houses, the village is worth a visit, not least for its sweeping views of the wooded hills and valleys that surround it. There are also a handful of sights to explore, including a 17th-century olive oil mill and a Renaissance château.

For a self-guided tour of Le Colorado Provençal, pick up a map of the walking route from the Maison du Colorado Visitor Centre. There are two routes to choose from. You can also book a tour of Le Lavage des Ocres, where descendants of the local *ocriers* (ochre workers), who owned the land, will show you how ochre was quarried, then washed and dissolved in water in channels and settling ponds before being made into paints, dyes and ceramic glazes.

← Visitor exploring the carved up landscape of the former ochre quarry

← Hiking trail through the multi-coloured ochre cliffs

EXPERIENCE Vaucluse

Did You Know?

At the peak of the ochre industry, the quarries of Luberon produced 40,000 tonnes of ochre a year.

↑ View from the edge of Le Colorado Provençal, over wooded hills and vales

EXPERIENCE MORE

8 L'Harmas de Fabre

A B3 **A** 445 rte de Orange, Sérignan-du-Comtat **O** 10am–6pm Mon, Tue, Thu & Fri; 2:30–6pm Sat & Sun **Q** 1 May **W** harmasjean henrifabre.fr

Bees buzz, cicadas sing and butterflies flutter by in the half-wild gardens that surround this pretty traditional farm-house. It was home to the remarkable Jean-Henri Fabre, scientist, writer and teacher, who bought it in 1879. The estate comprises of some fallow land ("harmas" means fallow land in the Provençal language), providing Fabre with an open-air laboratory for his studies. The hawthorn, lavender and rosemary he planted attracted plenty of insects for him to observe and record in his paintings.

Inside the house, now a museum dedicated to Fabre's life and work, you can see his vast collection of finds from the surrounding countryside, from bones and animal and bird skulls to shards of Roman and medieval pottery. There's also the laboratory where he conducted his entomological studies and a dining room with the harmonium on which he composed his music.

The gardens contain a pond, flower beds of French marigolds and lilies, heirloom vegetables and herbs, as well as an arboretum, with cedar, fig, sweet bay and pine trees.

9 Bollène

A B3 **A** **A** **i** 32 ave Pasteur; www.bollene tourisme.com

Despite being spread along the A7 autoroute, Bollène is pleasant, with airy boulevards and walks beside the river Lez, where there is a camping site. The narrow streets of the old quarter lead to the 11th-century Collégiale St-Martin, with its distinctive timber saddleback roof and Renaissance doorway.

The nearby Couvent Ursulines, built in the 17th century, also has some lovely features, including its magnificent chapel and staircase.

↑ Magnificent views from the walls of the Mornas fortress, outside Bollène

Bollène became famous in 1882, when Louis Pasteur stayed here and developed inoculation against swine fever. The Belvédère Pasteur garden above the town has views over the Rhône valley to the Cévennes, the Bollène hydroelectric power station and Tricastin nuclear power plant. The town hosts free open-air concerts from early July to August.

South of Bollène is the clifftop fortress of Mornas, built by the Earl of Toulouse, which was later fought over for its strategic position during the Wars of Religion. The steep climb is rewarded by spectacular views of the Rhône valley.

Between Bollène and Pierrelatte is the troglodyte village of Barry, on the side of a hill looking over Tricastin. Occupied in Neolithic times until the beginning of the 20th century, the soft rock of the caves was gradually dug out and the caves extended.

JEAN-HENRI FABRE

Renowned naturalist Jean-Henri Fabre (1823–1915) was the very first scientist to study the habits of insects in the wild at a time when entomologists collected dead specimens. With no formal schooling, the self-taught Fabre painstakingly unravelled the weird and wonderful life-cycles of the creatures of his native Provence, from tiny predators such as the praying mantis to shrill song-sters such as cicadas and crickets.

⑩

Carpentras

ⒶB3 **🚌** **ℹ**97 place 25 Août 1944; www.carpentras-ventoux.com

As the capital of the Comtat Venaissin, this picturesque market town is in the centre of the Côtes-du-Ventoux wine region. Boulevards encircle the old town, but the Porte d'Orange is the only surviving part of the medieval ramparts. In the Middle Ages, the town had a large Jewish community, and the 14th-century **Synagogue** is the oldest in France, now used by some 100 families. While not openly persecuted under papal rule, many Jews changed faith and entered the **Cathédrale-St-Siffrein** by its 15th-century south door, the *Porte Juive*. The cathedral is in the centre of the old town, near a smaller version of Orange's Arc de Triomphe. In it are Provençal paintings and statues by local sculptor Jacques Bernus (1650–1728). The town hall has a fine 18th-century pharmacy, and there are regional costumes in the **Musée Comtadin-Duplessis**.

Synagogue

ⒶPl Maurice Charretier **☎**04 90 63 39 97 **⊘**Mon–Fri **🗓**Jewish feast days

Cathédrale St-Siffrein

Ⓐ3 pl Saint-Siffrein **☎**04 90 63 08 33 **⊘**Tue–Sat

Musée Comtadin-Duplessis

⊘ **Ⓐ**234 blvd Albin-Durand **☎**04 90 63 04 92 **⊘**Apr–Sep: Wed–Mon **🗓**Public hols

←

Crowds in the square outside the Cathédrale-St-Siffrein in Carpentras

⓫ Caderousse

🅰B3 🛈 La Mairie, rue Berbiguier; www.orange-tourisme.fr

This bankside village lies at a point where Hannibal is said to have crossed the river Rhône with his elephants on his way to Rome in 218 BC. For centuries, Caderousse has endured the floods of the Rhône, and plaques on the town hall record the high levels of floodwater. By 1856, the villagers took action, and erected a dyke that is still in place. Its four entry points can close if floods should threaten again.

Caderousse has a Romanesque church, St-Michel, to which the Flamboyant Gothic chapel of St-Claude was added during the 16th century.

⓬ Châteauneuf-du-Pape

🅰B3 🚊 Sorgues, then taxi 🚌 🛈 3 rue de la République; www.chateauneuf-du-pape-tourisme.fr

The best-known of the Côtes-du-Rhône wine labels takes its name from an unassuming yellow stone village on a small hill, filled with cellars and restaurants selling the products of the local growers entitled to the *appellation d'origine contrôlée*. The **Musée du Vin – Maison Brotte** traces the history and current state of the local viniculture.

At the top of the village are the ruins of the Château des Papes, mostly burned down in the 16th-century Wars of Religion. From the remaining walls there is a superb view of Avignon and the vineyard-lined clay fields where smooth

↑ Châteauneuf-du-Pape wine displayed in the shop of a local vineyard

stones deposited by the Rhône reflect the sun's heat onto 13 varieties of grape. The château was built in 1317 by John XXII, an Avignon pope who planted the first vineyards, but it took some 400 years for the wine's reputation to spread. Today, there are 180 Châteauneuf-du-Pape domaines.

The nearby town of Pernes-les-Fontaines is known for its 40 fountains, in particular the 18th-century Fontaine du Cormoran. Until 1914, each of the fountains had an individual keeper.

Musée du Vin - Maison Brotte

🕐 🅰 Ave St-Pierre de Luxembourg, Châteauneuf-du-Pape 📞 04 90 83 59 44 🕐 Daily 🔒 1 Jan, 25 Dec

⓭ Fontaine-de-Vaucluse

🅰C4 🚌 Avignon 🛈 Résidence Jean Garcin, ave Robert Garcin; www.oti-delasorgue.fr

The source of the Sorgue river is one of the natural wonders of Provence. It begins underground, with tributaries that drain the Vaucluse plateau, an area of around 2,000 sq km (800 sq miles). In the closed valley above the town, water erupts from an unfathomable depth to develop into a fully fledged river. Beside the river is the **Moulin à Papier Vallis Clausa**, which produces handmade paper using a 15th-century method.

→ Mossy waterwheel in the canals that run through L'Îsle-sur-la-Sorgue

The mill sells maps, prints and lampshades. The town boasts an interesting underground museum, the **Ecomusée du Gouffre (Musée de Spéléologie)**, which features a speleologist's findings over 30 years of exploring Sorgue's caves and waterfalls. There is also the **Musée d'Histoire Jean Garcin 1939–1945**, which traces the fate of the Resistance during WWII and daily life under the Occupation. The **Musée Bibliothèque Pétrarque** was the house where the poet Francesca Petrarca lived for 16 years.

Moulin à Papier Vallis Clausa

🏛 🅰 Chemin du Gouffre
🕐 Daily 🗓 1–15 Jan, 25 Dec
Ⓦ moulin-vallisclausa.com

Ecomusée du Gouffre (Musée de Spéléologie)

🏛🏛🏛 🅰 Chemin du Gouffre
📞 04 90 20 34 13 🕐 Feb–15 Nov: daily

Musée d'Histoire Jean Garcin 1939–45

🏛 🅰 Chemin de la Gouffre
📞 04 90 20 24 00 🕐 Apr–Oct: Wed–Mon (pm only) 🗓 1 May

Musée Bibliothèque Pétrarque

🏛 🅰 Rive gauche de la Sorgue 📞 04 90 20 37 20
🕐 Apr–Oct: Wed–Mon
🗓 1 May

🔟 14
L'Île-sur-la-Sorgue

🅰 B4 🚌🚆 ℹ️ Pl de la Liberté
Ⓦ oti-delasorgue.fr

This attractive town lies on the river Sorgue, which once powered 70 watermills along its banks. Today, 14 idle wheels remain, and seven of the old buildings that once

↑ Sumptuous interior of the Baroque Notre-Dame-des-Anges

housed warehouses and weaving mills now house hundreds of antiques and vintage dealerships, making L'Isle-sur-la-Sorgue France's biggest antiques trading centre after Paris.

Dealers began to migrate to the area during the 1960s, attracted by affordable spaces for their stores. There were also rich pickings from local castles, farmhouses and village homes when their owners sold off unloved old possessions, which were soon to become pricey collectables. There are now around 300 antiques dealerships around the village.

Other highlights of the village include the ornate 17th-century Notre-Dame-des-Anges, with its attractive clock, and the Musée du Jouet et de la Poupée Ancienne, which displays antique toys and dolls.

> 💬 INSIDER TIP
> **Antiques hunt**
>
> For the best buys and biggest choice of antiques, visit L'Île-sur-la-Sorgue in mid August or at Easter, when the village turns into one huge antiques fair with a great selection of finds and bargains galore.

The spectacularly sited medieval village of Gordes ↑

15

Gordes

C3 **ℹ** Pl du Château; www.gordes-village-com

Expensive restaurants and hotels confirm the popularity of this hilltop village, which spills down in terraces from a Renaissance château and the church of St-Firmin. Its grand position is the main attraction, although its vaulted, arcaded medieval lanes are also lovely. The village has been popular with artists since the academic Cubist painter André Lhote began visiting in 1938.

The **Château de Gordes** was built in the 16th century on the site of a 12th-century fortress. One of the château's best features is an ornate 16th-century fireplace in the great hall on the first floor, decorated with shells, flowers and pilasters. In the entrance there is an attractive Renaissance door. The building was restored by the Hungarian-born Op Art painter Victor Vasarely (1908–97), and once housed a museum of his works. Today, the château hosts temporary exhibitions during the summer.

Outside Gordes is the **Village des Bories**, a museum of rural life and dry stone huts.

Château de Gordes
🏠 Pl du Château 📞 04 90 72 98 64 🕐 Apr–Oct: daily

Village des Bories
🏠 Rte de Cavaillon 📞 04 90 72 03 48 🕐 Daily 🚫 1 Jan, 25 Dec

16

Château Saumane

C4 🏠 Allée René Char 🕐 Times vary, check website 🌐 oti-delasorgue.fr

Looming on a hilltop above the village of Saumane, the massive medieval walls of this impressive fortress conceal a lavish interior graced by vaulted corridors, painted ceilings, marble fireplaces and stone stairways. The outer walls are almost 2 m (6 ft) thick, ensuring the interior is pleasantly cool, even in high summer.

Within is a mysterious labyrinth of hidden doorways and secret passages leading to a series of gloomy cellars and dungeons that once stirred the twisted imagination of the young Marquis Donatien de Sade (1740–1814), a notorious libertine and philosopher. He lived here as a guest of his

SHOP

Ocres de France
Discover more than 150 shades of authentic ochre-based paint and plaster on display in this historic factory and showroom.

C4 🏠 93 chemin des Ochres, Apt 🕐 Sat & Sun

La Compagnie des Ocres
Paints and pigments made from ochre and a rainbow of other traditional colorants are on sale here. You can ask for items to be sent to your home address.

C4 🏠 Sentier des Ocres, Roussillon 🌐 lacompagnie desocres.fr

→ Striking colourful landscape of the Sentier des Ochres

in and around the village, notably in the dramatic former quarries along the Sentier des Ochres. The entrance to the quarries – which are home to a bizarre series of landscapes that would look more at home in Arizona than in Provence – is to the east of the village, a 90-minute trip from the information office. The Conservatoire des Ocres et de la Couleur in the old factory *(open mid-Feb–Dec: daily)*, is well worth visiting. It displays a huge collection of natural pigments, and runs day courses on the subject.

A superb panorama to the north can be enjoyed from the Castrum, the viewing table beside the church in the main square.

---

uncle, the Abbé Jacques-Francois de Sade, between the ages of five and ten. The château was owned by the de Sade family until 1868. It was acquired by the regional council in 1982 and opened to the public.

17

Roussillon

⚑ C4 𝒊 Pl de la Poste; www.otroussillon. pagesperso-orange.fr

The deep ochres used in the construction of this hilltop community are stunning. Its hues come from at least 17 shades of ochre discovered

17

Cavaillon

⚑ B4 🚈🚌 𝒊 Pl François Tourel; www.luberon coeurde provence.com

The viewing table outside the Chapelle St-Jacques at the top of this town shows the Luberon range in perspective against Mont Ventoux and the Alpilles chain. In closer proximity are acres of fruit and vegetable plots, for

Cavaillon is France's largest market garden, an area especially well-known for its melons. Its local market competes with the one in Apt for renown as the most important in Vaucluse.

Colline St-Jacques was the site of the pre-Roman settlement that prospered under Rome. There is a 1st-century Roman arch in place Duclos nearby. Roman finds are on display in the **Musée Archéologique de l'Hôtel Dieu** in the grand rue, which leads north from the church, a former cathedral dedicated to its 6th-century bishop, Saint Véran. The **synagogue** in rue Hébraïque dates from 1772, although there has been one on this site ever since the 14th century. The **Musée Jouves et Juif Comtadin**, on the same road, commemorates its fascinating history.

Musée Archéologique de l'Hotel Dieu

⊛ ⚑ Hôtel Dieu, Porte d'Avignon 📞 04 90 72 26 86 🕐 May–Sep: Mon, Wed-Sat (pm only)

Synagogue & Musée Jouves et Juif Comtadin

⊛ ⚑ Rue Hébraïque 📞 04 90 71 21 06 🕐 Oct-Apr: Mon, Wed-Sat; May–Sep: Wed-Mon 🚫 1 Jan, 1 May, 25 Dec

19 Cadenet

🅐 C4 🚌 Avignon 🛈 11 pl du Tambour d'Arcole; www. luberoncotesud.com

Tucked underneath the hills in the Durance valley, the pretty village of Cadenet has 11th-century castle ruins and a 14th-century church with a square belltower. Its font is made from a Roman sarco-phagus. In the main square, which is used for Cadenet's bi-weekly market, is a statue of the town's heroic drummer boy, André Estienne, who beat such a raucous tattoo in the battle for Arcole Bridge in 1796 that the Austrian forces thought they could hear gunfire and retreated.

20 Apt

🅐 C4 🚌🚆 Avignon 🛈 788 ave Victor Hugo; 04 90 74 03 18

Apt is the northern entry to the Parc Naturel Régional du Luberon (*p183*). The **Maison du Parc**, a restored 17th-century mansion, has information on the area, including walks, *gîtes d'étapes* and flora and fauna.

The busy old town of Apt has a square for playing *boules*, and fountains and plane trees. Surrounded by cherry orchards, it claims to be the world capital of crystallized fruit. The **Musée de l'Aventure Industrielle** explains how the production of crystallized fruit, earthenware pottery and the extraction of ochre brought prosperity to Apt in the 18th and 19th centuries. The town is also famous for truffles and lavender essence. The Saturday market offers Provençal delicacies and enter-tainment, including jazz, barrel-organ music and stand-up comedy. Le Colorado Provençal (*p176*), the best ochre quarry site by the River Dôa, to the northeast, makes for an interesting excursion.

The medieval **Cathédrale Ste-Anne** lies at the heart of Apt's old town. Legend has it that the veil of St Anne was brought back from Palestine and hidden in the cathedral by Auspice, who is thought to have been Apt's first bishop. Each July her festival is cele-brated with a procession. The Royal Chapel commemorates Anne of Austria. She paid a pilgrimage to Apt to pray for fertility and contributed the funds to finish the chapel, which was finally completed

around 1669–70. The treasury inside the sacristy contains the saint's shroud and an 11th-century Arabic standard from the First Crusade (1096–9). In the apse is a 15th–16th-century window that depicts the tree of Jesse. Nearby is the 17th-century Hôtel d'Albertas.

The items on display in the **Musée d'Histoire et d'Archéologie** consist of prehistoric flints, stone implements, Gallo-Roman carvings, jewellery and mosaics. Just a few miles from Apt, **L'Observatoire Sirene** has an idyllic location and state-of-the-art technology, ideal for star-gazing.

Maison du Parc
🏠 60 pl Jean-Jaurès 🕐 Mon-Fri 🌐 parcduluberon.fr

Musée de l'Aventure Industrielle
⊘ 🏠 Pl du Postel 📞 04 90 74 95 30 🕐 Sep-Jun: Tue-Sat; Jul-Aug: Mon-Sat 🚫 Public hols, Jan

Cathédrale Ste-Anne
⊘🚫 🏠 Rue Ste-Anne 🕐 Tue-Sat 🌐 apt-cathedrale.com

←
The village of Cadenet with the castle ruins on the hillside above

Musée d'Histoire et d'Archéologie
⊗ 🏠27 rue de l'Amphi-théâtre 📞04 90 74 95 30 ⏰By appointment only

L'Observatoire Sirene
⊗ 🏠D34 Lagarde d'Apt ⏰Daily by appt 🗓Public hols 🌐obs-sirene.com

---

21 Ansouis

🅰C4 ℹ️Pl de la Vieille Fontaine; open Easter–Sep; www.luberon cotesud.com

One of the most remarkable things about the Renaissance **Château d'Ansouis** is that it was owned by the Sabran family from 1160 until 2008, when it was sold to a new owner. The Sabrans have a proven pedigree: in the 13th century, Gersende de Sabran and Raymond Bérenger IV's four daughters became queens of France, England, Romania and Naples, respectively. In 1298, Elzéar de Sabran married Delphine de Puy, a descendant of the Viscount of Marseille. But she had resolved to become a nun, so agreed to the marriage, but not to its consummation. Both were canonized in 1369.

The castle's original keep and two of its four towers are still visible. Its

gardens include the lovely Renaissance Garden of Eden, built on the former cemetery.

The **Musée Extraordinaire de Georges Mazoyer**, located south of the village, displays the work of artist Georges Mazoyer, as well as Provençal furniture and a re-created underwater cave, all in 15th-century cellars.

Château d'Ansouis
⊗ 🏠Rue du Cartel ⏰Apr–Oct: Thu–Mon for guided tours 🌐chateauansouis.com

Musée Extraordinaire de Georges Mazoyer
⊗⏰ 🏠Quartier de Columbier 📞04 90 09 82 64 ⏰Daily (mid-Sep–mid-Jun: pm only)

---

22 Pertuis

🅰C4 🚆🚌 ℹ️Le Donjon, pl Mirabeau; www.ville-pertuis.fr

Once the capital of the Pays d'Aigues, present-day Pertuis is a quiet town, whose fertile surroundings were gradually taken over by Aix-en-Provence. Pertuis was the birthplace of the philandering Count of Mirabeau's father, and the

13th-century clock tower is located in place Mirabeau. The Église St-Nicolas, re-built in Gothic style in the 16th century, has a 16th-century triptych and two 17th-century marble statues. To the south-west is the battlemented 14th-century Tour St-Jacques.

---

23 La Tour d'Aigues

🅰C4 🚌To Pertuis ℹ️Château de la Tour d'Aigues; www.luberon cotesud.com

Nestling beside the grand limestone mountain ranges of Luberon, and surrounded by scenic vineyards and orchards, this beautiful town takes its name from a historic 10th-century tower. The 16th-century castle completes the triumvirate of Renaissance châteaux in the Luberon (the others are Lourmarin and Ansouis). Built on the foundations of a medieval castle by Baron de Central, its massive portal is based on the splendid Roman arch at Orange (p166). The castle was damaged in the French Revolution (1789–9), but has been partially restored.

Château de la Tour d'Aigues
⊗⏰ 🏠BP 16 📞04 90 07 50 29 ⏰Daily for private tours only (call 04 90 07 42 10 to book)

←
Imposing entrance to the Château de la Tour d'Aigues

A CYCLING TOUR
IN VAUCLUSE

Length 48 km (30 miles) **Level** Easy
Start/finish point: Bédoin

Allow four hours in the saddle for this easy-going ride on
country roads and waymarked cycle trails lined with yellow
broom and wild almond, pine and oak trees. With plenty of time
for picnic stops, restorative coffees and a leisurely lunch break
in one of the pretty, red-tiled villages along the way, this tour
is a full day out from Avignon, Orange or Carpentras.

A Cycling Tour
in Vaucluse
VAUCLUSE

Locator Map
For more detail see p156

← View over Mazan,
with Mont Ventoux
in the distance

*Medieval townhouses line the
narrow streets of the village of
Mazan, where the aristocratic
dynasty that spawned the
infamous Marquis de Sade
(p180) had its roots.*

Mazan

D942

*Olive groves and cherry
orchards surround
Malemort-du-Comtat,
where you can stretch
your legs by ambling
around the tumbledown
remnants of medieval
towers and ramparts.*

Malemort-
du-Comtat

Did You Know?
—
Werewolves supposedly
preyed on Mazan's
ancient cemetery until
a chapel was built
to protect villagers.

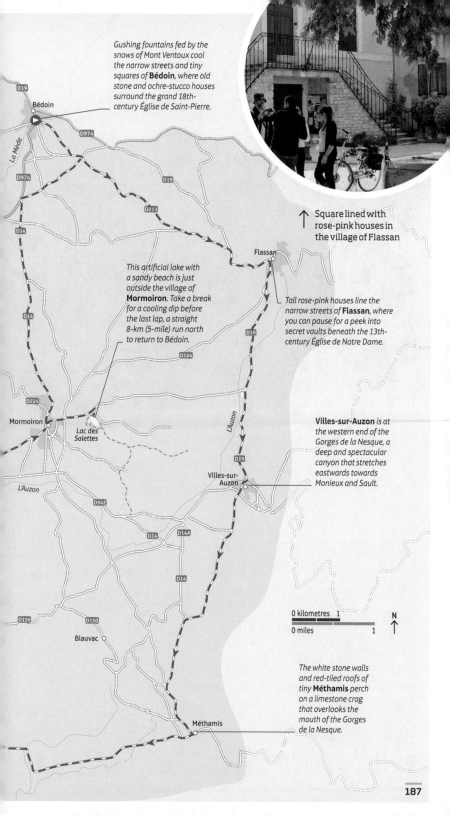

Gushing fountains fed by the snows of Mont Ventoux cool the narrow streets and tiny squares of **Bédoin**, where old stone and ochre-stucco houses surround the grand 18th-century Église de Saint-Pierre.

↑ Square lined with rose-pink houses in the village of Flassan

This artificial lake with a sandy beach is just outside the village of **Mormoiron**. Take a break for a cooling dip before the last lap, a straight 8-km (5-mile) run north to return to Bédoin.

Tall rose-pink houses line the narrow streets of **Flassan**, where you can pause for a peek into secret vaults beneath the 13th-century Église de Notre Dame.

Villes-sur-Auzon is at the western end of the Gorges de la Nesque, a deep and spectacular canyon that stretches eastwards towards Monieux and Sault.

0 kilometres 1
0 miles 1

N ↑

The white stone walls and red-tiled roofs of tiny **Méthamis** perch on a limestone crag that overlooks the mouth of the Gorges de la Nesque.

ALPES-DE-HAUTE-PROVENCE

In this, the most undiscovered region of Provence, agriculture is still the primary source of income. The Valensole plain is now the most important lavender producing area of France. Peaches, apples and pears have been planted in orchards only recently irrigated by the Durance, the region's main river, which has been tamed by dams and a hydro-electric power scheme. These advances have created employment and helped bring prosperity to the region. Another modern development is the Cadarache nuclear research centre, situated just outside Manosque. The town's population has grown rapidly to 22,100 inhabitants, overtaking the region's capital, Digne-les-Bains.

The region's history and architecture have also been greatly influenced by the terrain and climate. Strategically positioned citadels crown mountain towns such as Sisteron, which was won over by Napoleon in 1815, and the frontier town of Entrevaux. The design of towns and buildings has remained practical, mindful of the harsh winter and strong Mistral winds. Undoubtedly, the beauty of the region is revealed in the high lakes and mountains, the glacial valleys and the colourful fields of Alpine flowers.

ALPES-DE-HAUTE-PROVENCE

Must See
1 Gorges du Verdon

Experience More
2 Sisteron
3 Barcelonnette
4 Seyne-les-Alpes
5 Mont Pelat
6 Colmars
7 Digne-les-Bains
8 Lurs
9 Les Pénitents des Mées
10 Forcalquier
11 Manosque
12 Gréoux-les-Bains
13 Valensole
14 Riez
15 Moustiers-Ste-Marie
16 Annot
17 Castellane
18 St-André-les-Alpes
19 Entrevaux

VAUCLUSE
p154

HAUTES-
ALPES

ALPES-DE-HAUTE-
PROVENCE

ITALY

Chorges

*Lac de
Serre-Ponçon*

Saint-Vincent-
les-Forts

Meyronnes

Ubayette

D900

La Condamine-
Châtelard

Jausiers

Méolans-Revel

D900

3

BARCELONNETTE

D64

Saint-Martin-
lès-Seyne

Selonnet

Bayons

SEYNE-LES-ALPES

4

Pra-Loup

D902

Saint-Dalmas-
le-Selvage

ALPES-DE-
HAUTE-
PROVENCE

D900

Verdaches

Prads-Haute-
Bléone

MONT PELAT

5

St Etienne

D908

Allos

D2205

Barles

La Robine-
sur-Galabre

Bléone

La Javie

COLMARS **6**

> RIVIERA AND
ALPES-MARITIMES
p60

Marcoux

D900

Thorame-Haute

Verdon

ALPES-
MARITIMES

7 DIGNE-LES-BAINS

Valberg

*Montagne
de Coupe*

La Mure-Argens

Méailles

Guillaumes

Le Chaffaut-
Saint-Jurson

N85

Clumanc

ST-ANDRÉ-
LES-ALPES

D2202

Mézel

18

ANNOT **16**

Var

Saint-Jeannet

ENTREVAUX **19**

D907

Barrême

Sénez

Estoublon

Asse

*Lac de
Castillon*

N202

Vergons

Val-de-Chalvagne

*Parc Naturel Régional
du Verdon*

CASTELLANE

Saint-
Auban

Le Mas

MOUSTIERS-
STE-MARIE

15

17

Soleilhas

D952

GORGES DU
VERDON

Rougon

D952

Verdon

Valderoure

1

*Lac de
Ste-Croix*

D71

Séranon

D6085

D2

∨∨

VAR AND THE
ÎLES D'HYÈRES
p98

0 kilometres   10

0 miles   10

N
↑

❶

GORGES DU VERDON

🅐 E4 🛈 Parc Naturel Régional du Verdon, Domaine de Valx, Moustiers Sainte Marie; www.parcduverdon.fr

France's answer to the Grand Canyon, where the river Verdon slices through deep gorges beneath vertical cliff faces, is a paradise for adventurers and lovers of the great outdoors. Walking, kayaking, river rafting and rock climbing are among the numerous activities on offer in this breathtakingly beautiful ravine.

Castellane

At the east end of the canyon, Castellane is the gateway to the Gorges du Verdon, and bustles in summer with adventurers of all ages setting out on river trips by canoe, kayak and raft. Experiences range from gentle floats for families to hardcore white-water journeys along the full 24-km (15-mile) expanse of runs and rapids to Lac de Sainte-Croix, at the western end.

La Palud-sur-Verdon

La Palud is the start-point for a variety of walks in the gorges, from relatively easy-going strolls to much more challenging treks. The most popular and spectacular walk is the Sentier Blanc-Martel, which leads through wooded cliff paths and riverside tunnels.

←

Visitors sailing through the gorgeous Gorges du Verdon

→

A griffin flying over the river;
spectacular view over the
Gorges du Verdon *(above)*

↑ Climber tackling the face of a cliff
above the Gorges du Verdon

Pont d'Artuby

Only the brave dare to plummet 182 m (597 ft) from what is claimed to be the highest bungee jump in Europe, from the Pont d'Artuby, which spans a southern tributary of the Verdon. Less courageous visitors can enjoy fantastic views of forest-capped limestone cliffs that plummet to the blue trickle of the river far below.

L'Escales

More than 1,000 hardcore routes attract rock climbers to the Gorges du Verdon. The 400-m (1312-ft) crag of l'Escales is among the most renowned challenges. Non-climbers can watch in awe as experts tackle it using tiny holds.

Sainte-Croix de Verdon

After an adrenaline-powered journey in the Gorges du Verdon, this trendy, purpose-built resort on the shore of the vast, artificial Lac de Sainte-Croix is the perfect place to unwind. For families, there are sandy beaches with lifeguards on duty (in summer) and easy-going activities like paddle-boarding and pedaloes.

A DRIVING TOUR
OF THE ROUTE DES CRÊTES

ALPES-DE-HAUTE-PROVENCE

A Driving Tour of the Route Des Crêtes

Locator Map
For more detail see p190

Length 120 km (75 miles) **Stopping-off points**
La Palud-sur-Verdon has several cafés and Moustiers-Ste-Marie is a good place to stop for lunch

A driving tour of the Gorges du Verdon takes at least a day, and this route, made up of two loops, encompasses its most striking features. At its east and west points are the towns of Castellane and Moustiers-Ste-Marie. Parts of the tour are very mountainous, so drivers must be aware of hairpin bends and narrow roads with sheer drops. Weather conditions can also be hazardous and roads can be icy until late spring.

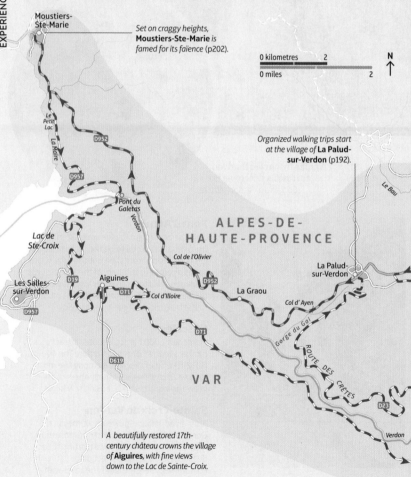

Set on craggy heights, **Moustiers-Ste-Marie** is famed for its faïence (p202).

Organized walking trips start at the village of **La Palud-sur-Verdon** (p192).

ALPES-DE-HAUTE-PROVENCE

Pont du Galetas

Lac de Ste-Croix

Col de l'Olivier

La Palud-sur-Verdon

Les Salles-sur-Verdon

Aiguines

Col d'Illoire

La Graou

Col d'Ayen

Gorge du Gal

ROUTE DES CRÊTES

VAR

Verdon

A beautifully restored 17th-century château crowns the village of **Aiguires**, with fine views down to the Lac de Sainte-Croix.

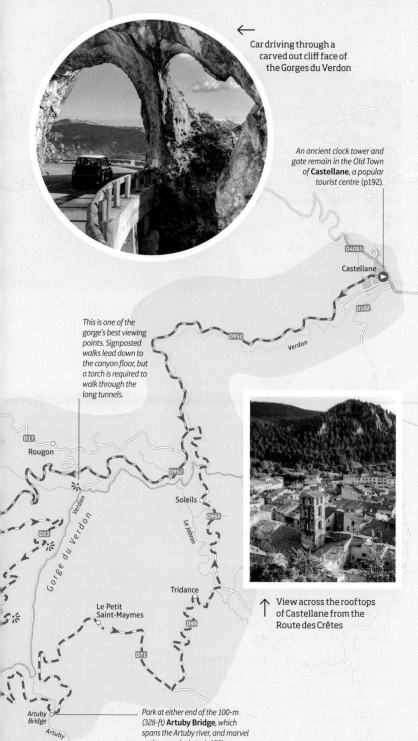

← Car driving through a carved out cliff face of the Gorges du Verdon

An ancient clock tower and gate remain in the Old Town of **Castellane***, a popular tourist centre (p192).*

D4085

Castellane

D102

D952   Verdon

This is one of the gorge's best viewing points. Signposted walks lead down to the canyon floor, but a torch is required to walk through the long tunnels.

D17
Rougon

D952

Soleils

D955

D23   Verdon   Le Jabron

↑ View across the rooftops of Castellane from the Route des Crêtes

Tridance

Le Petit Saint-Maymes

D90

D71

Gorge du Verdon

Artuby Bridge

Artuby

Park at either end of the 100-m (328-ft) **Artuby Bridge***, which spans the Artuby river, and marvel at the superb views (p193).*

↑ The stronghold of Sisteron along the bank of the Durance

EXPERIENCE MORE

2

Sisteron

▲D3 🚉🚌 ℹ1 pl de la République; www. sisteron-buech.fr

As you approach Sisteron from the north or south, it is easy to appreciate its strategic importance. The town calls itself the "gateway to Provence", sitting in a narrow valley on the left bank of the Durance river. It is a lively town, protected by the most impressive fortifications in Provence. However, it has suffered for its ideal military position, most recently with heavy Allied bombardment during 1944.

La Citadelle, built in the 12th century, dominates the town and affords superb views down over the Durance. These defences, though incomplete, comprise a keep, dungeon, chapel, towers and ramparts. It also offers a fine setting for the Nuits de la Citadelle, the summer festival of music, theatre and dance.

The cathedral in the main square, Notre-Dame et St-Thyrse, is an example of the Provençal Romanesque school, dating from 1160. At its east end, the 17th-century Chapelle des Visitandines houses the Musée Terre et Temps, a museum dedicated to the examination of time. In the Old Town, shops, cafés and bars line the narrow alleyways called *andrônes*. Rocher de la Baume on the opposite bank is a popular practice spot for mountaineers.

La Citadelle

◈ 🏛1 allée de Verdun, 04200 Sisteron ⏰Apr–11 Nov: daily 🖥 citadelledesisteron.fr

---

3

Barcelonnette

▲E3 🚌 ℹPl Frédéric Mistral 🖥barcelonnette. com

In the remote Ubaye Valley, surrounded by a demi-halo of snowy peaks, lies Provence's northernmost town. It is a flat, open settlement of cobbled streets, smart cafés and restaurants, and quaint gift shops, selling specialities such as raspberry and juniper liqueurs. The town was named in 1231 by its founder Raymond-Bérenger V, Count of Barcelona and Provence, whose great-grandfather of the same name married into the House of Provence in 1112. The town's Alpine setting gives it a Swiss flavour, but it also has a Mexican link: the Arnaud brothers, whose business in Barcelonnette was failing, emigrated to Mexico and made their fortune. Others followed, and on their return in the early 20th century, they built the grand villas which encircle the town.

Housed in one of the villas is the **Musée de la Vallée**, where the Mexican connection is explained through illustrations and costumes. There are four other branches of this museum in the Ubaye valley, at St-Paul, Jausiers, Val-d'Oronaye and Le Lauzet.

Mont Pelat

🗺 F3 🚉 Thorame-Verdon
🚌 Colmars, Allos 🛈 Pl
de la Coopérative, Allos
🌐 valdallos.com

This is the loftiest peak in the Provençal Alps, rising to a height of 3,050 m (10,017 ft). All around are mountains and breathtaking passes, some of them closed by snow until June. Among them are the Col de Cayolle, 2,327 m (7,635 ft) on the D2202 to the east, and the hair-raising Col d'Allos, 2,250 m (7,380 ft) on the D908 to the west.

South of Mont Pelat, in the heart of the Parc National du Mercantour, is the beautiful 50-ha (124-acre) Lac d'Allos. It is the largest natural lake in Europe at this altitude. The setting is idyllic, ringed by snowy mountains, its crystal-clear waters swimming with trout and char.

Another record-breaker is Cime de la Bonette, on the D64 northeast of Mont Pelat. At 2,862 m (9,390 ft) this is the highest pass in Europe. It also has what is perhaps the most magnificent view of this region's extraordinary mountain scenery.

In summer, there is an information point in the town for the Parc National du Mercantour (p80). The park stretches along the Italian border and straddles the Alpes Maritimes region in the south. It is a haven for birds, wildlife and fauna, with two major archaeological sites.

Musée de la Vallée

♿ 🚫 🏠 10 ave de la Libération 📞 04 92 81 27 15 🕐 Wed–Sat pm (Jul & Aug: daily) 🚫 Mid–Nov–mid-Dec

---

Seyne-les-Alpes

🗺 E3 🚌 🛈 Place d'Armes
🌐 blancheserreponcon-
tourisme.com

The small mountain village of Seyne dominates the Vallée de la Blanche, sitting 1,260 m (4,134 ft) above sea level. Horses and mules graze in the nearby fields, and there is a celebrated annual horse and mule fair in August.

Beside the main road is Notre-Dame de Nazareth, a 13th-century Romanesque church with Gothic portals, a sundial and a large rose window. The path by the church leads up to the citadelle, built by Vauban in 1693, which encloses the still-standing 12th-century watchtower. There are also ramparts visible, part of the original fortifications of this border town.

The village is also a centre for winter sports, with facilities nearby at St-Jean, Le Grand Puy and Chabanon.

NAPOLEON IN PROVENCE

In his bid to regain power after his exile on Elba, Napoleon knew his only chance of success was to win over Sisteron. On 1 March 1815, he secretly sailed from the island of Elba, landing at Golfe-Juan with 1,026 soldiers. With his troops, he scrambled across difficult terrain, and waited for news of the royalist stronghold of Sisteron. The arsenal was empty and he entered the town on 5 March. The people were, at last, beginning to warm to him.

6
Colmars

ⒶE3 🚍 🅘Ancienne Auberge Fleurie; www.colmarslesalpes-verdontourisme.com

Colmars is a fortified town, nestling between two 17th-century forts with 12-m (40-ft) ramparts, which look across oak-planked roofs. The town is named after the hill on which it is built, *collis Martis*, where the Romans built a temple to the god Mars. Vauban, the military engineer, designed its lasting look. On the north side, an alley leads to the 17th-century **Fort de Savoie**, a fine example of military architecture.

In summer, residents enjoy relaxing on their wooden balconies (*soleillades lit*, sun-traps), or strolling along alpine paths with beautiful views.

Fort de Savoie
⊛⊛ 🚹04370 Colmars 📞04 92 83 41 92 🕐Mid-Jun–mid-Sep: Sat-Mon pm (Jul-Aug: daily); mid-Sep–mid-Jun: by appt only

7
Digne-les-Bains

ⒶE3 🚉🚍 🅘Pl du Tampinet; www.dignelesbains-tourisme.com

A spa town fed by eight hot springs, the Thermes Digne-les-Bains is a short drive southeast of the town. Digne's boulevard Gassendi is named after local mathematician and astronomer Pierre Gassendi (1592–1655). Digne, the *"capitale de la Lavande"* hosts a five-day lavender carnival in August. The town is also a centre for modern sculpture.

The **Musée Gassendi**, in the old town hospice, holds 16th–19th-century paintings, contemporary art and 19th-century scientific instruments. Alexandra David-Néel, one of Europe's most intrepid travellers, died in Digne in 1969. Her house, *Samten-Dzong* (fortress of meditation), now the **Maison Alexandra David-Néel**, includes a Tibetan centre and a museum. The grand cathedral of Notre-Dame-du-Bourg, built between 1200–1330, is the largest Romanesque

church in Haute Provence. Relics in its archaeological crypt date from Roman times.

The **Jardin des Cordeliers**, an enchanting walled garden in a convent, has medicinal plants and a sensory garden.

Musée Gassendi
⊛⊛ 🚹64 blvd Gassendi 🕐Wed-Mon (Oct–mid-May: Sat & Sun pm only) 🚫Public hols, 25 Dec–2 Jan 🌐musee-gassendi.org

Maison Alexandra David-Néel
⊛⊛ 🚹27 ave Maréchal Juin 🕐Tue-Sun (Dec-Mar: pm only; Jul-Aug: daily, by guided tour only) 🌐alexandra-david-neel.fr

Jardin des Cordeliers
⊛ 🚹Couvent des Cordeliers, ave Paul Martin 📞04 92 31 59 59 🕐Mar-Nov: Mon pm-Fri 🚫public hols

---

TRAIN DES PIGNES
The Train des Pignes runs four times a day throughout the year from Digne-les-Bains to Nice. It is the remaining part of a network that was designed to link the Côte d'Azur with the Alps, built between 1891 and 1911. It is a popular service, used by locals going about their daily business as much as by tourists. It rattles along the single track at a fair pace, over 16 viaducts, 15 bridges and through 27 tunnels, and is sometimes a little bumpy. The journey takes about three hours each way and can be broken en route. Entrevaux *(p191)* is a good place to stop. Tickets can be booked online *(www.trainprovence.com)*.

8
Lurs

ⒶD4 🚍La Brillanne 🅘La Mairie; 04 92 79 95 24

The Bishops of Sisteron and the Princes of Lurs were given ownership of the town of Lurs in the 9th century by Emperor

↑ Other-worldly rock formations of the Pénitents des Mées

Charlemagne. The town was repopulated after World War II, mainly by printers and artists.

The old town is entered via the Porte d'Horloge, held in by medieval ramparts. North of the restored Château of the Bishop-Princes is the 300-m (900-ft) Promenade des Evêques (Bishops' walk), lined with 15 oratories leading to the chapel of Notre-Dame-de-Vie, with views over the sea of poppy fields and olive groves of the Durance valley.

The 12th-century **Prieuré de Ganagobie** has beautifully restored mosaics, inspired by oriental and Byzantine design. Offices are held several times a day by the monks – visitors may attend.

Prieuré de Ganagobie
🕐 🅰N96, 04310 🅾Tue-Sun pm 🗓1 week in mid-Jan 🔳abbaye-ganagobie.com

9

Les Pénitents des Mées

🅰D3 ✈Marseille 🚉St-Auban 🚌Les Mées 🅸La Mairie, 18 blvd de la République; 04 92 34 36 38

Les Pénitents des Mées is a row of columnar rocks more than 100 m (300 ft) high and over 2 km (a mile) long. This curious rock formation is said to be a cowled procession of banished monks. In local mythology, monks from the mountain of Lure pursued some Moorish beauties, captured by a lord during the time of the Saracen invasion in the 6th century. They were turned into stone as punishment for their sins.

The small village of Les Mées is tucked away at the north end. The chapel of St-Roch affords a great view of the rocks' strange formation of millions of pebbles and stones.

10

Forcalquier

🅰D4 🚌 🅸13 pl du Bourguet 🔳haute-provence-tourisme.com

Crowned by a ruined castle and domed chapel of the 19th-century Notre-Dame-de-Provence, this town is now a shadow of its former self, though it has a lively weekly market which attracts local artists and artisans.

There are some fine façades in the old town, but only one gate, the Porte des Cordeliers. The **Musée de Salagon**

preserves the history of the people and culture of Haute-Provence. The **Observatoire de Haute Provence** and the nearby Centre d'Astronomie are a must for star-gazers.

Musée de Salagon
✱✱🕐 🅰N100, Mane 🅾Daily (Oct-Apr: Wed-Mon) 🗓24, 25 & 31 Dec 🔳musee-de-salagon.com

Observatoire de Haute Provence
✱✱ 🅰St-Michel l'Observatoire 🅾Easter-1 Nov: Wed pm from the Office de tourisme only 🔳obs-hp.fr

↑ Medieval gate, Porte Soubeyran, leading into the town of Manosque

11
Manosque

🅰D4 🚆🚌 ℹ️Pl du Docteur Joubert; www.tourisme-manosque.fr

France's national nuclear research centre, Cadarache, has brought prosperity to Manosque, a town which has sprawled beyond its original hill site above the Durance. French skincare company L'Occitane has its headquarters here, which you can visit on a tour. The centre has 13th- and 14th-century gates, Porte Soubeyran and Porte Saunerie. The perfume shop in rue Grande was once the atelier of writer Jean Giono's mother. The second floor belonged to his father. The **Centre Jean Giono** tells the story of his life.

The town's adoptive son is the painter Jean Carzou, who decorated the interior of the **Couvent de la Présentation** with apocalyptic allegories of modern life.

Centre Jean Giono
🅰🅰 🅰3 blvd E Bourges 🅲04 92 70 54 54 🅾Tue-Sat (Oct-Mar: pm only) 🅾Public hols, 25 Dec–2 Jan 🆆centre jeangiono.com

Couvent de la Présentation
🅰🅰 🅰9 blvd Elémir Bourges 🅲04 92 87 40 49 🅾Apr-Oct: 10am–12:30pm & 2–6pm Tue-Sat; Nov-Mar: 2–6pm Wed-Sat 🅾Public hols, 23 Dec–2 Jan

12
Gréoux-les-Bains

🅰D4 🚌 ℹ️7 pl Hôtel de Ville; www.greoux-les-bains.com

The thermal waters of this spa town have been enjoyed since antiquity, when baths were built by the Romans in the 1st century AD. Gréoux flourished in the 19th century, and the waters can still be enjoyed at the Etablissement Thermal. This spa is on the east side of the village, on Avenue du Verdon, where bubbling, sulphurous water arrives at the rate of 100,000 litres (22,000 gallons) an hour.

The restored castle ruin of the Templars sits on a high spot and an open-air theatre is in the grounds. **Le Petit Monde d'Emilie** is a museum with 148 miniatures from 1832 to the present, including dolls, costumes and toy trains.

Le Petit Monde d'Emilie
🅰🅰 🅰16 ave des Alpes 🅲06 84 62 71 23 🅾Mid-Apr-Oct: Mon, Wed & Fri pm only 🅾Public hols

13
Valensole

🅰D4 ℹ️2 rue de Docteur Chaupin; www.valensole.fr

This is the centre of France's most important lavender-growing area. It sits on the edge of the Valensole plains with a sturdy-towered Gothic church at its height. Admiral Pierre-Charles Villeneuve, the unsuccessful adversary of Admiral Nelson at the Battle of Trafalgar, was born here in 1763. Signs for locally made lavender honey are everywhere, and just outside the town is the **Musée Vivant de l'Abeille**. This fascinating interactive museum explains the intriguing life of the honey bee, with informative demonstrations, photographs and videos. During the

→ Vibrant hues as the sun sets over lavender fields in Valensole

---

LAVENDER HONEY

Busy bees forage the fields, forests and farmland of Provence to contribute sweet and subtle flavours to local honey. For the best lavender honeys, seek the "Miel de Lavande et Lavandin" appellation d'origine contrôlée (AOC) label in stores, where you'll also find honeys tagged with the "Miel de Provence" and "Miel Toutes Fleurs", labels of authenticity. These are tinged with hints of herbs, broom, and wildflowers.

summer month, you can visit the beehives and see the beekeepers at work.

Musée Vivant de l'Abeille
📍 🏠 Rte de Manosque
📞 04 92 74 85 28 🕐 Tue–Sat 🚫 public hols

---

⑭
Riez

🅰 D4 🚌 ℹ️ Pl de la Mairie; www.ville-riez.fr

At the edge of the sweeping Valensole plateau is this unspoiled village, filled with small shops selling ceramics and traditional *santons*, honey

Did You Know?

At Musée Vivant de l'Abeille you can see 30,000 bees at work inside a glass hive.

and lavender. Its grander past is reflected in the Renaissance façades of the houses and mansions in the old town. This is entered through the 13th-century Porte Aiguyère, which leads on to the tree-lined Grand rue, with fine examples of Renaissance architecture at numbers 27 and 29.

The most unusual site is the remains of the 1st-century AD Roman temple dedicated to Apollo. It stands in the middle of a field by the river Colostre; the original site of the town where the Roman colony *Reia Apollinaris* lived. On the other side of the river is a rare example of Merovingian architecture, a small baptistry dating from the 5th century.

The village has a number of fountains: Fontaine Benoîte, opposite Porte Sanson, dates to 1819; Fontaine de Blanchon is fed by an underground spring – it was used to wash the clothes of the infirm in the days before antibiotics; and the soft waters of the spring-fed Fontaine de Saint-Maxime were believed to heal the eyes.

15 Moustiers-Ste-Marie

E4 Pl de l'Église; www.moustiers.fr

The setting of the town of Moustiers is stunning, high on the edge of a ravine, beneath craggy rocks. Situated in the town centre is the parish church, with a three-storey Romanesque belfry. Above it, a path meanders up to the 12th-century chapel of Notre-Dame-de-Beauvoir. The view across Lac de Sainte-Croix is magnificent.

A heavy iron chain, 227 m (745 ft) in length, is suspended above the ravine. Hanging from the centre is a five-pointed, golden star. Although it was renewed in 1957, it is said to date back to the 13th century, when the chevalier Blacas hoisted it up in thanks for his release from captivity during the Seventh Crusade of St Louis.

Moustiers is a popular tourist town. The streets are crowded in summer due to its pretty setting and its ceramics. The original Moustiers ware is housed in the **Musée de la Faïence**, while modern reproductions can be bought in the town. The new Musée de la Préhistoire in Quinson, 40 km (25 miles) south, is a must.

Musée de la Faïence

Le Village, rue du Seigneur de la Clue, Moustiers-Ste-Marie 04 92 74 61 64 Apr-Oct: Wed-Mon; Feb, Mar, Nov & Dec: Sat & Sun

16 Annot

E4 Place du Germe annot-tourisme.com

The town of Annot, on the Train des Pignes railway line *(p198)*, has a distinct Alpine feel. Annot lies in the Vaïre valley, crisscrossed by icy waters streaming down from the mountains. The surrounding scenery, however, is a more unfamiliar pattern of jagged rocks and deep caves.

MOUSTIERS WARE

The distinctive glaze of Moustiers faïence was first established in the late 17th century by Antoine Clérissy, a local potter who was given the secret of faïence by an Italian monk. The first pieces had a luminous blue glaze and were decorated with hunting or mythological scenes. In 1738, Spanish glazes and brightly coloured floral and fauna designs were used. A number of potters continue the tradition, and can be seen in their ateliers.

Vast sandstone boulders, known as the *grès d'Annot*, are strewn around the town, and local builders have constructed houses against these haphazard rocks, using their sheer faces as outside walls. The old town lies behind the main road, where there is also a Romanesque church. The tall buildings that line the narrow streets here have even retained some of their original 15th- to 18th-century carved stone lintels.

Most Sundays (May–Oct) in summer, a 1909 belle époque steam train chugs its way from Puget-Théniers up to Annot, providing a pleasant way for visitors to enjoy the unspoiled countryside.

17 Castellane

E4 Rue Nationale; www.castellane-verdon tourisme.com

This is one of the main centres for the Gorges du Verdon, surrounded by campsites and

←

The little steam train crossing a viaduct on its way to Annot

↑ The picturesque town and citadel of Entrevaux, built into the rocky hillside

Did You Know?

Visitors in Entrevaux who walk up to the citadel pass through 20 fortified doorways.

caravans. Tourists squeeze into the town centre in summer and, in the evenings, fill the cafés after a day's hiking, climbing, canoeing and white-water rafting on the rapids of the Verdon. It is a well-sited town, beneath an impressive 180-m (600-ft) slab of grey rock. On top of this, dominating the skyline, is the chapel of Notre-Dame-du-Roc, built in 1703. A strenuous, 30-minute walk from behind the parish church to the top is rewarded with superb views. Castellane was once a sturdy fortress, and repelled invasion several times. The lifting of the siege by the Huguenots in 1586 is commemorated every year with firecrackers at the Fête des Pétardiers (last Sun in Jan).

The town's fortifications were completely rebuilt in the 14th century after most of the town, dating from Roman times, crumbled and slipped into the Verdon valley. Most social activity takes place in the main square, place Marcel-Sauvaire, which is lined with

small hotels that have catered for generations of visitors.

All that remains of the ramparts is the Tour Pentagonal and a small section of the old wall, which lie just beyond the 12th-century St-Victor church, on the way up to the chapel.

---

⑱ St-André-les-Alpes

⚐E4 🚉🚌 ℹ Place Marcel Pastorelli; saintandreles alpes-verdontourisme.com

Lying at the north end of the beautiful Lac de Castillon, where the river Isolde meets the river Verdon, is St-André. It is a popular summer holiday and leisure centre, scattered around the sandy flats on the lakeside. The lake is man-made, formed by damming the river by the 90-m (295-ft) Barrage de Castillon, and is a haven for rafting, canoeing and kayaking, as well as swimming and fishing.

Inland, lavender fields and orchards make for picturesque walks. Hang-gliding has become so popular here that one of the local producers advertises its wine as "the wine of eagles".

⑲ Entrevaux

⚐F4 🚉🚌 ℹPorte Royale du Pont Levis; www. tourisme-entrevaux.fr

It is easy to see why Entrevaux is called a "fairy-tale town" as you cross the drawbridge and enter through the Porte Royale. The dramatic entrance is flanked by twin towers and from here you enter the Ville Forte, inside which, the streets are narrow and dark.

Fortified in 1690 by the military engineer Vauban (1633–1707), Entrevaux became one of the strongest military sites on the Franco-Savoy border. Even the 17th-century cathedral, Notre-Dame l'Assomption, was skilfully incorporated into the turreted ramparts.

Unlike most military strong-holds, the citadel was not built on top of a hill, but strategically placed on a rocky outcrop. It was last used in World War I as a prison for German officers. A steep track leads to the citadel, 156 m (511 ft) above the village. The 20-minute climb to the top, past basking lizards, should not be made in the midday heat.

NEED TO KNOW

Coastal road to Villefranche-sur-Mer

BEFORE YOU GO

Forward planning is essential to any successful trip. Be prepared for all eventualities by considering the following points before you travel.

AT A GLANCE

CURRENCY
Euro

AVERAGE DAILY SPEND

ON A BUDGET	MODERATE SPENDER	SPLASH OUT
€60	€165	€300+

BOTTLED WATER	COFFEE	BEER	DINNER FOR TWO
€1.00	€2.50	€5.00	€60

ESSENTIAL PHRASES

Hello	Bonjour
Thank you	Merci
Please	S'il vous plaît
Goodbye	Au revoir
Do you speak English?	Parlez-vous anglais?
I don't understand...	Je ne comprends pas

ELECTRICITY SUPPLY

Power sockets are type C and E, fitting two-pronged plugs. Standard voltage is 230 volts.

Passports and Visas

EU nationals and citizens of the US, Canada, Australia and New Zealand do not need a visa for stays of up to three months. Consult your nearest French embassy or check the **France-Visas** website if you are travelling from outside these areas.
France-Visas
w france-visas.gouv.fr

Travel Safety Advice

Visitors can get up-to-date travel safety information from the Foreign and Commonwealth Office in the UK, the State Department in the US, and the Department of Foreign Affairs and Trade in Australia.
AUS
w smartraveller.gov.au
UK
w gov.uk/foreign-travel-advice
US
w travel.state.gov

Customs Information

An individual is permitted to carry the following within the EU for personal use:
Tobacco products 800 cigarettes, 400 cigarillos, 200 cigars or 1 kg of smoking tobacco.
Alcohol 10 litres of alcoholic beverages above 22 per cent strength, 20 litres of alcoholic beverages below 22 per cent strength, 90 litres of wine (60 litres of which can be sparkling wine) and 110 litres of beer.
Cash if you plan to enter or leave the EU with €10,000 or more in cash (or the equivalent in other currencies) you must declare it to the customs authorities prior to departure.

Insurance

It is wise to take out an insurance policy covering theft, loss of belongings, medical problems, cancellations and delays.
To receive discounted or free emergency medical care in France, EU citizens should ensure

they have an **EHIC** (European Health Insurance Card) with them when travelling around. Visitors from outside the EU must arrange their own private medical insurance.
EHIC
🅦 gov.uk/european-health-insurance-card

Language

English is spoken in all large hotels, but not in all smaller establishments, shops, bars and cafés, so mastering a few niceties could go a long way. Major attractions offer multilingual audio guides and guided tours, and there are foreign language guided tours and walks in most cities.

Vaccinations

No inoculations are needed for France.

Booking Accommodation

Accommodation ranges from campsites and farmhouse-style gîtes to luxury hotels, family-run *chambres d'hôtes* and villas with pools. Book well ahead if you plan to visit during the summer (June to August) or during events such as the Avignon Festival or Cannes Film Festival.

Listings and links to booking sites can be found on official regional tourist information websites. **The Hotel Guru** is a hotel review and booking site featuring personally curated and inspected boutique hotels, guesthouses and B&Bs all over Provence, and throughout France. **Gîtes de France** lists almost 2,500 rural self-catering holiday rental properties, *chambres d'hôtes* and campsites in Provence.
🅦 **The Hotel Guru**
thehotelguru.com
Gîtes de France
🅦 gitesdefrance.com

Money

Major credit and debit cards are accepted in most hotels, shops and restaurants. US-style cards that do not use chip-and-PIN technology are less widely accepted. Cash machines can be found in banks, airports and train stations, shopping areas and on most main streets. Most taxi drivers and market traders, as well as many smaller bars and restaurants, accept only cash, so do carry a small amount with you at all times.

Travellers with Specific Needs

Most museums and galleries are wheelchair-accessible and offer audio tours and induction loops for people with hearing disabilities. **Bespoke Holidays** specializes in accommodation for wheelchair users and people with learning disabilities and their carers.

Fully supported activity holidays are offered by **Go Provence**. To find out about accessible public transport, visit the **Vianavigo** website. SNCF also offers **Accès Plus**, which accompanies travellers with specific needs on rail journeys.
Bespoke Holidays
🅦 bespokefrance.com
Go Provence
🅦 goprovence.co.uk
Vianavigo
🅦 vianavigo.com/en
Accès Plus
🅦 accessibilite.sncf.com

Closures

Lunchtime Most shops and businesses close for an hour or two from around noon. Very few restaurants serve lunch after 2pm.
Monday Some museums, smaller shops and many upmarket restaurants close for the day.
Sunday Most shops are closed.
Public holidays Post offices, banks, public services and shops close. Museums and attractions are also likely to be closed, notably on 1 January, 1 May and 25 December.

PUBLIC HOLIDAYS	
1 Jan	New Year's Day (Jour de l'An)
Mar/Apr	Good Friday (Vendredi Saint)
Mar/Apr	Easter Sunday (Pâques)
Mar/Apr	Easter Monday (Lundi de Pâques)
1 May	Labour Day (Fête du Travail)
8 May	VE Day (Victoire 1945)
30 May	Ascension
9 June	Pentecôte
14 July	Bastille Day (Fête Nationale)
15 Aug	Assumption
25 Dec	Christmas Day (Noël)

GETTING AROUND

You'll find it easier to explore most of the historic towns and villages of Provence on foot. Here's how to get around Provence like a local.

AT A GLANCE

PUBLIC TRANSPORT COSTS

AVIGNON

€1.40

Single bus journey

MARSEILLE

€1.70

Single bus, metro or tram journey

NICE

€1.50

Single bus journey

TOP TIP

Avoid on-the-spot fines by stamping your ticket to validate your journey.

SPEED LIMIT

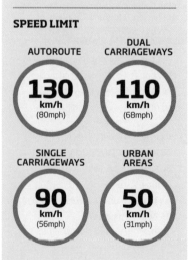

AUTOROUTE

130 km/h (80mph)

DUAL CARRIAGEWAYS

110 km/h (68mph)

SINGLE CARRIAGEWAYS

90 km/h (56mph)

URBAN AREAS

50 km/h (31mph)

Arriving by Air

Provence has five international airports in Avignon, Marseille, Nice, Nîmes and Toulon-Hyères; all are near their respective cities, with good bus services to the city centres. A free shuttle bus connects Marseille airport with Vitrolles TER station for trains to the city and to Arles, Avignon and Nîmes. Monaco has no airport but has a city centre heliport with a helicopter shuttle service to Nice International Airport, taking seven minutes with **Heli Securite**. For information on getting to and from Provence's main airports, see the table opposite.

Heli Securite

🅦 helisecurite.fr

Train Travel

International Train Travel

High-speed TGV trains connect Provence with the UK, Italy, Spain and Switzerland, and most TGV stations are in city centres. Reservations for these services are essential as tickets are booked up quickly. Visit the **RENFE-SNCF** or **Thello** websites for tickets, depending on your route.

You can buy tickets and passes for multiple international journeys via **Eurail** or **Interrail**, however, you may still need to pay an additional reservation fee. Always check that your pass is valid on your chosen service before boarding.

Students and those under 26 and over 60 can benefit from discounted rail travel both to and within France. Visit the Eurail website for details.

Eurail

🅦 eurail.com

Interrail

🅦 interrail.eu

RENFE-SNCF

🅦 renfe-sncf.com

Thello

🅦 thello.fr

Regional Train Travel

SNCF's high-speed TGV trains connect major towns and cities all over France. Regional TER trains stop at every station on local and suburban routes.

GETTING TO AND FROM THE AIRPORT

Airport	Distance to City	Taxi Fare	Public Transport	Journey Time
Avignon	10 km (6 miles)	€25	TCRA 30 bus	40 mins
Marseille	27 km (17 miles)	€50	L91 Navette Aéroport coach	25 mins
Nice	7 km (4 miles)	€35	Lignes d'Azur route 98 and 99 Airport Express coach	20 mins
Nîmes	20 km (12 miles)	€25	Navette Aéroport coach	25 mins
Toulon-Hyères	24 km (15 miles)	€55	102 Navette Aéroport coach	30 mins

JOURNEY PLANNER

This map plots the fastest driving routes to help you plan your car journeys between Provence's main towns and cities. Tolls apply on most routes.

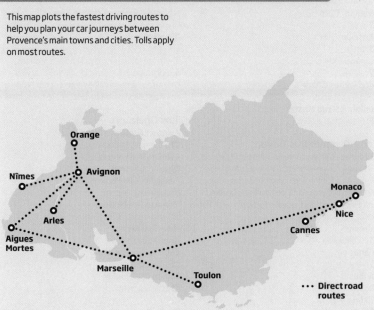

••• Direct road routes

Avignon to Aigues Mortes	1 hr	**Aigues Mortes to Marseille**	1.75 hr
Avignon to Arles	0.75 hr	**Marseille to Nice**	2.5 hr
Avignon to Nîmes	0.75 hr	**Marseille to Toulon**	1 hr
Avignon to Orange	0.5 hr	**Nice to Cannes**	0.75 hr
Avignon to Marseille	1.25 hr	**Nice to Monaco**	0.5 hr

Public Transport

Each urban area in Provence has its own public transport system extending from the city centre to the outer suburbs. City bus networks are complemented in Marseille by Métro and tram lines, and in Nice by Tramway de Nice. A second Tramway route is set to open in Nice in summer 2019, linking Nice's port and airport. In Avignon, a new tramway is also scheduled to open in summer 2019.

City Transport

TCRA is the local transport authority for Avignon and its suburbs, including Villeneuve-les-Avignon. Hop-on, hop-off electric shuttles (Baladines) trundle around the medieval centre.

In Marseille, **RTM** co-ordinates bus, Métro and tram lines. **CAM** operates buses within Monaco and to Nice and Menton, and seven lifts and escalators connect its waterfront with the upper urban level. **Lignes d'Azur** is the public transport operator for Nice, Cannes and Alpes-Maritimes, including Tramway de Nice. **Réseau Mistral** is Toulon's city and suburban bus network.

Avignon: TCRA
🅦 tcra.fr
Marseille: RTM
🅦 rtm.fr
Monaco: CAM
🅦 cam.mc
Nice: Lignes d'Azur
🅦 lignesdazur.com
Toulon: Réseau Mistral
🅦 reseaumistral.com

Long-Distance Bus Travel

Eurolines coaches connect points in Provence, including Aix-en-Provence, Avignon, Marseille, Nîmes and Toulon with London, Brussels and other major European cities. **Isilines**, **Ouibus**, and **Flixbus** connect cities in Provence with Paris and other French cities.

Eurolines
🅦 eurolines.eu
Isilines
🅦 isilines.fr
Ouibus
🅦 ouibus.com
Flixbus
🅦 flixbus.com

Tickets

Buying tickets or transport passes before boarding is always cheaper than buying from the driver when boarding. Carnets (books of up to 10 tickets) and multi-trip passes valid for one or more days are available on all urban transport networks and can be bought at rail and bus stations, designated stores and city tourist information offices.

In Marseille, a Transtick card can be purchased which allows users two or more trips with connections across the RTM network.

Remember to always purchase a ticket as ticket inspections are common.

Country Buses

Beyond major towns, local bus routes are served by private companies under regional authority governance. Timetables are geared to the needs of local school pupils and shoppers, and are not always convenient for visitors. **PACA Mobilité** is the one-stop shop for local transport across the region.

PACA Mobilité
🅦 pacamobilite.fr

Trams

Trams can be more efficient than buses in Provence's cities. Marseille's tramway operates over three lines, and tickets must be purchased in advance. Nice has a two-route tram system and tickets can be bought from machines at the tramstop. Avignon is in the process of developing a tram system for the city, scheduled for completion in June 2019.

Taxis

There are taxi ranks at rail and bus stations, airports and in most main squares in towns and cities. You can also call or text for taxis. Visitors can ride pillion on motorbike "moto taxis" in Nice.

Taxi Operators

Avignon: Provence Cab
🅦 provencecab-paca.fr
Cannes: Taxi Cannes
🅦 taxi-cannes.net
Marseille: Taxi Radio Marseille
🅦 taximarseille.com
Monaco: Taxi Monaco
🅦 taximonaco.com
Nice: Taxi Riviera
🅦 taxis-nice.fr
Cab Express Taxi Moto
🅦 cab-express.com
Toulon: Taxi Toulon
🅦 taxi-toulon.fr

Driving

Driving to Provence

It takes 9-10 hours to drive to Avignon from the Channel ferry ports via the A26 and A27 autoroutes. Driving from Bilbao in Spain, which is served by ferries from the UK, takes around 8 hours. To take your own car into France, you will need proof of registration, valid insurance documents, a full, valid driving licence and your passport.

Car Rental

To rent a car in France you must be 21 years or over and have held a valid driver's licence for at least a year. You will also need to present a credit card. Driving licences issued by any of the EU member states are valid throughout the EU.

International driving licences are not needed for short-term visitors (up to 90 days) from North America, Australia and New Zealand. Visitors from other countries should check with their local automobile association.

Driving in Provence

Driving in Provence can be a pleasure, but plan your journey carefully to avoid traffic bottle-necks on rural and coastal roads in summer. For a fast point-to-point journey, the A8 *autoroute* cuts across the Camargue from Menton to Aix-en-Provence, near which it meets the A7 "Autoroute du Soleil", so you can drive on *autoroutes* all the way across Provence from the Italian border to Orange in just over 3 hours. The same journey avoiding *autoroutes* takes more than 6 hours but costs less, as the A8 is the most expensive toll road in France.

Routes départementales are the narrowest and slowest roads, but in hinterland regions such as Alpes-de-Hautes-Provence they may be your only option. Bison Futé *(p213)* signs indicate routes avoiding heavy traffic and can be useful during peak French holiday periods.

Driving in the historic centres of Provençal towns is not recommended. Finding your way isn't easy as there are many one-way streets, and parking is difficult and expensive. In summer, traffic on the coast road between Hyères and Nice, and especially the section between Nice and Cannes, is often excruciatingly slow.

Rules of the Road

Always drive on the right. Unless otherwise signposted, vehicles coming from the right have right of way, and cars on a roundabout usually have right of way as well.

At all times, drivers must carry a valid driver's licence, registration and insurance documents. In case of a breakdown, it is compulsory to carry one red warning triangle and a luminous vest. Seat belts must be worn, and it is prohibited to sound your horn in cities. For motorbikes and scooters, the wearing of helmets and protective gloves is compulsory. It is against the law to drive in urban bus lanes. France strictly enforces its drink-drive limit *(p212)*, and random breath testing at mobile checkpoints is common.

Parking

Park only in areas with a large "P" or a *Payant* sign on the pavement or road, and pay at the parking meter with cash or contactless debit or credit card. Avignon, Marseille, Nice and Toulon have numerous underground car parks, signposted by a white "P" on a blue background, and overground car parks are usually located on the edge of historic town centres. Some city hotels have private parking.

Cycling

Most towns (except Nice and Monaco) have few hills and bike rental is widely available. In the hot summer months, or for less energetic riders, electric-boosted e-bikes take less effort. Avignon, Marseille and Nice have bike-sharing schemes with multiple docking stations around each city. Bicycles may be taken on most trains, but the service must be booked in advance on TGV trains. To take your bike on a local train, look for the bicycle symbol on the timetable. Wearing a helmet is not compulsory but is strongly advised.

Bike Rental and Bike Sharing

Aix-en-Provence: Aixprit Vélo
w aixpritvelo.com
Avignon: Vélopop
w velopop.fr
Marseille: Le Vélo
w levelo-mpm.fr
Nice: Vélobleu
w velobleu.org

Boats and Ferries

A free *navette fluviale* (river shuttle), also called the *bac à traille*, crosses the Rhône between Quai de la Ligne in Central Avignon and Île de la Barthelasse. **Réseau Mistral** operates *bateau-bus* (water taxi) services from Toulon to La Seyne-sur-Mer and Les Sablettes and to the Îles d'Hyères. **Bateliers de la Rade** and **Bateliers de la Côte d'Azur** also sail from Toulon to the Îles d'Hyères. **RTM** operates ferries from Marseille's Vieux Port to Pointe-Rouge and l'Estaque. TLV ferries sail from Saint-Pierre Marina in Hyères to the Îles d'Hyères. In Monaco, **CAM** electric bus-boats connect Quai Kennedy with the cruise ship terminal.

Maritima Ferries (formerly SNCM) sail from Marseille, Toulon and Nice to Corsica and Sardinia. **Corsica Ferries** sail from Nice and Toulon to Corsica and Sardinia and from Toulon to Majorca.

Réseau Mistral
w reseaumistral.com
Bateliers de la Rade
w lesbateliersdelarade.com
Bateliers de la Côte d'Azur
w bateliersdelacotedazur.com
Maritima Ferries
w maritima-ferries.eu
Corsica Ferries
w corsica-ferries.fr

PRACTICAL
INFORMATION

A little local knowledge goes a long way in Provence. Here you will find all the essential advice and information you will need during your stay.

AT A GLANCE

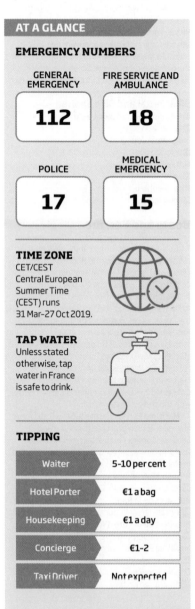

EMERGENCY NUMBERS

GENERAL EMERGENCY	FIRE SERVICE AND AMBULANCE
112	**18**

POLICE	MEDICAL EMERGENCY
17	**15**

TIME ZONE
CET/CEST
Central European
Summer Time
(CEST) runs
31 Mar–27 Oct 2019.

TAP WATER
Unless stated otherwise, tap water in France is safe to drink.

TIPPING

Waiter	5–10 per cent
Hotel Porter	€1 a bag
Housekeeping	€1 a day
Concierge	€1–2
Taxi Driver	Not expected

Personal Security

Provence is generally a safe region and most visits are trouble-free. However, beware of pickpockets and bag-snatchers on public transport, and on buses and trams during the rush hour and in major tourist areas. If possible, avoid using public transport late at night in the outlying areas of Marseille and Toulon. If you have anything stolen, report the crime as soon as possible to the nearest police station, and bring ID with you. Get a copy of the crime report in order to claim on your insurance. Contact your embassy or consulate if your passport is stolen, or in the event of a serious crime or accident.

Health

If you fall sick during your visit, pharmacists are an excellent source of advice – they can diagnose many health problems and suggest appropriate treatment. Phone 3237 to find the nearest pharmacy.

EU nationals holding a European Health Insurance Card (EHIC) are entitled to use the French national health service (p207). Patients pay for treatments but can reclaim most of the cost from the local Caisse Primaire D'Assurance Maladie (CPAM) office. You must provide proof of treatment, your EHIC, your address of residence and your bank details. EHIC is not a substitute for travel insurance, so all travellers should purchase an appropriate travel policy.

Non-EU nationals must have full private medical insurance while in France and pay for services, claiming their costs back from their insurer.

Smoking, Alcohol and Drugs

Smoking is prohibited in all public places, but is allowed on open-air restaurant, café and bar terraces. Possession of illegal drugs could result in a prison sentence.

Unless stated otherwise, alcohol consumption on the streets is permitted.

France has a strict limit of 0.05 per cent BAC (blood alcohol content) for drivers.

ID

While not obligatory, it is advisable to carry your passport or ID card at all times as police or transport officials may ask you for identification at any time. If you don't have it with you, the police may escort you to wherever your passport is being kept so that you can show it to them.

Local Customs

Etiquette *(la politesse)* is everything in France. Upon entering a store or café, you are expected to say *bonjour* to staff, and when leaving to say *au revoir*. Be sure to add *s'il vous plaît* (please) when ordering something and *pardon* (sorry) if you accidentally bump into someone.

The French shake hands when meeting someone for the first time. Friends and colleagues who know each other well usually greet each other with a kiss on each cheek. If you are unsure, wait to see if they offer a hand or a cheek.

Visiting Churches and Cathedrals

Dress respectfully: cover your torso and upper arms, and ensure your knees are covered.

Mobile Phones and Wi-Fi

Free Wi-Fi hotspots are available in a number of public spaces like libraries, gardens and parks. Almost all hotels and many cafés and restaurants offer free Wi-Fi for patrons.

Visitors with EU mobile phone contracts can use their devices in Provence without additional data roaming charges. Users will be charged the same rates for data, SMS and voice calls as they would pay at home.

Mobile phone coverage in most cities, towns and villages is adequate but mobile and GPS reception in some mountainous areas is patchy.

Post

Stamps *(timbres)* can be bought at post offices and tabacs, or online via **La Poste**. Most post offices have self-service machines to weigh and frank your mail, to save queuing at the counter.
La Poste
W laposte.fr

Taxes and Refunds

A sales tax (TVA) of 20 per cent is imposed on most goods and services. Non-EU residents can reclaim the TVA they pay on French goods at shops displaying the Global Refund Tax-Free sign, as long as they spend more than €175 in the same shop in one day, and take the goods out of France. The retailer will generally supply a form and issue a détaxe receipt at the time of purchase. Make sure that you have your passport with you to prove non-resident status.

Discount Cards

City and regional passes can help you cut the cost of sightseeing and public transport. With the **Avignon Passion** pass, free from the city tourist office, you pay the full ticket price for the first attraction you visit, with 20–50 per cent off others in Avignon and Villeneuve-les-Avignon. The **French Riviera Pass** allows free access to many sights, tours and activities, and free travel on public transport throughout the Nice Côte d'Azur metropolitan area. The **City-Pass Marseille** offers free public transport, free admission to museums and galleries and other discounts. Buy it at the city tourist office and metro stations.
Avignon Passion
W avignon-tourisme.com
French Riviera Pass
W en.frenchrivierapass.com
City-Pass Marseille
W marseille-tourisme.com

WEBSITES AND APPS

Bison Futé
Official road journey website and app for smartphones and tablets.
W bison-fute.gouv.fr

OUI SNCF
Buy and download rail tickets direct to your phone or tablet with this app.

PACA Mobilité
Official app for public transport through Provence-Alpes-Côte d'Azur area.

ViaMichelin
Free app for real-time road travel planning, including costs, journey times and traffic information.

Index

PHRASE BOOK

IN AN EMERGENCY

Help!	**Au secours!**	*oh sekoor*
Stop!	**Arrêtez!**	*aret-ay*
Call a	**Appelez un**	*apuh-lay uñ*
doctor!	**médecin!**	*medsañ*
Call an	**Appelez une**	*apuh-lay oon*
ambulance!	**ambulance!**	*oñboo-loñs*
Call the	**Appelez la**	*apuh-lay lah*
police!	**police!**	*poh-lees*
Call the fire	**Appelez les**	*apuh-lay leh*
brigade!	**pompiers!**	*poñ-peeyay*
Where is the	**Où est le téléphone**	*oo ay luh tehlehfon*
nearest telephone?	**le plus proche?**	*luh ploo prosh*
Where is the	**Où est l'hôpital**	*oo ay l'opeetal luh*
nearest hospital?	**le plus proche?**	*ploo prosh*

COMMUNICATION ESSENTIALS

Yes	**Oui**	*wee*
No	**Non**	*noñ*
Please	**S'il vous plaît**	*seel voo play*
Thank you	**Merci**	*mer-see*
Excuse me	**Excusez-moi**	*exkoo-zay mwah*
Hello	**Bonjour**	*boñzhoor*
Goodbye	**Au revoir**	*oh ruh-vwar*
Good night	**Bonsoir**	*boñ-swar*
Morning	**Le matin**	*matañ*
Afternoon	**L'après-midi**	*l'apreh-meedee*
Evening	**Le soir**	*swar*
Yesterday	**Hier**	*eeyehr*
Today	**Aujourd'hui**	*oh-zhoor-dwee*
Tomorrow	**Demain**	*duhmañ*
Here	**Ici**	*ee-see*
There	**Là**	*lah*
What?	**Quoi, quel, quelle?**	*kwah, kel, kel*
When?	**Quand?**	*koñ*
Why?	**Pourquoi?**	*poor-kwah*
Where?	**Où?**	*oo*

USEFUL PHRASES

How are you?	**Comment allez-vous?**	*kom-moñ talay voo*
Very well, thank you.	**Très bien, merci.**	*treh byañ, mer-see*
Pleased to meet you.	**Enchanté de faire votre connaissance.**	*oñshoñ-tay duh fehr votr kon-ay-sans*
See you soon.	**A bientôt.**	*byañ-toh*
That's fine.	**C'est bon**	*say bon*
Where is/are...?	**Où est/sont...?**	*ooay/soñ*
How far is it to...?	**Combien de kilometres d'ici à...?**	*kom-byañ duh keelometr d'ee-see ah*
Which way to...?	**Quelle est la direction pour...?**	*kel ay lah deer-ek-syoñ poor*
Do you speak English?	**Parlez-vous anglais?**	*par-lay voo oñg-lay*
I don't understand.	**Je ne comprends pas.**	*zhuh nuh kom-proñ pah*
Could you speak slowly please?	**Pouvez-vous parler moins vite s'il vous plaît?**	*poo-vay voo par-lay mwañ veet seel voo play*
I'm sorry.	**Excusez-moi.**	*exkoo-zay mwah*

USEFUL WORDS

big	**grand**	*groñ*
small	**petit**	*puh-tee*
hot	**chaud**	*show*
cold	**froid**	*frwah*
good	**bon/bien**	*boñ/byañ*
bad	**mauvais**	*moh-veh*
enough	**assez**	*assay*
well	**bien**	*byañ*
open	**ouvert**	*oo-ver*
closed	**fermé**	*fer-meh*
left	**gauche**	*gohsh*
right	**droite**	*drwaht*
straight on	**tout droite**	*too drwaht*
near	**près**	*preh*
far	**loin**	*lwañ*
up	**en haut**	*oñ oh*
down	**en bas**	*oñ bah*
early	**de bonne heure**	*duh bon urr*
late	**en retard**	*oñ ruh-tar*
entrance	**l'entrée**	*l'on-tray*
exit	**la sortie**	*sor-tee*
toilet	**les toilettes, le WC**	*twah-let, vay-see*
free, unoccupied	**libre**	*leebr*
free, no charge	**gratuit**	*grah-twee*

MAKING A TELEPHONE CALL

I'd like to place a long-distance call.	**Je voudrais faire un appel á l'étranger.**	*zhuh voo-dreh fehr uñ apel a laytroñ-zhay*
I'd like to make a reverse charge call.	**Je voudrais faire une communi-cation en PCV.**	*zhuh voo-dreh fehr oon komoonikah-syoñ oñ peh-seh-veh*
I'll try again later.	**Je rappelerai plus tard.**	*zhuh rapeleray ploo tar*
Can I leave a message?	**Est-ce que je peux laisser un message?**	*es-keh zhuh puh leh-say uñ mehsazh*
Hold on,	**Ne quittez pas, s'il vous plaît.**	*nuh kee-tay pah seel voo play*
Could you speak up a little please?	**Pouvez-vous parler un peu plus fort?**	*poo-vay voo parlay uñ puh ploo for*
local call	**la communication locale**	*komoonikahsyoñ low-kal*

SHOPPING

How much does this cost?	**C'est combien s'il vous plaît?**	*say kom-byañ seel voo play*
I would like ...	**Je voudrais...**	*zhuh voo-dray*
Do you have?	**Est-ce que vous avez**	*es-kuh voo zavay*
I'm just looking.	**Je regarde seulement.**	*zhuh ruhgar suhlmoñ*
Do you take credit cards?	**Est-ce que vous acceptez les cartes de crédit?**	*es-kuh voo zaksept-ay leh kart duh kreh-dee*
Do you take travellers' cheques?	**Est-ce que vous acceptez les cheques de voyages?**	*es-kuh voo zaksept-ay leh shek duh vwayazh*
What time do you open?	**A quelle heure vous êtes ouvert?**	*ah kel urr voo zet oo-ver*
What time do you close?	**A quelle heure vous êtes fermé?**	*ah kel urr voo zet fer-may*

This one.	Celui-ci	suhl-wee-see
That one.	Celui-là	suhl-wee-lah
expensive	cher	shehr
cheap	pas cher,	pah shehr,
	bon marché	boñ mar-shay
size, clothes	la taille	tye
size, shoes	la pointure	pwañ-tur
white	blanc	bloñ
black	noir	nwahr
red	rouge	roozh
yellow	jaune	zhohwn
green	vert	vehr
blue	bleu	bluh

TYPES OF SHOP

antique	le magasin	maga-zañ
shop	d'antiquités	d'oñteekee-tay
bakery	la boulangerie	booloñ-zhuree
bank	la banque	boñk
bookshop	la librairie	lee-brehree
butcher	la boucherie	boo-shehree
cake shop	la pâtisserie	patee-sree
cheese shop	la fromagerie	fromazh-ree
chemist	la pharmacie	farmah-see
dairy	la crémerie	krem-ree
department store	le grand magasin	groñ maga-zañ
delicatessen	la charcuterie	sharkoot-ree
fishmonger	la poissonnerie	pwasson-ree
gift shop	le magasin de	maga-zañ duh
	cadeaux	kadoh
greengrocer	le marchand	mar-shoñ duh
	de légumes	lay-goom
grocery	l'alimentation	alee-moñta-syoñ
hairdresser	le coiffeur	kwafuhr
market	le marché	marsh-ay
newsagent	le magasin de	maga-zañ duh
	journaux	zhoor-no
post office	la poste,	pohst,
	le bureau de poste,	booroh duh pohst,
	le PTT	peh-teh-teh
shoe shop	le magasin	maga-zañ
	de chaussures	duh show-soor
supermarket	le supermarché	soo pehr-marshay
tobacconist	le tabac	tabah
travel agent	l'agence	l'azhoñs
	de voyages	duh vwayazh

SIGHTSEEING

abbey	l'abbaye	l'abay-ee
art gallery	la galerie d'art	galer-ree dart
bus station	la gare routière	gahr roo-tee-yehr
cathedral	la cathédrale	katay-dral
church	l'église	l'aygleez
garden	le jardin	zhar-dañ
library	la bibliothèque	beebleeo-tek
museum	le musée	moo-zay
railway station	la gare (SNCF)	gahr (es-en-say-ef)
tourist	les renseignements	roñsayn-moñ
information	touristiques,	toorees-teek,
office	le syndicat	sandee-
	d'initiative	ka d'eenee-syateev
town hall	l'hôtel de ville	l'ohtel duh veel
closed for	fermeture	fehrmeh-tur
public holiday	jour férié	zhoor fehree-ay

STAYING IN A HOTEL

Do you have a	Est-ce que vous	es-kuh voo-zavay
vacant room?	avez une chambre?	oon shambr
double room,	la chambre à deux	shambr ah duh
with double bed	personnes, avec	pehr-son avek un
	un grand lit	groññ lee
twin room	la chambre à	shambr ah
	deux lits	duh lee
single room	la chambre à	shambr ah
	une personne	oon pehr-son
room with a	la chambre avec	shambr avek
bath, shower	salle de bains,	sal duh bañ,
	une douche	oon doosh
porter	le garçon	gar-soñ
key	la clef	klay
I have a	J'ai fait une	zhay fay oon
reservation.	réservation.	rayzehrva-syoñ

EATING OUT

Have you	Avez-vous une	avay-voo oon
got a table?	table de libre?	tahbl duh leebr
I want to	Je voudrais	zhuh voo-dray
reserve	réserver	rayzehr-vay
a table.	une table.	oon tahbl
The bill	L'addition s'il	l'adee-syoñ seel
please.	vous plaît.	voo play
I am a	Je suis	zhuh swee
vegetarian.	végétarien.	vezhay-tehryañ
Waitress/	Madame,	mah-dam,
waiter	Mademoiselle/	mah-demwahzel/
	Monsieur	muh-syuh
menu	le menu, la carte	men-oo, kart
fixed-price	le menu à	men-oo ah
menu	prix fixe	pree feeks
cover charge	le couvert	koo-vehr
wine list	la carte des vins	kart-deh vañ
glass	le verre	vehr
bottle	la bouteille	boo-tay
knife	le couteau	koo-toh
fork	la fourchette	for-shet
spoon	la cuillère	kwee-yehr
breakfast	le petit	puh-tee
	déjeuner	deh-zhuh-nay
lunch	le déjeuner	deh-zhuh-nay
dinner	le dîner	dee-nay
main course	le plat principal	plah prañsee-pal
starter, first	l'entrée, le hors	l'oñ-tray, or-
course	d'oeuvre	duhvr
dish of the day	le plat du jour	plah doo zhoor
wine bar	le bar à vin	bar ah vañ
café	le café	ka-fay
rare	saignant	say-ñoñ
medium	à point	ah pwañ
well done	bien cuit	byañ kwee

MENU DECODER

apple	la pomme	pom
baked	cuit au four	kweet oh foor
banana	la banane	banan
beef	le boeuf	buhf
beer, draught	la bière, bière	bee-yehr, bee-yehr
beer	à la pression	ah lah pres-syoñ
boiled	bouilli	boo-yee

bread	**le pain**	*pan*
butter	**le beurre**	*burr*
cake	**le gâteau**	*gah-toh*
cheese	**le fromage**	*from-azh*
chicken	**le poulet**	*poo-lay*
chips	**les frites**	*freet*
chocolate	**le chocolat**	*shoko-lah*
cocktail	**le cocktail**	*cocktail*
coffee	**le café**	*kah-fay*
dessert	**le dessert**	*deh-ser*
dry	**sec**	*sek*
duck	**le canard**	*kanar*
egg	**l'oeuf**	*l'uf*
fish	**le poisson**	*pwah-ssoñ*
fresh fruit	**le fruit frais**	*frwee freh*
garlic	**l'ail**	*l'eye*
grilled	**grillé**	*gree-yay*
ham	**le jambon**	*zhoñ-boñ*
ice, ice cream	**la glace**	*glas*
lamb	**l'agneau**	*l'anyoh*
lemon	**le citron**	*see-troñ*
lobster	**le homard**	*omahr*
meat	**la viande**	*vee-yand*
milk	**le lait**	*leh*
mineral water	**l'eau minérale**	*l'oh meeney-ral*
mustard	**la moutarde**	*moo-tard*
oil	**l'huile**	*l'weel*
olives	**les olives**	*leh zoleev*
onions	**les oignons**	*leh zonyoñ*
orange	**l'orange**	*l'oroñzh*
fresh orange juice	**l'orange pressée**	*l'oroñzh press-eh*
fresh lemon juice	**le citron pressé**	*see-troñ press-eh*
pepper	**le poivre**	*pwavr*
poached	**poché**	*posh-ay*
pork	**le porc**	*por*
potatoes	**les pommes de terre**	*pom-duh tehr*
prawns	**les crevettes**	*kruh-vet*
rice	**le riz**	*ree*
roast	**rôti**	*row-tee*
roll	**le petit pain**	*puh-tee pañ*
salt	**le sel**	*sel*
sauce	**la sauce**	*sohs*
sausage, fresh	**la saucisse**	*sohsees*
seafood	**les fruits de mer**	*frwee duh mer*
shellfish	**les crustaces**	*kroos-tas*
snails	**les escargots**	*leh zes-kar-goh*
soup	**la soupe, le potage**	*soop, poh-tazh*
steak	**le bifteck, le steack**	*beef-tek, stek*
sugar	**le sucre**	*sookr*
tea	**le thé**	*tay*
toast	**pain grillé**	*pan greeyay*

vegetables	**les légumes**	*lay-goom*
vinegar	**le vinaigre**	*veenaygr*
water	**l'eau**	*l'oh*
red wine	**le vin rouge**	*vañ roozh*
white wine	**le vin blanc**	*vañ bloñ*

NUMBERS

0	**zéro**	*zeh-roh*
1	**un, une**	*uñ, oon*
2	**deux**	*duh*
3	**trois**	*trwah*
4	**quatre**	*katr*
5	**cinq**	*sañk*
6	**six**	*sees*
7	**sept**	*set*
8	**huit**	*weet*
9	**neuf**	*nerf*
10	**dix**	*dees*
11	**onze**	*oñz*
12	**douze**	*dooz*
13	**treize**	*trehz*
14	**quatorze**	*katorz*
15	**quinze**	*kañz*
16	**seize**	*sehz*
17	**dix-sept**	*dees-set*
18	**dix-huit**	*dees-weet*
19	**dix-neuf**	*dees-nerf*
20	**vingt**	*vañ*
30	**trente**	*tront*
40	**quarante**	*karoñt*
50	**cinquante**	*sañkoñt*
60	**soixante**	*swasoñt*
70	**soixante-dix**	*swasoñt-dees*
80	**quatre-vingts**	*katr-vañ*
90	**quatre-vingt-dix**	*katr-vañ-dees*
100	**cent**	*soñ*
1,000	**mille**	*meel*

TIME

one minute	**une minute**	*oon mee-noot*
one hour	**une heure**	*oon urr*
half an hour	**une demi-heure**	*oon duh-mee urr*
Monday	**lundi**	*luñ-dee*
Tuesday	**mardi**	*mar-dee*
Wednesday	**mercredi**	*mehrkruh-dee*
Thursday	**jeudi**	*zhuh-dee*
Friday	**vendredi**	*voñdruh-dee*
Saturday	**samedi**	*sam-dee*
Sunday	**dimanche**	*dee-moñsh*

ACKNOWLEDGMENTS

The publisher would like to thank the following for their kind permission to reproduce their photographs:

Key: a-above; b-below/bottom; c-centre; f-far; l-left; r-right; t-top

123RF.com: deymos 181tr; Iakov Filimonov 34bl; Andrea Izzotti / Malizia © Kees Verkad 72clb; Zdenek Matyas 26–7t; mikeosphoto 8cla; olrat 32tl.

4Corners: Jordan Banks 2–3; Matteo Carassale © The Estate of Alberto Giacometti (Fondation Annette et Alberto Giacometti, Paris and ADAGP, Paris), licensed in the UK by ACS and DACS, London 2018 79tr; Hans-Georg Eiben 142bl; Susanne Kremer 16, 60–1; Sandra Raccanello / exterior *Vasarely Foundation Building* © ADAGP, Paris and DACS London 2018 131bl; Maurizio Rellini 134–5t; Giovanni Simeone 103tr.

Alamy Stock Photo: Adventure Pictures / Marcin Jamkowski 45b; AEP 74cr; AGE fotostock 26tl, 53crb, 97br, 118tl; ALLSTAR Picture Library 75cra; ALLTRAVEL / Finn Jaschik 138br; Andia 49br; Arco Images GmbH 146t; ART Collection 161ca; Arterra Picture Library / Clement Philippe 105crb; ASK Images 49tr; andy aughey 122t; BIOSPHOTO 175tr; Clearview 198bl; Matjaz Corel 176bl; Ian Dagnall 56br, 136t; David Noton Photography 40b, 96–7t; Werner Dieterich 43br; Mark Dunn 41ca; Adam Eastland 52crb, 107cla; eFesenko 74–5b; Endless Travel 8clb; escapetheofficejob 159tr; F1online digitale Bildagentur GmbH 11cr; FedevPhoto 192bl; Kirk Fisher 158br; Jan Fritz 80–1b; funkyfood London - Paul Williams 145cr; Stephane Gautier 22clb; Granger Historical Picture Archive 161tc; guichaoua 109tr; Susana Guzman 139tr; Hackenberg-Photo-Cologne 93cl; Hardyuno 8cl; ML Harris 166t; Chris Hellier 54bc, 117tr, 119tr; Hemis 20t, 20crb, 25cla, 26cla, 30tr, 31cl, 35cla, 35cr, 39tl, 42–3b, 46bl, 69t, 69br, 90tr, 93tr, 114tl, 119b, 178bl, 198–9t, 202bl; hemis.fr / Giovanni Bertolissio 83br, / Denis Caviglia 171cla, / Jean-Pierre Degas 158–9t, / John Frumm 161cra, / Pierre Jacques 130t, / Lionel Montico 18bl, 154, Camille Moirenc 87b, 104cl, 186cla, / © Architects Rudy Ricciotti & Roland Carta / Mucem 18tl, 124–5; Historic Images 56–7t, 107tl; Horizons WWP / TRVL 26–7ca; / Peter Horree *Field of Mars* (1954) by Marc Chagall ® / © ADAGP, Paris and DACS, London 2018 37tl; IanDagnall Computing 197br; imageBROKER/ Foster + Partners 25tr, 38–9b, 47cb, 52cra, 200tl; / Christian Hütter 165cla, i / Sergio Pitamitz 87cl; Imageplotter / Musee Matisse / *Fleurs et Fruit* (1952–3) by Henri Matisse © Succession H. Matisse/ DACS 2018 66–7b; INTERFOTO 67tl; Ivoha 52cr, 144bl; Brian Jannsen 43tr, 51cr; Jon Arnold Images Ltd / Walter Bibikow 137b; David Jones 162bl; David Keith Jones 49cl; John Kellerman 33cl; Keystone Pictures USA 113cl; Nathan King / *Le Buffle* by Yves Klein © Succession Yves Klein c/o DACS 2018 36tl; Jason Knott 82clb; Laurent Koffel 52cl; Art Kowalsky 82bl; Lanmas 36cra; Lebrecht Music & Arts 168bl; Hervé Lenain 29cl, 115tr; Lightworks Media 175cra; LOOK Die Bildagentur der Fotografen GmbH 180tc; Manjik photography 70–1; Stefano Politi Markovina 179bl; mauritius images GmbH / Klaus Neuner 165tr; Rod McLean 120–1b; Ian Middleton 117br; Tim Moore 40–1t; Serge Mouraret 107br; niceartphoto 113tr; John Norman 113tr; parkerphotography 187tr; Doug Pearson 76–7t; philipus 173br; The Picture Art Collection 36br; Eric D Ricochet69 136bc; robertharding 20cr, 95t; Norbert Scanella 24–5t, 164–5b; Shawshots 54t; StevanZZ 28bl, 148bl; Boris Stroujko 105tl; travellinglight 145b; travelstock44 Hero, sculpture of Nimeño II by Serena Carone © ADAGP, Paris and DACS, London 2018 20bl, 47bl, 82clb, 96bl; Frédéric Vielcanet 52clb.

AWL Images: Christian Heeb / © Architects Rudy Ricciotti & Roland Carta / Mucem 132bl; Hemis 169tr; Camill Moirenc 111crb; Marco Simoni 19, 188.

Bridgeman Images: 55br; AGIP 67cra; Centre Historique des Archives Nationales, Paris, France 55cr; De Agostini Picture Library / G. Dagli Orti 22cr.

Depositphotos Inc: bbsferrari 142–3; gevision 64t; Labemax 196–7t; SergiyN 108t.

Dreamstime.com: Aaa187 11br; Alexirina27000 / *Sculpture Loch Ness Monster* by Niki de Saint Phalle, © Niki de Saint Phalle Charitable Art Foundation / ADAGP, Paris and DACS, London 2018 64br; Gordon Bell 136cla; Benkrut 128–9t; Oleksandr Berezko 41tr; Ryhor Bruyeu 22t; Drewrawcliffe 33tr; Darius Dzinnik 172–3; Eddygaleotti 29tr; Emicristea 182–3t; Steve Estvanik 161tl; Fcobosp 178–9t; Fotografiecor 195crb; Prochasson Frederic 200–1b; Giuseppemasci 111tl; Rostislav Glinsky 57crb; David Hughes 116–7b; Irina88w/ *L'Oiseau Lunaire* (1968) by Joan Miró © Successió Miró / ADAGP, Paris and DACS London 2018 79br; Izanbar 195tl; Wieslaw Jarek 150b; Jeromaniac 85b; Kumax 102t; Horst Lieber 147b; Masr 163tl; Zdeněk Matyáš 28–9b; Milosk50 167cra; Martin Pelanek 81cr; Porojnicu 81tr; Fesus Robert 170–1; Alessandro Sarasso 193cr; Benjamin Sibuet 52cla; Stevanzz 54crb; Larysa Uhryn 31tr; Ivonne Wierink 173bl; Robert Zehetmayer 169tl.

François Fernandez: *Nu bleu IV* by Henri © Succession H. Matisse / DACS 2018 66bl.

Getty Images: AFP / Anne-Christine Poujoulat 48–9t, 53tr, / Jean Christophe Magnenet/ Matisse Museum, Nice / *Jeannette III* (1911) by Henri Matisse © Succession H. Matisse / DACS 2018 66crb, / Pascal Pavani 53tl; Christian Alminana 12crb; Bettmann 72br; Bloomberg / Balint Porneczi 57cra; Tibor Bognar 163br; Fanny Broadcast 55tl; Gareth Cattermole 11tl; Christophel Fine Art 56cb; DEA / G. Dagli Orti 56tl,165cl; Danita Delimont 6–7; duncan1890 55tr; P. Eoche 107; Patrick Escudero 48bl; EyeEm / Jean-Franois Monnot 33br; Iggi Falcon 10clb; Chuck Fishman 65tr; Found Image Holdings Inc 56cr; Franz-Marc Frei 10ca; Gamma-Rapho / Jean-Patrick Deya 78clb, / Raphael Gaillarde 83cl; genekrebs 38tl; GitoTrevisan 106cra; Elodie Gage 110bl; Ken Glaser 90bl; Christian Heeb 114–5b; hemis.fr / Franck Chaput 17, 98–9, Camille Moirenc 149t, / Rene Mattes 122–3b; Francesco Riccardo Iacomino 8–9; Imagno 37b; Johner Images 51crb; Keystone-France 57bl; Markus Lange 112cl; Raimund Linke 138–9t; Elena Liseykina 204–5; LL 57tr; Linda McKie 34–5t; James O'Neil 30–1b, 192–3t; Kevin Pronnecke 81crb; Jim Richardson 55cla; Zoya Stafienko 13cr; Guillaume Temin 174–5; Ivan Vdovin 91t; WaterFrame / Borut Furlan 112clb; Westend61 72–3t, 89tr; Konrad Wothe 50–1b; Yann Guichaoua Photos 12t; Jean-Marc Zaorski 53cl, 53clb.

Grotte Saint Cezaire: Benjamin Celier 89br.

iStockphoto.com: AGaeta 141crb; Allard1 203t; andrzej63 121tr; aprott 84tl; AygulSarvarova 58–9; btrenkel 46–7t; Bunyos / Hero, sculpture of Nimeño II by Serena Carone © ADAGP, Paris and DACS, London 2018 128br; Byrdyak 24–5ca; cristianoalessandro 81cra; drevojan 175tl; eddygaleotti 76br; EdoTealdi 193bl; gianliguori 94bl; GitoTrevisan 51tl, 107cr, 150–1t, 184t; Janoka82 153b; LiliGraphie 10–1b; lucentius 39cb; manjik 92–3b; Marcobarone 177; merc67 31crb; peterleabo 41br; pipalana 141b; PJPhoto69 140bl; PK-Photos 67cr; princegarik 28tl; republica 50t; spooh 183b; SvetlanaSF 27cla; tichr 134bl; trabantos 55clb; Flavio Vallenari 171tr, 180–1b; Noppasin Wongchum 132–3t.

The Metropolitan Museum of Art: Catharine Lorillard Wolfe Collection, Wolfe Fund, 1913 13br.

Musées de Grasse: 86t.

Oceanographic Museum of Monaco: 44–5t.

Parc Spirou Provence: 44br.